Development Dramas

Development Dramas

Reimagining Rural Political Action in Eastern India

Dia Da Costa

Routledge
Taylor & Francis Group
LONDON NEW YORK NEW DELHI

First published 2010
by Routledge
912 Tolstoy House, 15–17 Tolstoy Marg, New Delhi 110 001

Simultaneously published in the UK
by Routledge
2 Park Square, Milton Park, Abingdon, Oxon, OX14 4RN

Routledge is an imprint of the Taylor & Francis Group, an informa business

Transferred to Digital Printing 2010

Typeset by
Star Compugraphics Private Limited
D–156, Second Floor
Sector 7, Noida 201 301

British Library Cataloguing-in-Publication Data
A catalogue record of this book is available from the British Library

ISBN: 978-0-415-55373-5

Contents

List of Tables and Figures

Tables

Figures

Acknowledgements

This book began as a dissertation project conducted between 1999 and 2003 in the Department of Development Sociology at Cornell University. It is the outcome of ten years of research and relationships. In the academic world, my thanks go first and foremost to my dissertation committee members — Philip McMichael, Shelley Feldman, and John Forester. They were exemplary advisors who inspired me to think and write in new ways. Questions and discussions from my dissertation defense were wired into my brain despite my ritualised efforts at forgetting them. I have asked Phil for feedback far too often during and since the dissertation. I am grateful for his infectious belief in my work, for suffering my syntax, and for helping me ground ideas in this world when I was on cloud nine. I thank Shelley for her incisive questions which continue to push me towards greater clarity in thinking and writing. And I thank John for pushing me to find my own telescope rather than rely on a series of other people's telescopes.

I am grateful to Srilatha Batliwala for telling me about Jana Sanskriti's work, and to Sanjoy Ganguly for giving in to my dogged persistence to make Jana Sanskriti the subject of my research. I thank especially Sanjoy, Sima, and Shujoy Ganguly who have opened their home and family life to me repeatedly for the past ten years. The only thing that made this feel somewhat normal for me is that they have opened their home to countless others and lived public lives. Sanjoy Ganguly's vision, political passion, and care combined to challenge my notions of democracy, class struggle, and generosity. Sima Ganguly is an inspirational actress and person and I am so thankful that she made me feel at home as often as she pushed me out of my comfort zone. Rohini Mukherjee's commitment and quiet, unfailing, efficiency enabled everyone else's work to go on unhindered. Inadvertently, she showed me the limits of my own commitment to enter new worlds and live new commitments, and helped me be honest with myself and others.

This book simply would not have existed without the talent, kindness, generosity, and intelligence of activists and actors at Jana Sanskriti. In particular I am grateful to Kavita Bera, Renuka Das, Brindavan Haldar, Pritilata Mondol, Sadananda Mondol, Maheshwar Nahiya, Satyaranjan Pal, and Pradeep Sardar for helping me conceptualise questions and consider anomalies within particular research topics. They and their families repeatedly let me stay in their homes. Renuka Das in particular has been my companion and research assistant since 1999 when she made me feel at home during the theatre workshop in Bagda. Also since 1999, Satyaranjan Pal, more than anyone else, put up with my questions, moods, insensitivities, and ignorance. I thank him for doing so with equal amounts of grace and brutality.

The Social Movements Research Working Group at the Polson Institute for Global Development at Cornell University has provided me with an incredible forum for collective thought and exchange. In different ways and at different times, each of its members — Nosheen Ali, Rachel Bezner-Kerr, Alexandre Da Costa, Kelly Dietz, Andreas Hernandez, Gayatri Menon, Philip McMichael, Karuna Morarji, Rajeev Patel, Emelie Peine, Alicia Swords, Hannah Wittman, and Anna Zalik — have helped me rethink my work and for that I am very grateful. Without this space to reflect, share ideas, and develop my work, negotiating the post-dissertation landscape without 'cohorts' would have felt even more alienating.

Nosheen Ali, Alexandre Da Costa, Philip McMichael, and Karuna Morarji have been my closest interlocutors, readers, and friends. Without them, the process of writing a first book would have been much less fun and certainly more disconcerting. Rustom Bharucha always gave me good advice, read my work over the years, and gave me confidence that theatre was worth studying. I also owe a considerable debt to the following people for reading one or more chapters in this book and for offering perceptive comments and useful suggestions: Jason Cons, Aparna Dharwadker, Ann Grodzins Gold, Suzan Ilcan, Aditya Nigam, Ian Petrie, Arild Engelsen Ruud, and Juliana Saxton. Finally, I am grateful to those who have challenged my thinking and taken the time to read and comment on my work as conference discussants, journal editors, or colleagues: Amita Baviskar, Cynthia Caron, Rajarshi Dasgupta,

Sudhanva Deshpande, Saurabh Dube, Anjan Ghosh, Jeff Harrod, Ron Herring, Farhana Ibrahim, Dip Kapoor, Nita Kumar, Adriane Lentz-Smith, Craig Jeffrey, Rebecca Klenk, David Lelyveld, Kirin Narayan, Dunbar Moodie, Rajeev Patel, Patricia Paton, Vijay Prashad, Chris Powell, Mahesh Rangarajan, Kanchana Ruwanpura, K. Sivaramakrishnan, Susanne Soederberg, Ajantha Subramanian, Nandini Sundar, Marcus Taylor, and Heloise Weber. Having said this, the views and analysis expressed in this book are mine and are not necessarily shared by anyone who has helped shape my thinking.

The research for this book was conducted with funding from the following institutions: the Department of Rural Sociology, The Mario Einaudi Center for International Studies, Women's Studies Program, and the Polson Institute for Global Development, all at Cornell University; Ford Foundation Interdisciplinary Training Grant on Nationalism, Citizenship, and Identity Formation (2000–01); the Taraknath Das Foundation at Columbia University; Provost's Office at Hobart and William Smith Colleges (HWS); and the Office of Research Services at Queen's University. I acknowledge their support with sincere thanks. I am also grateful to the library staff at National Library in Kolkata, the Natya Shodh Sansthan in Salt Lake, Kolkata, Centre for Studies in Social Sciences, Kolkata, the Kroch, Olin, Uris, and Mann libraries at Cornell University, Ithaca, the HWS Library, Geneva, and the Stauffer Library at Queen's University for their assistance.

I thank my students at the Department of Anthropology and Sociology, HWS and the Department of Global Development Studies at Queen's University for asking good questions and making the classroom a significant site through which I developed my analysis.

I acknowledge with gratitude permission granted by a number of journals and publishers to reprint in revised form sections of my articles originally published as the following:

'"Spoiled Sons" and "Sincere Daughters": Schooling, Security, and Empowerment in rural West Bengal, India', *Signs: Journal of Women and Culture,* 33(2) 2008: 283–308.

'Tensions of Neo-liberal Development: State Discourse and Dramatic Oppositions in West Bengal', *Contributions to Indian Sociology* 41(3) 2007: 287–320.

Mohan, D. (2004a). 'Re-imagining Community: Scripting Power and Changing the Subject through Jana Sanskriti's Political Theatre in Rural North India', *Journal of Contemporary Ethnography,* 33(2): 178–217.

Mohan, D. (2004b). 'Jana Sanskriti's Theatre and Political Practice in Rural Bengal: The Making of Popular Culture', *South Asian Popular Culture,* 4(1): 39–53.

I am very grateful to Nilanjan Sarkar, the Publishing Manager at Routledge, for his diligent efforts in seeing this book through reviews and editing. I thank the two anonymous reviewers at Routledge for their helpful comments on the manuscript. I am also grateful to other editorial and design staff at Routledge, New Delhi, for their work to make this book accessible. I am especially grateful to Amitabh Mukherjee for his patient work with copy-editing the manuscript to give it greater clarity.

My final thanks are reserved for everyone in my family in India, London, and Pittsburgh. My new family in Pittsburgh is a world where the Emboaba Da Costas envelope me with their love and sense of fun, making me feel at home in a place that I never imagined could be home. In India, I am grateful to all members of the Jha family for distracting me constantly, and for their moral support, generosity, and interest through the years. In Kolkata, my *mama* and *mami* Samar and Anjana Jha, my cousins, Shreya and Anshumaan Jha, and my *mashi,* Soma Jha provided homes during various bouts of fieldwork. I could not have survived my time in West Bengal without the home food and family loving! Aditi Sen introduced me to interesting books, gave me lists of initial contacts, shipped books for me, and helped me overcome my fear of reading Bengali. Soma Jha procured books, journals, and films for me, guided by a shared sense of outrage and passion about contemporary history in India. Kolkata always meant *mamabari* — a space for younger generations to experience delicious food and unbounded kindness from older generations. I received a lot of admiration and moral support from my grand-uncles and grand-aunts for the unknown work I did 'in the villages'. And thank you Bonumashi for your timely gift of *The Colonial Staged!*

My thanks to my brother Aakash Mohan and sister-in-law Shalini Kukreja for various forms of support and encouragement over the years. Additionally, I thank Shalini for being the first family member who could share with me the thrills and pressures of academic work. Alexandre Da Costa has read this book in its entirety a few too many times, questioning logic and argument alike. I realise that I am the queen of misplaced commas. I thank him for his generous spirit, for reading my work with such patience, for helping me bring clarity to it, and maintain integrity within it. I think of our office as my safe haven: a den of good music, sounding-board for half-baked ideas, and an ideal hub of procrastination. My final words of gratitude are reserved for my mother, Sushmita Jha. I will humiliate myself, borrow from Peter Cetera, and say that you are my inspiration. You inadvertently had me imagining what it would be like to grow up as a *subziwali*'s daughter. Through that story and through the strength, grace, and love with which you live your life you taught me the core lesson of this book — the power of our imaginations. This book is dedicated to you.

Part I

Introduction

Reimagining Development and Rural Political Action

This book is about the work of rural political theatre in an iconic electoral democracy — West Bengal, India. Till the 2009 elections, rural Bengalis unfailingly voted the Left Front Government (LFG) — made up of a coalition of parties led by the Communist Party of India (Marxist) or the CPM — back into power since 1977. In the 2009 parliamentary elections, the LFG suffered a significant setback as it won 15 seats out of a total of 42 while the opposition won a total of 25 seats combining the victories of the Indian National Congress and the regional political party, Trinamul Congress. With an 81.3 per cent voter turnout in West Bengal, the mandate for change seems decisive. However, in the past three decades of LFG rule and consistent electoral success, rural Bengali citizens had consolidated an image and reality of being iconic beneficiaries of LFG agrarian reforms and political decentralisation in the countryside, while also being extensively educated in the cultural and political ideologies of the Left. Contesting the meaning of development, democracy, and political action appeared to be moot in this seemingly emblematic government of and by the rural poor. To be sure, in part, the redundancy of reimagining development and rural political action in West Bengal is an outcome of progressive LFG legal and agricultural policy. In equal part, however, the seeming redundancy is an outcome of conceptualising development and political action in the sphere of policy rather than giving equal attention to the everyday cultural politics, practices, meanings, and processes of development and political action. This book redresses the latter omission by looking through the lens of political theatre in order to analyse grounded constructions and critiques of development forwarded in everyday rural political action on- and off-stage in West Bengal.

Counting on decades of electoral legitimacy in the countryside, CPM leaders embraced private capital investment to correct the trends of capital flight, unemployment, and declining working-class vote since the 1980s. Along with the rest of India, the ruling Left undertook reforms to rejuvenate industry in the 1990s, proposing to acquire agricultural land for industrialisation in the early 2000s by invoking the colonial Land Acquisition Act of 1894. Notwithstanding consistent electoral success, land acquisition for industrial development incited militant public protests both against capital–state collaboration to dispossess land and against the land protection movement. About 997 acres of multi-crop land were acquired by the CPM and leased to the Indian conglomerate Tata to build a 'people's car' factory.[1] Inducing industrial development, voices within the CPM suggested, was necessary for variously addressing the problems of land fragmentation and agrarian livelihoods. Such livelihoods, as they viewed it, could no longer absorb the growing population in rural West Bengal. This in turn adversely impacts growth, job creation, welfare, and possibilities for eventual socialism. While land reform was the mantra that generated government action and electoral legitimacy through the 1980s and 1990s, the current Chief Minister of West Bengal, Buddhadeb Bhattacharya who came into power in 2001, had a new catchphrase manifesto for the 2006 state elections: 'Agriculture is our foundation, industry our future' (P. P. Basu 2007: 294).

Development thinking and Marxism tend to share the chief minister's ultimately disdainful vision of peasants and rural culture as base, history, and legacy, but not future. As one professor of economics puts it, 'West Bengal's comparative advantage must lie with industry and services and not with agriculture. [...] Since land is anything but abundant in West Bengal, efficiency requires that the state imports agricultural goods from the rest of India selling in return services and industrial goods' (A. Sarkar 2007: 1438). Such calculations of comparative advantage and efficiency are loyal to a market episteme claiming it as the only realistic and therefore normative formulation of development in West Bengal.[2] These views construct agriculture and industry in a zero-sum game where the development of one can only be constructed by displacing extant livelihoods and modernising the other.

When the assembly elections in 2006 swept the LFG back into power, commentators claimed that the traditional rural vote bank had voted in spite of the reforms, because the 'reformist orientation is firmly cushioned by decades of solid support in rural West Bengal' (P. P. Basu 2007: 31). This claim of solid support is an overstatement as recent protests demonstrate and as a complex view of the past three decades might reveal. Since 2006, the West Bengal countryside has witnessed protests, violent state repression, and heightened politicking demonstrating a crisis of hegemony precisely among the Left's prized historic vote-base of rural citizens. Development Dramas considers the socio-historical formation of this crisis rather than viewing this as a recent and sudden reaction to new policies that privilege industry as future. It does not assume that Leftist electoral legitimacy and policies on agrarian reform were ultimate testimony of democracy and development. Therefore, rather than view the LFG victory and defeat as a matter of traditional rural base versus new urban middle-class base mirroring a tradition versus modernity binary, or even a development versus post-development paradigm, this book calls for a more complex view of development and political action in contemporary Bengal. This book is about ways in which one organisation, Jana Sanskriti (People's cluture), has contributed to revealing the formation of CPM's hegemonic political society and the ongoing normalisation of the market episteme that underlies prevailing notions of development in West Bengal. Jana Sanskriti's (henceforth JS) rural political theatre practiced since 1985 offers a rare opportunity to understand and address ongoing processes through which the multiple meanings of development, political action, and rural future are cut down to size. Their on-stage political theatre and off-stage political action feed each other to reveal the processes through which electoral success and agrarian reforms benefitting the dispossessed have ironically enabled structural and subjective closure on alternate visions, dispossessing multiple and contextual meanings of rural futures, collectivity, and social transformation.

Rather than view elected leaders as the distant state, farmers in the JS play *Unnayan* (Development) say, 'No matter what, behind the clothes lies a human being we elected.'[3] The play was written in the aftermath of recent land acquisitions and dramatic protests. It begins by identifying the difference between feudal lords of the pre-colonial past who controlled and took away land at will and the government today with a similar ability to take away land.

The difference, as one character on-stage puts it, is that '[T]he government does not keep the land. They give it to Tata. That's it, isn't it?' Tata is the conglomerate that will set up a 'people's car' factory on multi-crop agricultural land. The play depicts the transition from past to present land relations by showing yesterday's feudal lord as today's chief minister, while Tata has become today's feudal lord with sycophants like the chief minister at their beck and call.

The play reveals a thoroughly compromised Leftist chief minister — an emperor with no clothes — who cannot find his 'decent attire' (the ideals of Communism) because he has sold the red flag. The entity that bought the red flag is Tata. For the chief minister, this factory represents 'people's development'. Tata is pleased to be participating in a '[N]ew history for Bengal. [...] Let the people of the world see how Communists love capitalists'. The play depicts Tata loaning the red flag to the chief minister on occasions when the minister has to face farmers in public forum. *Unnayan* is a critique of the expedient use of Leftist ideological rhetoric of a 'people's car' for people's development to mask a process of neoliberal transition to aggressive capitalism.

Figure 1: A scene from JS play *Unnayan* depicting Tata controlling the West Bengal Chief Minister (left) and Industry Minister (right) in a puppet dance*

When Jana Sanskriti protests the dispossession of rural livelihoods and meanings, their aim is not to suggest that West Bengal does not need capital investment, development, or rural employment. Rural Bengalis, including JS members, certainly want employment, they want capital investment in rural Bengal, they want their sons and daughters to get an education so that they can become engineers and doctors, and many want employment in villages without displacement from their rural homes. The fact that a majority of landowners took monetary compensation in exchange for their multicrop land in Singur suggests that many in Singur also envision factories on what used to be their agricultural land. Numerous citizens across India want a future beyond the fields. I also do not wish to suggest that such normative aspirations are evidence of villagers' false consciousness. Nor is JS using the idea of primordial rural cultural difference to 'disguise relations of inequality' (Ferguson 2006: 20). As James Ferguson has recently argued, we need to go beyond anthropological relativising in the debates on 'mental colonisation or capitulation to cultural imperialism' and instead take seriously the meaning and power of African yearnings for a rectangular modern house over an ecologically sensible thatched one, among other 'yearnings for cultural convergence' (*ibid.*). Ferguson argues that claiming cultural difference and denying certain material advancements as ill-conceived development are statements of privilege which serve to reinforce categorical and material subordination of the African, exploited and dominated in global history.

In critiquing dispossession of land and meanings, JS members are not making a claim for cultural difference and economic isolation. Nor am I. For example, on the one hand, there is a palpable fear of cultural pollution regarding arenas of commodification and exploitation associated with transgressive consumption enabled by the insertion of new media in rural areas. On the other, cultural globalisation also absorbs rural male youth in new 'economies of desire', counteracting the abstract 'narrative of doom' associated with globalisation (Menon and Nigam 2007: 83). Rural youth's particular experience of unemployment and dead end futures is caught between transitioning economic realities. Indeed, rural Bengalis have long been part of global history and what Gidwani and Sivaramakrishnan have called 'regional modernity', which has 'elements of a Gramscian counter-hegemonic praxis: a symbolic and material vocabulary for challenging ruling ideologies' as villagers move across rural and urban spaces of living and working (Gidwani and Sivaramakrishnan 2003: 187). The significance of growing unemployment across urban India, cycles of capital insertion and capital flight which haunt rural and urban landscapes in many developed parts of the world, and the fact that their rural homes represent *some* measure of security in comparison with a deeply insecure urban housing environment is not lost on rural Bengalis. The disregard and insecurity rural migrants have faced in urban centres is a reality which competes with the experience of the dispossessed value and decreasing viability of rural livelihoods. To many, the competition between these realities does not spell a foregone conclusion about their place in the future.

As a *consequence* of this regional modernity, JS members critique dispossession of land and meanings. They reveal the ongoing categorical and material subordination of villagers, whereby rural life and agriculture are made visible as base, legacy, and past but unviable as adequately productive future. JS questions the assumption that protecting rural values and futures amounts to a romantic assertion out of sync with rural aspirations to become urban citizens. For JS, the question is: For whom is it romantic to claim belonging to a rural life-world? In a phone interview conducted in November 2008, Sanjoy Ganguly, Director of JS, quoted data gathered from cultivators in Singur. People interviewed in Singur by JS members said that those who sold their land for compensation sold it for a price, not to enable a new move into an urban future but to add to income from an existing job in Kolkata. Still others claimed that 'How are you saying there is no profit in farming. What does profit mean? I grow rice, vegetables, lentils from my land. With this I can eat, I live here, I employ a whole family, and I get my children married.' Far from a romanticised view, these are calculations, however tenuous and partial, of profit and security. Cultivators in Singur claimed that those who exchanged land for compensation were relatively educated, with jobs in Kolkata, for whom this land was not the only source of security.[4] JS insists that they only happen to be combating the CPM and Tata in this particular moment and context. Their battle is with any undemocratic government that colludes to promote an aggressive capitalism.

Where development planning is devoted to increasing productivity and profit-making through coercive dispossession of land and meanings, they critique dispossessing a diversity of values, skills, and futures as the *condition* for normalising an alluring promise of generating jobs while satisfying new aspirations and urban futures. By 'dispossession of meaning', I refer to representational inequality situated in political–economic inequalities and enforced through processes of rule. Dispossessing the value of rural social life, livelihood, and future further naturalises the very meaning of development while rendering other existing meanings and practices of life and livelihood politically unthinkable and economically unviable.

JS represents some rural Bengalis who are asking whether addressing material inequality has to come with displacement, deskilling, and devaluing extant skills, livelihoods, and life-worlds. Developing Ferguson's question and following JS's lead, I ask whether the 'aspiration to overcome categorical subordination' and material inequality has to be accomplished with material and symbolic dispossession (Ferguson 2006: 20)? JS is combating the way in which comparative advantage of West Bengal's industrialisation and profit-making has to be realised by invoking a colonial law, using a police force, and ruling out other historically existing and possible ways of defining rural futures. The promise of reskilling the dispossessed for a new economy rings false to rural Bengalis who have lived with decades of shoddy rural schooling.

The assertion that 'another development is possible' might strike the social scientist and political realist as idealism, even elitism. But the idea that factory work is the only realist perspective on employment, that comparative advantage must rule social relations, and that industrialisation through ecological and social disregard is the tragic necessity of our times are the bankrupt corpus of ideas that perpetuate the dispossession of alternate notions of work, value, and future, further closing off existing possibilities. As Menon and Nigam have put it, as we normalise in policy and discourse the daily degradation of lives and denials of dignity, we can count on reminders that 'at every stage of the long and dark history of development, alternatives were always available' (2007: 74). The theatre activists, who brave a battle against the constant normalisation of a world of shrinking possibilities and social relations, are rendered idealists while those who acquiesce to neoliberal capital's normalisations are considered realists. The plays, mobilisations, and commitment documented in this book pays homage to those who engage in the productive work of refusing normative closures, rethinking the cultural persuasion of capitalism, and the masquerade of the state. These actors reimagine development and rural political action by questioning the ideological and hierarchical divides between 'real' choices and 'idealistic' visions of development.

Post-colonial Development Dramas

The dispossession of rural life and future from conceptions of development in West Bengal is a particular outcome of the larger political history of capitalism. David Harvey (2000) has described 'spaces of hope' as the processes that reimagine development against the workings and spaces of capital. Although he pays explicit attention to spaces of hope, his concept of 'accumulation by dispossession' takes as given the desire and desperate need for capital, rather than considering when and where such a hegemony captures an audience or fails to have such efficacy in the subjectivities, aspirations, and politics of a particular context and time (*ibid.*: 2003: 154).[5] Harvey's understanding resonates with our times because capital insertion is every government's 'need'. His view also echoes with the Polish economist Kalecki's idea that '[T]he tragedy of capital is that it is necessary' (cited in Prashad 2005: 120). But this view about the need for capital investment rings true at least in part because Kalecki constructs as proof the only pudding that counts ideologically and institutionally — procuring capital investments.[6] Despite this ruling market episteme, the massive protests in West Bengal since 2006 put the brakes on indiscriminate expropriation of agricultural land despite the lure of capital insertion. Protestors against it were aware that the expropriation would bring capital insertion and some jobs. But some of the protestors wondered in whose vision and in what way capital investment comes to be necessary. In whose terms of living and future then does the need for and procurement of capital constitute a tragedy?

Post-colonial development policy is emblematic in constructing such 'tragedy' as inevitable, thus mastering epistemic exclusions while upholding the rhetorical value of political representation. The normalisation of development as productive industrial employment is not an overnight outcome of globalisation and recent land acquisitions. The dispossession of agrarian livelihoods and meanings is an ongoing process that has made it more persuasive, rational, and institutionally viable to choose a life beyond the fields.

Independent India followed political non-alignment in the Cold War and a mixed economy under the Nehruvian plan. In principle, the Five-Year-Plans were committed to overcoming some of the inequalities of feudal and colonial capitalism's distribution of public and private resources and attempt to bridge the city–country divide.

Scholars have argued that the development regime is an institutional complex 'created by colonial capitalism and bourgeois nationalism' (Ludden 1992: 249) and that the development state uses the rhetoric of inclusive development and liberal democracy to mask its continuity with the colonial state (P.Chatterjee 1993). Sudipta Kaviraj (1989) has argued that the promise of revolution that galvanised masses in the anti-colonial struggle was displaced by a passive revolution in the planning process, legal and governance structures which assumed a bourgeois reformist agenda that pursued industrialisation at the expense of radical agrarian reform. In Sugata Bose's (1997) terms, the post-colonial Indian state used development planning as a principle mode for garnering legitimacy for state rule. The definition and implementation of 'development' by Indian state officials relied on geopolitical, historical, and indigenous structures of power and relations of rule embedded in hierarchies of class, caste, religion, and gender. Infrastructural developments, for example, were repeatedly implemented through the sacrifice of peasants and indigenous populations for the greater common good (Baviskar 1995).

This is not to say that agriculture and peasants did not matter in these conceptions of development. On the contrary, as Ludden (Ludden 1992: 276) puts it, '[T]he farming culture of India's development regime is that of a diverse and differentiated agrarian petty bourgeoisie, which has been rising in economic and cultural power since late pre-colonial times, in constant interaction with the state, whose powers are integral to its own'. At the same time, agrarian interventions are not invariably outcomes of radical land struggles, but have also been modes of accomplishing governmentality through administrative control (Herring 1983). Nor can the rise of peasant power and agrarian populism be understood without appreciating in it the protest against cultural exclusion and representational inequality privileged by 'the normative world and etiquette of Western modernity' and the urban English-educated Indian (Menon and Nigam 2007: 7; see Gupta 1998). Not surprisingly then, to daily-wage workers who became leaders within JS like Prasad Sardar, both policies which undermine agrarian futures on the logic of 'greater common good' *and* policies that institute reform for the rural poor seem to be founded on a suspiciously similar principle of minimal regard. Prasad, whose family depends on a combination of daily agricultural labour on shrimp farms and selling goods on local trains, puts it like this:

> I have my suspicions whether our government or the people in power actually consider villagers human. We live like cows and goats. *Somehow* think of the absolute minimum needs and give it to them, (*pause*) or deny them these things. Give it or not, it all speaks of the same [attitude] (*Dile o dao, na dile o na, byapar ta eki*). And yet, it is with villagers that they constitute their collective (*othocho gramer lokeder niye-i oder shongothon*).

Prasad's critique is damning indictment of the accumulating attitude to peasants. In an echo of Prasad's critique, a recent description characterises the Indian peasantry's 'gruesome fate of being slowly killed while being kept artificially alive' (Baviskar and Sundar 2008: 87).

Despite and through this dehumanisation, the idea of 'development' effects coercive force, it constitutes a mode of accomplishing rule that takes away freedoms as often as it grants them (Jeffrey et al. 2007; Li 1999a, 1999b). The neoliberal mandate of inviting private capital investment for development further strengthens state complicity in processes of capital accumulation and normalises development as 'accumulation by dispossession' (Harvey 2003: 137–82). Now more than ever, the developmental state eloquently constructs its economic nationalism via a patriotic duty to generate employment opportunity by competing for prospects in the global and domestic market. On the one hand, by constructing India as an emerging giant in the world market, urban, middle-class optimism, and development policy glosses over constitutive material and representational inequalities within the nation. On the other hand, the multiple insurrections, secessionist movements, and armed warfare in the countryside in India testifies to the simmering 'crisis of secular-nationalism', all of which belie the assumed 'nation' of economic nationalism and the optimism of 'India Shining' (Needham and Sunder Rajan 2007; Nigam 2006).

Like other governments in developing contexts worldwide, the Left Front government of West Bengal needs capital investment to rejuvenate employment. Unlike many other governments, especially in India, it is faced with the unenviable task of persuading citizens that inviting capital to take over agricultural land has citizen welfare in mind and is the only logical next step in its own progressive history of development and reform. I have argued elsewhere that recently the CPM has done a great deal of hard work to persuade its critics and citizens that what it is engaged in is state-guided capital investment for industrial development, not neoliberal development (Da Costa 2007a). The CPM also argues that without this investment in industrialisation, Bengalis are being denied the opportunity to participate in a competitive global market, be liberated from scarcity, and get relief from a saturated agricultural sector. At the same time, they argue that capitalist development takes us one step closer to socialism (*People's Democracy*, 4 February 2008).[7] Ultimately, the CPM claims that as regional government, it does not control the processes through which development is defined nor structure the field of possibility to usher future socialism. As such, this regional government is bound by the tragic need to procure capital via the rules and constraints set by a bourgeois central government. As discussed in chapter three, if the CPM cannot go against the central government in any fundamental sense, then what exactly does it mean to be a conduit of capitalism while expecting a vote on the basis of being a regional anti-capitalist force that will bring future socialism? While the CPM defines its delimited spaces of control and political action, the organic relationship between capital investment at one place and time, with dispossession in another, comes as no surprise to those rural citizens who live next to rusting factory buildings that have been empty since the 1980s when capital vacated the premises. It is not easy to justify to all farmers why empty factory buildings neighbouring their agricultural land are less attractive options for setting up factories than fertile soil and people's homes.

Moreover, governments such as the LFG in West Bengal are not alone in facing the trials of constructing 'development' in a context of shrinking possibilities and inordinate constraints. JS participates in the 'transnational governmentality' that confounds the spatial understanding of a state as encompassing a delimited territory (Ferguson and Gupta 2005: 106). Not only does JS help constitute 'processes through which the conduct of a population is governed' (*ibid.*: 114), they are also situated in transnational circuits of capital although they do not have NGO status and are unable to receive organisational funding from foreign sources. They rely on donations from friends situated all over the world, grants from domestic organisations, and grants from agencies such as MacArthur Foundation won by individuals within the organisation. For the past 29 years, JS has done its best to resist becoming a service-providing NGO even though this would give them financial security. Their focus on representational struggle is not an accident, but a conviction and vision.

However, in 2001, they did build a preschool programme which takes on the neglected governmental duty of providing rural education. For this work they are funded by Tata and ICICI Bank. Thus, JS also negotiates the bind of procuring capital investment in rural areas while they critique the impositions of aggressive capital in cases where dispossession of agricultural land is enforced to procure capital for building a car factory. In other words, JS cannot be romanticised as cultural difference or political–economic autonomy just because it is grassroots theatre and activism by villagers.

As they view it, JS does the work of questioning hegemonic control over democratic processes as embodied in LFG electoral success. For example, Ganguly researched into the basic inequities highlighted by agricultural workers to ask why a more equitable distribution of *existing* government revenues has not been possible. He asks, 'Why has the salary of a government rural school teacher, with a Masters degree, why has their salary increased from Rs 340 to Rs 30,000 since 1977 while the wage of agricultural workers increased from Rs 30 to Rs 75 in the same time period?' Villagers participating in JS work propose a more equitable revenue distribution by the government so that the agricultural worker is actually valued. Far from asking the state to get out of the way and not play a role in generating employment, they propose that the state do more to control and define the purpose of capital insertion and recommit to principles of Leftist politics. For example, an alternative path than capital insertion for a 'car factory' would be to invest capital that rejuvenates productivity of weaving and other artisanal skills, to generate employment through infrastructural development — building roads, hospitals, schools, and colleges.

It strikes me that the 'alternative' suggested by JS can hardly be characterised as post-development or rural autonomy. They do however insist that it is time to construct development by encouraging capital investment towards rural livelihoods, food security and sovereignty, and sustainable futures — making these both valuable and viable. The representational inequality that views these goals for capital as unprofitable and unproductive are the kinds of dispossession of meaning that JS aims to highlight and combat. JS has procured capital investment for pedagogical, cultural, and political work in rural areas while questioning the categorical and material dispossessions of a regional government and capitalism. JS's work of combating representational inequality mobilises and publicises the possibility of viewing theatrical labour, political activism, cultural work and teaching in rural schools as work with an exchange value but not reducible to it. They view their work as worth valuing and remunerating, as worthy employment and significant vision of rural future.

The Question of Culture

The question of culture looms large in constructions and critiques of development. The inability to trust culture as political process and to accept praxis as foundation of collectivity has to be understood as a constitutive tension of our present. The cultural turn of development has been characterised as the institutional and intellectual recognition that the study of development and institutional practices conceived economically is not enough. There is resounding institutional legitimacy for culture within development imaginaries today. Yet, in the current conjuncture of food crises, wars, and displacement, what effect can culture have on material crises and resource struggles? Seen from the JS perspective, what exactly does it mean for culture and 'substantive freedoms' to matter to development? Notwithstanding the programmatic attention to a world beyond markets, at the capitalist extreme, neoliberal incorporation showcases and commodifies culture, reducing praxis and process to generalisable nuggets of wisdom for development statements on best practice.

On the other hand, in a post-Cold War world, analysis of development and social change is still anxious that size of collectivity and change matters. Small spaces of hope are received with healthy doses of scepticism for fears of succumbing to communitarian culture, or as moments of creative battle that signify minimal structural transformation, if at all. Fragmented criticism is assumed to be decontextualised and depoliticised, merely 'local' voices missing the larger structural picture. Indeed, despite the cultural turn, ultimately, mobilising collectivity based on redistributing the means of representation rather than the means of production faces all the baggage of being 'merely cultural' (Butler 1998: 33) and 'merely politic' (Yúdice 2003). In this book, I assume that the expedient incorporation of culture within institutions of governance and development is significant reason for scholarly analysis of cultural work. As demonstrated here, 'invisible' audiences for multiple expressions and histories of power are present and visible, whether we, as scholars, call them spaces of hope or not, and whether we are looking or not (Harvey 2000; Mitchell 2002).

The Nobel Laureate economist Amartya Sen (2004) sees the pendulum swing — from ignoring culture to cultural determinism — as equally problematic reifications of culture. For him, culture must be understood as one important constituent element of substantive freedoms at the same time that culture can produce exclusionary practices. This is a laudable theoretical suggestion, but what does it mean in practice? In an interview in the Kolkata daily *The Telegraph*, Sen justifies the expropriation of agricultural land in Singur by invoking Bengal's history as a centre of industry. He argues that the recent post-colonial de-industrialisation of Bengal can and must be corrected to return Bengal to its glorious industrial heritage of pre-colonial and colonial times. Moreover, in his view, dispossession of agricultural land for industrialisation has always competed with agriculture for fertile land in the history of development. He says:

> It is also very important to recognise that production of industrial goods was based on the banks of the Hooghly and the Ganges, which are fertile areas anyway. So to say that 'this is fertile agriculture land and you should not have industry here' not only goes against the policy of the West Bengal government but also against the 2,000-year history of Bengal.
>
> This is where industry was based because even though the land may be very fertile, industrial production could generate many times more than the value of the product produced by agriculture. The locations of great industry, be it Manchester or Lancashire, these were all on

> heavily fertile land. Industry has always competed against agriculture because the shared land was convenient for industry for trade and transportation. (Saha with Sen 2007)

While industry wins in this competition, it does so through a circular logic, holding European developments as ideal, ignoring the oppressive inequalities of feudal and colonial systems, and through a definition of current value that is captive to a market episteme. Other values and substantive freedoms such as rural livelihoods, skills, and futures do not seem to matter here. Using the examples of the US, Canada, and Australia, Sen argues later in the interview that these countries have prosperous agriculture today because there is simultaneously a very small population in agriculture and widespread industry to absorb those displaced from agriculture. In other words, industry must be generated because the people displaced from agriculture must be absorbed.

In the interest of restoring Bengal's glorious industrial heritage and ensuring development of industry, Sen contradicts his own philosophical discourse on progress as freedom, one that is celebrated worldwide as a transition in development thinking that takes culture into account. Sen (1999) has identified development as 'substantive freedoms', or those freedoms that 'enable people to participate in the determination of what they should value and/or enable people in effect to construct their opportunities' (Da Costa and McMichael 2007: 591). Critics have argued that his 'model presumes the very thing it claims to deliver' (*ibid*). Sen also undermines the very freedoms that he claims development will deliver because he denies viability to critiques against industrialisation in Singur on account of the claim that agriculture does not generate as much (market) value as industry would.

On 5 October 2008, the Tata car factory was moved from West Bengal and welcomed by Chief Minister Narendra Modi and farmers in Gujarat. This move from the iconic Leftist state to Gujarat, the state with a right-wing Hindu government further delegitimises public opposition to Tata in West Bengal. Tata's departure reinforces the terms of the ideological battle: the choice is to want 'development' as capital will have it, or not at all. The dispossessed meanings of development are quite simply invisible and inadmissible in these debates. Sen's position on Singur contributes to this logic of the neutrality of market value and capital movement.

Sen's philosophical thoughts appear to give agency and opportunity to the poor to choose a life they have reason to value. Yet, in a world where philosophical discourses of choice, freedom, and agency remain theoretical commitments while policies assume that there is no alternative to capitalist development, Karuna Morarji's (2007: 3) question to Sen gets to the kernel of contradiction in Sen's theories when she asks: '[A]gency and choice to do what: what kinds of lives do people have reason to value?' For Morarji, people's aspirations are socialised through a 'political economy of aspirations' encouraging certain types of lives and futures (*ibid.*). In other words, while the ideal of development as freedom suggests a world of possibility, Sen himself participates in dispossessing certain meanings and futures of value when he suggests that market values are the important ones. While Sen is celebrated for attending to culture and human development, his view maintains the ideological boundary between the global macro-space of capital and the local micro-space of culture while neglecting to highlight capitalism as cultural formation (Kapoor 2008).

These are questions of agency and freedom which are particularly fraught in light of the need and desire for capital on the one hand and the realities of cultural imperialism and political–economic coercion on the other (Ferguson 2006; Da Costa 2007a). This has direct bearing on how we conceptualise the relationship between culture and development. Arguably, the issue is not just whether or not culture is commodified, but also how the commodification of culture and politics contributes to naturalising certain modes of participating and belonging in society, normalising certain constructions of being and becoming, and making viable certain definitions of social justice and social change while ruling out others (Rajagopal 2001). Here, culture is not just that which is being incorporated into capital; it is the constitutive and persuasive force of the market episteme despite and through capital's interaction with other histories of power.

Viewing culture as a thoroughly encompassed mode of conducting imperialism, dispossession, and practice of accumulation, my task is to historicise multiple practices of rule. At the same time, recognising that '"everyone" is a philosopher' in Gramsci's terms, I show that the accomplishment of hegemonic rule is always a struggle (1971: 330). In this book, culture is understood as a whole way of struggling over the naturalisation of the market episteme as *the* relation of rule which dispossesses other meanings and modes of living as anomalous and anachronistic. Any study of cultural work and struggle has to wrestle with the possibilities of agency and pedagogical power embedded in cultural practices of meaning-making on the one hand, while attending to the ways in which cultural work constitutes and remains subject to relations of power, capital accumulation, and rule which depoliticise creativity and commodify agency on the other.

Not only does JS wrestle with the contradictions of cultural work and funding for it, they stage this wrestle for their audience. In the play *Unnayan,* the first thing farmers say in a collective voice mocks the value of performing a play in the midst of land expropriations, 'Performing a play? Two days after the land is gone, there's no telling what I will be able to eat, and they are performing a play here?! We have to mobilise a movement. Yes, yes. We will build a movement. Performing a play!' Staging this self-critique of political theatre as political action in a publicly performed play about land expropriation at the site of protests against land expropriation allows JS to highlight their core strategy of mutually constituted political activism off-stage and political theatre on-stage.

Cultural work, as I conceptualise it, provides a lens into the relationship between processes of meaning-making and the continuing formation of multiple histories of power. *Development Dramas* documents the ongoing dispossession of meanings and reimagines development and political action by taking the labour of meaning-making seriously and assuming that there are multiple histories of power. I show *how* certain modes of subjection and agency come to congeal as the legitimate, valuable sources for conceiving future and development despite the historical existence of multiple sources of persuasion and coercion that constitute material life and life-worlds and despite the availability of other available opportunities and authorities. The cultural work of struggling over meaning-making may be out of sight in the conceptualisation of development, but that speaks of blinkers that rule academic vision.

This book is founded in a method of historical and cultural sociology that asks how development and political action are constituted in places and at times when we are not looking. This analysis of JS's rural political action and political theatre contributes to the growing literature that studies the evolving and contentious relationship between culture, development, and dispossession in an effort to consider how the workings of power materialise 'development' in rural West Bengal. Instead of reading rural protests against the coalition of capital and CPM as reactionary, communitarian, or isolated fragments, this book reimagines development and rural political action by historicising alienation expressed by some within the prized rural vote-base of a government. This book argues that daily alienation and representational inequality can be studied as a trace on the political–economic exclusions/inclusions and the epistemic violence that constitutes what counts as political action and development.

Ethnography of Development and State

In this section, I show how I came to conduct this research on rural political theatre and articulate my methodological rationale for seeing theatre as a significant focus for studying rule, politically organised subjection, and reimagining rural political action.

Justifying land acquisitions in 2006, Chief Minister Bhattacharya rhetorically asked the Bengali public, 'Should the son of a farmer always remain a farmer?' Rural Bengali citizen, Mahesh Pal, whose family depends on an agricultural livelihood, offered a hypothetical response to this question by saying: 'Well, no but that is what I know how to do. Would Buddhadeb start farming tomorrow? No. There are such things as bodies and skills.'[8] Pal's question, 'Would Buddhadeb start farming tomorrow?' is likely to resonate with those urban, middle-class Indians such as myself who came of age in a new world struggling to reconcile the tug of multiple realities — the much publicised failures and corruption of empirical Communism, and the imperialist belief embedded within neoliberal development that the world will be increasingly and inevitably free of alternatives to capitalist ideologies. There are wars of ethnic and racial hatred as well as the increasing corporatisation of social relations. There are powerful appeals to altruistic principles and a problematic sense of superiority embedded in it. How and where I see 'development' in West Bengal and analyse possibilities for constructing development is inevitably shaped by the appeal of ideological equality and freedom, knowing that historically, liberal promises came with imperialist domination, exploitation, and exclusion. In part for this reason, critiques of capitalist and imperialist formation *and* post-structural critiques of universal history and unitary subjectivity are equally compelling and problematic sources of knowledge.

Given the multiple perspectives, crises, and compromises in India's post-colonial development experience described earlier, the idea of 'development' was never completely secure. My socialisation in urban, middle-class India taught me that India was a divided country — some people were modern, some were on their way there, and some were stubbornly backward and traditional. Stages of modernity were echoed in the categories of underdeveloped, developing, and developed — three worlds within one country, let alone the world at large. But being raised by a single mother and in the course of my education, I began to question these sacred and authoritative categories of post-colonial subjectivity. The stability of 'development' was increasingly challenged for me. I began to wonder who among the faces I saw on the streets, newspapers, and landscapes of India fit into these reductive yet powerful classifications by which we organised lives and understood our pasts and futures.

A vivid memory retrospectively appears as my first encounter with development as dispossession of meaning. On a fieldtrip with classmates in Delhi, I traveled to Silvassa, in western India, for an undergraduate research methodology class. There was a tax holiday for businesses to invest in the region. This was also a region of the country that had a large *adivasi* (translated variously as tribal, indigenous, or Scheduled Tribes) population. When we got there, we could literally see what dispossession of land meant. I saw young *adivasi* boys with four, sometimes six and seven wristwatches lining their arms. While the businesses and the state addressed tribal welfare with monetary compensation, *this* is what the money meant to the *adivasi* boys. Stirred by the insanity of the situation and assuming naive and romantic visions about how *adivasis* truly defined wealth or time, I embarked on a mission to conduct interviews with people working in the new factories.

I spent one morning talking with some women. I noticed that they were clad in plastic jewellery, bright plastic hair clips, and polyester saris. They told me of the changes in their lives as a consequence of industrial development in their region — growth of jobs, lack of safety for women around factories, and the availability and convenience of the products they were wearing. In the end, one of the women insisted on asking me a question. This is the question that stayed with me: 'Why are *you* wearing khadi?' Most Indians know khadi as the home and handspun fabric popularised by Gandhi as a symbol of self-sufficiency during the freedom struggle. In India today, it is manufactured to meet popular demand for the urban middle-class. According to the woman, what I really should have been wearing — as the epitome of modernisation and urbanisation to her — was what industrialisation had brought to them, namely plastic and polyester. Perhaps the women were asking what romantic notions of development did *khadi* embody for me. This experience not only cut my middle-class morality and romanticism down to size but it also made me realise that development was a historical, complex, varied, and uneven experience. It had to be questioned rather than assumed to be a historical inevitability. Most importantly, in order to comprehend it, it had to be understood in people's lives.

Now I realise that citizens across a broad spectrum are variously invited, persuaded, or forced to participate in the ongoing dispossession of meaning that undergirds development processes. At the same time, there are also life-worlds that are judged inadequate to modernity that people continue to deem worth living. To say this is not to return to a romantic past and cultural isolation, but to understand a complex and grounded history of development that is tied to the political history of capitalism, and also to other histories of representation and material life.

Seeing Development Relationally: Figure and Ground

In graduate school at Cornell University's Department of Development Sociology, I found expression for these thoughts about studying development at multiple levels through Terence Hopkins' (Hopkins 1979) development of Marx's methodological analogy of the camera obscura and the need to choose a focus on the figure or the background. Applying this analogy of a focusing camera lens, development can be seen as an outcome of human action and historical process. The minute the camera lens focuses on the macro-level of world-historical relations, the subjects of development and their actions blur out of focus. Yet it is precisely the blurred existence of a mass of people trying to survive hardship and marginality that makes the clarity of development as a world-historical project possible. And when we foreground and focus on the subjects of development, this project blurs into the background as if people's biographies, desires, and needs have nothing to do with the powerful history of capitalist development. For me, the work of sociological reconstruction of development and its dispossessions in any given context require elaborating the relation between figure and ground.

As I use it in this book, Hopkins' world-historical method of studying figure and ground relationally is first and foremost a method of studying the construction of development in macro- and micro-scale. In his book, *Spaces of Hope*, David Harvey (Harvey 2000: 15) argues that 'Globalization is the most macro of all discourses that we have available to us while that of "the body" is surely the most micro from the standpoint of understanding the workings of society [...] But little or no systematic attempt has been made to integrate "body talk" with "globalization talk"'. To address alienation in the world today, Harvey (*ibid.* 2000: 49) argues, 'Ways have to be found to connect the microspace of the body with the macrospace of what is now called "globalization"'. Studying rural political theatre allows analysis of the practice of bringing the micro-space of the body into direct public confrontation with the macro-processes of state power and neoliberal globalisation.

But for me, studying development relationally is also a political and epistemic framework for problematising 'development' as an outcome of coercive relations of rule on the one hand and seeing it simultaneously as an incomplete hegemonic process always subject to tensions, struggles, and historical difference on the other. In this sense, to study development relationally, historicises the agency of Pal's question, protest plays, and the apparently fragmented criticisms of daily alienation which I argue expose and refuse epistemic closures of rule and hegemonic development. Studying figure and ground relationally, my larger research problematic is to consider the possibility of conducting an ethnography of the developmental state through the lens of political theatre.[9]

In suggesting this use of Hopkins world-historical methodology, I am guided by Philip Abrams' (1988: 58–89) methodological approach studying the state where rather than reify *the* state as those institutions that claim official state status as legitimate makers of state in society, he suggests studying processes of 'politically organised subjection'. Along with Foucault's concept of governmentality and Gramsci's vision that power is a practice and struggle rather than simply a capacity and ability to enforce will that is located in some place, body, or structure, Abrams' notion founds much of the de-centred scholarship on state-formation. The centrality of subjection in this decentralised view of power retains focus on the coercive and disciplinary force of state practices while rendering the notion of 'structure' as 'a matter of process in time' (Abrams 1982: xv).[10]

Recognising that hegemony is never complete, the state-formation literature variously blurs the boundaries between state and society, inviting analyses of practices of constructing state efficacy and the inevitable contingency and struggle of accomplishing rule (Joseph and Nugent 1994; Li 1999a; Mitchell 1991b, 1999). In the historical sociology and anthropology of state-making, legitimate authority is seen as the outcome of a struggle among people who claim equally legitimate meanings and values (Gupta 1998; Sivaramakrishnan 1999). In his book *Postcolonial Developments*, Akhil Gupta (1998) understands development and state practices as socially diffuse, contested, and negotiated processes shot through simultaneously with governmental and oppositional agrarian populism, indigenous modernity, and global governmentality.While Gupta's study of agriculture is rich in cultural politics, my ethnography of the developmental state studies rural lives and livelihood, agrarian place and futures through the lens of rural *cultural* histories, work, and practices.

What Philip Abrams'(1988) essay suggesting the analysis of 'politically organised subjection' meant to me was that I ought to be prepared to be doing an ethnography of the developmental state when I least expected that I was 'looking' at the state or development. Fiction, veil, and fetish notwithstanding, sociologists continue to know the state when they see it thus giving the state empirically bounded reality. Rural political theatre offers profound insights for studying and reimagining political action because political theatre is the labour of refusing epistemic and material closure accomplished and compromised to varying degrees. Thus, I view it as a significant mode of understanding the relationship between micro-space of the body and the macro-space of globalisation. Theoretically speaking, bringing Judith Butler's conception of performativity in relation to David Harvey's discussion of the body as accumulation strategy allows me to understand development dramas relationally — attending to micro-space and macro-space while revealing the incomplete consent given for hegemonic coercions and rule.

Disloyal Enactments: Refusing the Body as Accumulation Strategy

David Harvey's (2000) discussion of the micro-space of the body describes the body as an accumulation strategy which makes it both a space of capital as well as hope. He draws on Marx to argue that the labouring body is an essential strategy of capital accumulation as the body labours to produce surplus value. For this, the body must be disciplined into the rhythm and requirements of the working day, to the denials and dogma of individualism, and dissuaded from the possibility of collective organisation. Crucially echoing the larger argument in Marx's *Capital*, Harvey shows that the body is not just a strategic force for *producing* surplus value, but rather, the body is also reproduced by the fraction of such value that is *consumed* by the worker enabling the labourer to return to work and maintain the production of this value and capital accumulation. The marginal consumption of surplus value then enables the labouring body to be a force within the accumulation strategy. Harvey highlights the importance of capital accumulation to argue that recent studies of the body tend to focus on discourse, discipline and subjection without adequate attention to body as a space and strategy of capital accumulation. On the other hand, Harvey's understanding limits conceptualisations of power to the history of capital.

Seen in Harvey's terms, JS's political theatre is situated in circuits of capital, but they do not treat theatrical work or labour as an accumulation strategy. Their theatre is not performed for a price and their international theatre festivals are organised and paid for through fees which cover basic costs. The roughly one dozen members of the coordinating team are employees of JS. Funds granted to individuals such as Sanjoy Ganguly are poured into organisational work rather than accumulated as personal wealth. While their work is absolutely central to JS's reputation, survival, and strength, the modest salaries of JS employees cannot be characterised as capital accumulation. Their theatrical work questions the normalisations, disciplines, and shrinking possibilities for the villager in the contemporary conjuncture.

The theatrical form practiced is 'Theatre of the Oppressed' which is Augusto Boal's innovative translation of pedagogy of the oppressed into a theatrical vocabulary. Among Boal's techniques used commonly by JS, 'Forum Theatre' refers to the process of scripting plays by weaving together images portraying daily experiences enacted by participants in theatre workshops. Often Ganguly, and increasingly actors from agricultural backgrounds, weave these stories told in kinetic form during workshops into a short play on given social issues. The themes of plays build upon the political campaigns at any given time. The play is performed for an audience. A second enactment of the play uses a 'joker' who prompts the audience to re-script the play at any given stage of its telling. In the Forum Theatre format, audience members are encouraged to step on-stage to rescript roles, norms, and taken-for-granted interactions of daily life that lead to the extraordinary social issues being discussed. Boal's term for an audience member who intervenes in the play is spect-actor. I have on occasion witnessed 10-minute first enactments turn into three hours of discussion with scores of interventions from the audience. With these routine, kinetic debates witnessed publicly, JS aims to generate debate on alternate social norms and potentialities and make imagined possibilities daily material realities.

Boal's (1979: 127) theatrical methods aim to combat the 'muscular alienation' of oppressed bodies which serve capital accumulation. Scholars such as Philip Auslander (1994: 130) have rightly questioned whether it is possible for the body to exist outside ideological encoding. At the same time, the body in Boalian theatrical practice is perpetually in movement where the goal is to try on different masks, different ideological encodings (*ibid.*: 1994: 131). In JS's practice, the goal of trying on different masks is not multicultural inclusion, but rather to nurture critical and collective embodied thinking. Engagement in 'Theatre of the Oppressed' becomes a mode of questioning and problematising one's *particular* muscular alienation and ideological encoding.

Looking at rural cultural and political action to understand development as lived experience de-centres knowledge and power. Judith Butler (1992: 3–21) has argued that power has 'contingent foundations' and that any category (such as sex or state or consciousness) that we imagine to be foundational, stable, and embodied is only coherent and unified because people look for intelligibility, origins, and causes. Her study of repetitious enactments emphasising the performative constitution of gender identity highlights the fact that embedded in repetition is the possibility of refusing to play normative scripts loyally (Butler 1990). While scholars have applied Butler's theories to the study of racial and gendered discourse and identity formation, I am interested in applying performativity to analyse the structure and rule of the market episteme. Moreover, while Butler privileges the off-stage, I am interested in the relation between everyday performativity and staged performativity.

Looking through Butler's lens, definitions of 'development' can be seen as acquiring hegemonic status as an outcome of daily materialisation of regulatory norms. Like reified gender identity which rules daily actions, 'development' through the market episteme is a 'compelling illusion, an object of belief' created through daily normative practices of power with the outcome of organising subjection and with punitive consequences for transgressing dominant epistemic norms (Butler 1990: 271; see Abrams 1988).[11] As Timothy Mitchell has argued, the people, processes, and 'mechanisms that set up the separations' and punitive consequences for transgression 'precede [...] the separation itself' (Mitchell 2002: 6). The embodied materialisation of regulatory norms reaffirms the political authority of a market episteme for ruling a complex and diverse social world — making capital the most realistic, relevant, viable, and powerful optic and episteme.

JS's political theatre challenges the very mechanisms, people, and processes that set up the separations that constitute normative discourses. The theatrical labour and political work that JS is engaged in disrupts the seamless incorporation and use of the body as accumulation strategy. Despite their 'low' place in dominant political and economic scales, its workers encourage each other and audiences to refuse to play normative scripts loyally. Here collective engagement with theatre is the grounds for constructing solidarity. For example, choosing theatrical work over the structurally enabled path of 'cheap labour', asserting the right of peasants and farmers to intellectually debate the terms of development rather than acquiesce to structured impositions, questioning the exclusion of domestic violence from definitions of 'material distress', questioning the disregard for communal and private wellbeing, ethics, and emotional stability when provisioning rural employment — each of these are ways in which JS disrupts the loyal enactment of scripts of development in West Bengal. In so doing, they disrupt the performative materialisations that reinforce epistemic rule which in turn constructs appropriation and accumulation of surplus value as *the* goal of work.

While we attend to historical complexity and difference however, Hopkins' use of Marx's camera metaphor and Ferguson's cautioning reminds us of the post-structuralist trap of relativism.[12] Studying political theatre as power allows us to appreciate how, when, and why certain histories of power and pedagogy are rendered marginal or used within social and political formations. Since JS's theatrical technique of 'Theatre of the Oppressed' in theory assumes a stable position of 'the oppressed' while disrupting the category in practice, their work offers the opportunity to analyse a 'quest for collectivities of protest and transformation with a rejection of fixed, reified identities' (Sarkar 1998: 89). As I show in depth in chapter four, JS's practice however is not always about transgressing domination, hierarchy, and oppression from the assumed position of 'the oppressed'. Rather, JS's on-stage work stages each person as always and potentially 'oppressor' *and* 'oppressed'; their off-stage relationships show that reciprocity and hierarchy can construct affirmative social relationships and at other times be sources of division and individualism; that playing with representational power can be formative of struggle and can contribute to reifying structure. In so doing, they reveal the limits of hegemonic norms. They also publicly exhibit the 'dead ends' that actors and activists face in transgressing norms thereby revealing the limits of extending freedom. In this, they themselves historicise 'agency'. Viewing political theatre in this way as 'everyday forms of collaboration' (White 1986: 56) as much as everyday forms of disloyal enactments and refusals to play normative scripts loyally allows us to critically scrutinise 'those who want to limit freedom' as well as 'those who want to extend it' (Mahmood 2005: 10).

At Home, Out There

This book is based on multiple periods of fieldwork from 1999 to 2008. Two of these periods of fieldwork were conducted for dissertation research stretching from June through July, 1999 and the second from August 2000 through August 2001. The rest of the research was conducted during the summers of 2004, 2005, and 2006, as well as a two-month period in early 2008. During these phases of fieldwork, I travelled across various villages with JS theatre teams who engaged in two integral practices: performances and fieldwork. I conducted research in two districts of West Bengal — South 24 Parganas and North 24 Parganas. The ethnographic data of village life was collected in Pathar Pratima, Mathurapur, and Kulpi blocks of South 24 Parganas. Evidence of JS's administrative and organisational centre was collected in Badu, North 24 Parganas.

Every month, the coordinating theatre team comprised the most artistically skilled, those most able to give their time regularly to performances, and most invested in the making of JS's practice from various theatre teams came to Badu for workshops, rehearsals, and performances. This team routinely performed in Kolkata and outside West Bengal, showcased and represented the group's work to people who were not familiar with it.

While travelling was a routine part of capturing this group's work, I also visited and stayed for a week- or two-week stretches (at the most) in villages that I call Tarinipur, Kultala, Mehekpur, Lakshmipur, Sriramkrishnapur, and Chandpara in South 24 Parganas. These villages have been variously under Congress, CPM, and Trinamul Congress (the main oppositional party with the acronym TMC) panchayat leadership in the last four decades. They are dominated by Scheduled Caste populations. Tarinipur, Sriramkrishnapur, and Kultala are an hour's walk from the main highway that runs from Kolkata to Ramganga. Mehekpur is an hour-and-a-half walk from the main highway that runs from Kolkata to Kakdwip. Lakshmipur and Chandpara are also directly on this highway. Although the data also comes from other villages, these are the main sites of my research.

In each place, my social location and those of my research assistants no doubt shaped my interaction with people I interviewed. For example, while in Tarinipur I stayed at the Pal household which was the nerve center of JS activity there.They claimed Tarinipur as their site of success and this is where I first began my research. My perspective and insights into caste, class and party political relations in rural Bengal are shaped by living with the Pal's. Their neighbourhood was mainly middle-caste, lower middle-class in an area of South 24 Parganas district which has historically supported the Congress party and has increasingly shifted to the TMC. Rather than relying on one research assistant since 1999, I have had the privilege of drawing on the knowledge and generosity of multiple JS leaders, actors, and political activists. I used this strategy of multiple research assistants given practical exigencies as well as to draw on varied perceptions from regions historically dominated by the Congress and the CPM, variously animated by the memories of the Tebhaga movement, and CPM agrarian reform.

I often found myself feeling at home in these places which were alien to me. I was considered the authority about 'American' life and held equally accountable for its hegemony. I was supposed to know the going rate of domestic labour, vegetables, rice and clothes in Delhi. At the same time, people slipped quite seamlessly into the assumption that being Bengali, I understood what they meant. I was daily made aware of the fact that I was neither native nor outsider or perhaps that I was both. Through this constantly shifting position, I succeeded and failed in equal measure to understand what my presence amongst them meant. Mahesh Pal, more than anyone else and consistently, forced my theoretical commitment to reflexivity to take some concrete form. We walked miles and crossed many bumpy fields on his cycle. I say more in chapter four about his insistence that I learn how best to reciprocate what JS gave me. Yet I know that such reciprocity in our relationship (whatever form it has taken and will take over time) remains partial considering that research subjects could not have inverted this power relationship, stepped into my world and studied me.

When I was not in the villages, or Badu, or with the travelling troupe, I stayed alternately with family or in a rented room in south Kolkata.[13] I was thus able to seek solace and distance routinely. The lives and worlds in this book are a construct of hours spent in rooms in Kolkata, or later snowed in upstate New York winters, and still later surrounded by a beckoning new town in Kingston, Canada. In Kolkata, I periodically spoke to theatre critics and did research in the National Library, the library at the Centre for Studies in Social Sciences, and the *Natya Shodh Sansthan* in Salt Lake. But my primary source of data comes from my understanding of JS's cultural and political work and perspectives.

The types of primary data I collected include handwritten texts of plays, video-recordings of performances, photographs, semi-structured interviews, and field notes on performances, rehearsals, meetings, and protests. I also collected secondary source data such as survey reports and census data gathered by government institutions such as the Census Bureau, The Pratichi Trust, and the Women's Commission. Regardless of the range of this data, readers looking for a comparative study of CPM and JS's cultural work will not find it here. This book does not directly address what makes the LFG persuasive to most rural Bengalis. My approach to rural Bengali agency is to study everyday anomalous political action and everyday collaborations in constructing relations of rule, dispossessions of meaning, and epistemic exclusion. I do not claim that mine is the story of all or most rural Bengalis. But it is a story of many dispossessed meanings and epistemic exclusions that are rendered 'merely cultural' and too small to matter. For this reason, I focus on what I learned from observing and travelling with JS. Nor will theatre scholars looking for aesthetic analyses of plays find this in this book. I am constrained by my disciplinary training and I do not attempt an art historical analysis of dramatic texts that moved me in different ways. For example, while there is much scope for analysing the ways in which JS's plays draw upon multiple indigenous traditions and contemporary forms, I do not offer an analysis of how any given play is constituted. Rather I focus my analysis on the implications of their hybrid form on their cultural work.

Staging What is to Come

This study of development as 'dispossession of meanings' is cast in a number of different ways to understand the material and cultural processes through which rural life, collectivity, and future is constituted, battled, and comes to rule dramatic texts and ethnographic contexts in West Bengal. The study of dispossession of meanings is an effort to highlight what counts as 'material' and 'cultural' in the very process of defining development and reimagining political action in a given time and place.

In this analysis of dispossessed meanings and reimagined possibilities, three particular forms of dispossession constitute core thematic threads. These are (1) the dispossession of rural life, livelihood, and skills as valuable and possible ways of defining development in present West Bengal; (2) the exclusion of cultural practices and work (specifically political theatre) within conceptualisations of development, political action, and productive work in scholarly and political analysis; and (3) the misrepresentation and marginalisation of particular social formations, actions, and collectivities as religious or non-progressive and therefore outside the definition of 'development' by seeing these variously as expressions of complete subjugation, given to reactionary communitarianism, or autonomous indigenous practices vestigial to capitalist post-colonial modernity. The vehicle and focus for representing dispossessions of meaning in this book are the on-going struggles and practices that reimagine collectivity, development, and political action in Bengal.

This book reimagines rural political action, first and foremost, by questioning the normative conceptualisation of political action and democracy as an interaction between economic production indicators, government policies, and electoral victories. Tracing a short history of the use of theatre in anti-colonial struggles, nation-building, and post-colonial developments in India, in chapter one entitled 'Development Dramas and World-Historical Anomalies' I show how rural cultural practices have been written into and written out of the present and future. This chapter details my rationale for writing this book through the lens and focus of the political theatre and activism of JS. I characterise JS's theatre as rural political theatre which is singular for having nurtured theatre teams in villages, where rural citizens are actors and scriptwriters on-stage and these teams become nodes of generating political activism off-stage.

Their work combines multiple indigenous theatre forms with a technique called 'Theatre of the Oppressed' which is their primary method of performance. Neither 'street theatre' nor 'folk culture,' JS belies categorisation and invites routine misrepresentation. Moving away from prescribing certain ideological collectivities as agit-prop theatre had done, theatre of the oppressed gives 'spectators themselves opportunity to discover their own solutions to their collective problems' (Schutzman and Cohen-Cruz 1994: 2). I end the chapter describing JS's formation and types of activity to show that their rural political theatre is an anomaly that exists despite being written out of the categorical and historical canon of Indian political theatre.

In chapter two, entitled 'The Work of Political Theatre in a Democratic Place', I shift focus to academic debates in development and theatre studies. Undervaluing political theatre as an ephemeral form of safety valve action assumed to ultimately reinforce structure is an inadequate interpretation of the power and productivity of cultural and political work. Against these views, I argue that rural political theatre must be seen as productive work, political action, and recognised for its contribution to 'class' struggles in agrarian life. In the rest of the book, I show what we can learn about development, dispossession, and class struggle when we situate dramatic texts, modes of livelihood in agrarian societies, vote banks, and government policies in ethnographic contexts.

The second way in which this book reimagines rural political action is by valuing ambiguity and complexity in rural citizens' relationship to agrarian reforms and rural development as constructed by the CPM. So, for example, in chapter three, entitled 'Political Society in Formation: Staging Early Critiques', I show that decentralised development through the institutions of local governance and representation are both valued and contested. In this chapter, I study three JS plays each about various political collectivities that mirror Left Front governmental organisations — trade unions in the industrial sector, panchayats in the rural sector, and women's committees in the gender sector. These early plays show that although these bodies were objective organisational bases of constituting collectivity, the LFG bartered votes for welfare by normalising paternalistic, often compromised, and mercy politics — the hallmark of Partha Chatterjee's (2002, 2004) concept of political society. He has defined political society as the democratic politics of the urban and rural poor distinguished from civil society to which the middle class has access. But, unlike Chatterjee who by his own admission does not dwell on the 'dark side of political society', JS's plays and off-stage political activism insists on staging political society as the formation of its 'dark side'.

The second section of the book focuses on practice and ethnographic context. This book values the ambiguity *within* JS's goals, practice, and accomplishments as well as people's relation to their work. Chapter four entitled 'Spect-Actors of History' focuses on JS's practice and wrestles with a driving concept of Boalian theatre — spect-actors — who are engaged audience members that step on-stage to rescript plays in the forum theatre format. This chapter suggests the importance of situating spect-actors on-stage within socio-historical and life-historical contexts. These actors are not examples of the subaltern voice. Rather, JS's spect-actors of history inherit and grapple with, battle against and sometimes strengthen the regulatory norms of distance and deference inculcated through the multiple socialisations of urban–rural, class, caste, religion, and gender. The tensions in JS's consciousness-raising and pursuit of equality in everyday interactions and representations highlight the very nature of becoming a spect-actor of history as a contingent process of negotiating a world of representational inequality and dispossession.

This chapter also reimagines development and political action by seeing them as constituted by multiple sources of ethical action — from ethics leaned through faith to ethical norms socialised within the Bengali Hindu family. Fighting the political commonsense of secular political action as *a priori* liberation and familial relations and authority as *a priori* domination, JS leaders draw on these resources of social action, interaction, and relation for battling the normative temptations of a 'political society'. I study expressions of faith as it finds presence in JS's work as well as when it is inadvertently excluded from JS practice. To reiterate, representing faith is not an effort to recuperate subaltern authenticity. Rather than assume that such spaces of action are invariably communitarian claims, I am interested in the ongoing formation and intersection of various histories of power in India (Chakrabarty 2000; Dube 2002a; Ludden 2001; Sarkar 1998). Revalourising the time of gods in the time of capital is imperative (Chakrabarty 2000). However, I also focus on moments when development becomes mobilised as faith rather than reason (Dube 2002a) while showing how gods compel collectivity and solidarity within and against the structures of class and caste power (see chapter seven).

This brings me to the third way in which this book reimagines rural political action. That is, by taking seriously complexities within subjectivity and agency among rural Bengali citizens which do not neatly calibrate with the political economic positions and structures that would suggest coherence within subjectivities of 'class', 'gender', 'oppressed', 'the religious' and so forth. Perhaps this is because of the unrealistic expectation of coherence made of people to fit such categories of analysis. This is not to replace attention to political economic structures with methodological individualism. But rather, to take seriously the epistemic exclusions that reinforce normalisation and the refusals to live with closure that reveal political–economic 'structure' as malleable.

In the last three chapters, a methodological juxtaposition of off-stage and on-stage, text and context, official statistics and life historical narratives present a complex view on the ambiguous recent history of development in West Bengal. Focusing on people's experience of schooling, liquor production as mode of livelihood and revenue generation, and rural health care systems, I show that these building blocks of development assumed to be good and even sources of freedom, have ambiguous and contradictory value in rural citizens' words and worlds.

In Chapter five, entitled '"Spoiled Sons" and "Sincere Daughters"', I join others in contesting Amartya Sen's enthusiastic celebration of education as the first step towards development. Schooling is not an autonomous sphere of social life that inevitably leads to security and empowerment. This chapter studies the meaning of schooling in rural Bengali lives as it comes to be constructed through the structural realities of fragmenting agricultural land and family. The massive institutional push towards 'education for all' in India, and worldwide, focuses specifically on girls' enrollment in schools. While this initiative has increased enrollment and literacy rates, such outcomes must be situated within the ethnographic complexity of the contexts within which they are realised. I juxtapose statistical and survey reports of growing literacy rates, domestic violence, marital desertion, informalisation, and high unemployment rates with ethnographic evidence from JS's forum theatre performances to analyse the emergent speech about 'spoiled sons' and 'sincere daughters'. I show the dead end futures produced by schooling boys and by marrying girls off. I also reveal the re-scripted futures enacted on-stage that echo the ambivalent attitudes to schooling I encountered off-stage.

Chapter six entitled 'Have they disabled us?' addresses the sphere of production and income generation in agrarian households. In the context of capital flight, land and family fragmentation, in 2003, the CPM liberalised licenses for liquor production. As a lucrative business, actual liquor production far exceeds the available licenses producing a business that is as often illegal as it is legal. This chapter draws on interviews with liquor producers, anti-liquor protestors and liquor consumers' wives to argue that the compromised political society that the CPM has constructed in rural Bengal has led to a privileging of certain definitions of material distress over others, selective punishment of illegal action, and encouragement of certain forms of political action affecting others. Ultimately, JS encourages a fundamental rethinking of the parameters of choice in the contemporary historical moment. They dramatise the material distress of liquor consumers' wives to highlight the fact that the political choice to mobilise around the material distress of liquor producers and not liquor consumers' wives reveals the kind of collectivity the CPM constructs and the alternative that JS constructs. In so doing, they reveal the ways in which an anti-patriarchal praxis can construct a political collectivity, and class struggle that takes relational account of the material distress in the private and public household (*sansar*).

In the final substantive chapter entitled 'The Snake-Goddess and her Antidote', I highlight one basis of collectivity to which both the Leftist government and JS have a complicated relation — lived religion. Notwithstanding the spiritual lives of JS leaders and actors described in Chapter four, this chapter implicitly reveals the limits of JS's and my attention to religion. In this chapter, I follow a line from the play *Song of the Village*, 'Snakes live in the village, and the antidote lives in cities' off-stage into life-historical contexts where villagers respond to widespread death from snake bites, defunct rural health systems, and worship of *Manasa*, the snake-goddess. Modernising projects worldwide insisted that culture and tradition are antithetical to development. Today, spirited neoliberal projects want to take culture into account. They cannot fathom however, how snake goddesses can be antidotes for snake bites. When push comes to shove, the 'stubbornly superstitious' villager remains guilty of 'blind' beliefs. Drawing on field notes, secondary survey data, and interviews I show that the secularism of development blinds critical examination and dispossesses the meaning of lived religion.

Chapters five, six and seven highlight ambiguously valued development goods to show that certain forms of political action are rendered unthinkable and as lacking value precisely because goals such as livelihood, health, and education are mobilised articles of faith conceptualised through a narrow vision in development thinking. In West Bengal, commodifying and trading welfare by nurturing criminality and normalising the 'dark side' of political society contributes to excluding substantive transformation of inequality and violence. JS views the constitution of the dark side of political society as a primary means of CPM's divisive rule which combines with the individualising relations of the market episteme to effect power in West Bengal. They question the insidious and pervasive political negotiations which compel individual political aggrandisement, corrupt incomes, and criminal and violent means of survival as the dominant modes through which development and democratic political action intersect in Bengal. JS argues that normalising this kind of 'mercy politics' of political society dispossesses existing collectivities of their value and power by accepting violent and criminal relations among the poor.

JS attempts to construct a critical and collective political society that scripts modernity through practices of consciousness-raising and universalising citizenship. Yet their construction of modernity also self-consciously invokes divine histories of power and ethical practices from familial life to collectively protest the corruption of modern social relations and rational political collectivities. The conventional epistemic exclusions of these extant forms of political action amount to dispossession of meaning, limiting and coercing particular norms and conventions for 'development' in rural West Bengal. This book goes against the grain of dispossessions of meaning to rethink what counts as development and political action. JS leaders attempt to strike a balance between civil society which remains inaccessible to most rural and urban poor, and political society, which tends to make criminality and violence the viable core of social relations among the poor. They do so by reimagining and constructing an alternate political society which represents complex and ambiguous voices as valuable, thinkable, and legitimately possible grounds for fortifying new social relations and futures.

✷

Notes

* All photographs in the book are courtesy the author.

1. Tata has emblematic place in India's post-colonial development history as makers of everything from steel to tractors.
2. There are others who argue that the problem should not be treated as industry versus agriculture since the reality is far more complex where rural areas are not merely spaces of agricultural livelihoods (Mohanty 2007). But ultimately, in these views, 'development' remains captive to a market episteme defined as increasing 'productivity alongside full employment' (Mohanty 2007: 739). A stated assumption then is that development is about a shift from the relatively lower productivity of agriculture to relatively higher productivity of industry (*ibid.*).

3. All translations are my own.
4. This perspective sharply contrasts the argument made by Mritiunjoy Mohanty who claims that those who refuse compensation and protest land acquisition are part of the rural bourgeoisie (2007). According to Mohanty, Singur is an agriculturally prosperous region with a mere 17% of the population classifiable as peasants or farmers (Mohanty 2007: 78). Here, it is the rural bourgeoisie who stand to lose by accepting compensation for expropriation whereas small holders have accepted compensation since they have nothing much to lose. Even for Mohanty, the success of displacement as strategy for development depends on the ability to generate employment for the displaced which remains a deferred goal rather than a concrete end in sight, especially among populations less diversified in skills than Singur.
5. Dispossession is of course at the very origin of capitalist development. Karl Marx argued more than a century ago that the forceful expropriation of peasant populations from land through primitive accumulation produces a landless proletariat, privatised land, and the original impetus for the formation of capitalism, expanded reproduction, and growth. In his essay on 'Accumulation by Dispossession,' David Harvey (2005) brings Marx's ideas to the present to describe contemporary processes and forms of ongoing robbery. 'Accumulation by dispossession' describes the process of expropriation as an ongoing, stabilising mechanism which requires investing over-accumulated capital in one space, only to dispossess that place and its people down the road by investing in other spaces and people. The mobility of capital between sectors, spaces, and people as the fountainhead of ongoing accumulation produces a constant search for 'new' frontiers of dispossession
6. I am grateful to Vijay Prashad for helping me understand Kalecki's quote with greater clarity.
7. http://pd.cpim.org/2008/0204_pd/02042008_agriculture.htm
8. All names of people apart from Sanjoy Ganguly, Rima Ganguly and Rohini Mukherjee have been changed from the original. All names of villagers have been changed from the original.
9. Akhil Gupta (1995) coined the term 'ethnography of the state' focusing on interactions between lower level village officials and citizens in rural India.
10. Historians of the subaltern studies school have focused on ideologies of development as subjection suggesting how these ideologies have remained captive to an epistemological legacy of Western thought. They argue that modes and definitions of social engineering naturalised as legitimate definitions of development, equality and freedom inherit their supremacy and epistemic privilege by dint of Eurocentric colonial capitalism.

11. Suzan Seizer has shown how drama actresses in Tamil Nadu have fought the stigmas of public performance to reconfigure dominant definitions of good women, respectable wives, and Tamil women's relation to public space (Seizer 2000).
12. For example, Saba Mahmood studies women in the pietist movement in Egypt (2005: 40–43 and 65–66), but as Nosheen Ali (2005) puts it, Mahmood's study of the relationship ethics and politics nonetheless 'profoundly ignore[s] how state politics have impacted the ethical Islamic discourses that are practiced and promulgated in contemporary Egypt'. For Mahmood to pay attention to the differences and continuities between the pietist movement in Egypt and other uses of religion would not undermine claims of agency so much as historicise them within multiple cultural registers, social imaginaries and relations of rule.
13. For the sake of uniformity, I am using the new name of the city Kolkata as opposed to Calcutta even though some of the events and the research in the book took place prior to the change.

Chapter One

Development Dramas and World-Historical Anomalies

In conventional narratives of nationalist history and post-colonial development, rural citizens are seen as transmitters of indigenous knowledge, folk, or traditional culture by populists, Marxists, and conservatives alike. They are key political constituents in national elections, focal points of departure for modernisation theories, and subject to radical transformation in socialist narratives of history. Although they occupy a central place in the material and cultural formation of modern India, their agency in constructing political action and scripting development is largely occluded. In these representational conventions for conceptualising political action and development, rural political theatre stands out as politically and practically unthinkable. In this chapter I unravel the politics of representing rural cultural practices in colonial and post-colonial India, and the constructions of political action and development embedded in them. In so doing, I theorise the anomaly — rural political theatre — and situate it within material and representational inequalities.

I realised that rural political theatre is a world-historical anomaly through my research of the non-partisan cultural group, Jana Sanskriti (JS), working in the Indian state of West Bengal since 1985. While my focus is on JS, there are other such groups which perform primarily for rural audiences and whose work remains invisible to metropolitan audiences and cultural intelligentsia despite their popularity in rural and non-metropolitan areas (P. Guha 1996). JS's theatre invites routine misrepresentation and defies ready categorisation. For example, in March 2001, JS was invited to perform their plays in Kolkata by organisers of the 'Concern for Kolkata' Festival. This festival was held in the parking lot of the New Market in central Kolkata on a Sunday when the market was closed. The convenient location provided an opportunity for the middle- and upper-classes to attend the event. At this festival, JS shared space with other displays of Bengal's diverse artisans and their crafts — the *bankura* horse, *bat-tala* prints, *kantha* embroidery, brightly painted wooden toys, *batik* wall-hangings, and so on. JS members object to such showcased display of 'folk' culture and certainly do not characterise JS as such. At the end of the evening, there was a brief interview with the JS director, Sanjoy Ganguly, for the evening television news. The festival organisers, however, framed the interview by describing JS as a street theatre (*path natak*) group — another misrepresentation.

But to be fair to the event organisers, JS is not easy to recognise and categorise. Their work does not resonate with the connotations of either 'street', 'indigenous' or folk theatre. On the one hand, their actors are from agricultural households, and primarily perform for rural audiences, which is why they distance their work from the connotation of urban performance written into 'street theatre'. Although they do not characterise JS's cultural form as 'folk', individual actors and the group itself, they are immersed in and draw upon histories and practices of indigenous cultural forms. On the other, even though they draw upon myriad folk cultural traditions in their plays and perform primarily in rural areas, they cannot be characterised as indigenous theatre either, because they draw equally on some Brechtian methods while using Augusto Boal's 'theatre of the oppressed' as a principle mode of performance and politics. Their use of these forms makes JS's theatrical form recognisably more diverse than any one of its aesthetic and political sources.

Hybridity is hardly a surprising feature of modernity and contemporary cultural practice (Canclini 1995; S. Chatterjee 2007). Yet, the ongoing difficulty of recognising rural political theatre for the hybrid that it is suggests that rural culture is expected to fit squarely into the fold of tradition (see de Bruin 2001 for a similar characterisation of *kattaikuttu* performances in Tamil Nadu, and Seizer 2005 for the hybrid form of Special Drama in Tamil Nadu). The script of postcolonial development in India reads rural citizens performing in urban (or rural) space by default as performers of folk or indigenous theatre. I argue that this is because a particular categorical history and political vision makes rural political theatre an anomaly in India, and arguably, worldwide.

Showcased in post-colonial Indian cultural policy, regional folk forms in West Bengal have received patronage from the central and state governments since the 1950s. Some have interpreted this centralisation move as means for encouraging a 'race for recognition and integration into the mainstream' which in turn divided and conquered theatre workers among themselves (Arambam 2008: 5).[1] Seeing rural artists as embodiments of indigenous cultures incorporated into national museums, tourism, commodification, and ultimately distinct from modernity leaves little room for recognising rural cultural practices as contemporary political action. Rural Bengalis in particular are not supposed to be doing political theatre to question the political ideology and common sense in West Bengal. It is worth remembering that West Bengal is known for the loyal politics of its rural citizens who have kept the regional Leftist government in power for three decades. On the one hand, they are iconic beneficiaries of land reform, privileged constituencies of the Leftist government, and educated in cultural and political ideologies of the left.

On the other hand, in the political culture of West Bengal, unlike patronised and protected folk or indigenous culture, political theatre is seen as the enlightened politics of social transformation and consciousness-raising — the work of urban middle-class cultural and political intelligentsia. Political theatre scripted by urban directors has been performed in agricultural settings before — most innovatively in the work of the Indian People's Theatre Association (IPTA), and theatre directors such as Badal Sircar and Utpal Dutt in West Bengal (Bharucha 1983; Bhatia 2004; M. Bhattacharya 1983, 1989; Biswas and Banerjee 1997; Dharwadker 2005; Pradhan 1979, 1982, 1985). Nonetheless, here the role of directing and even acting was reserved for urban middle-class professionals and students; professional actors who played the roles of rural citizens. In this kind of political theatre, rural Bengalis themselves were rarely seen as actors, directors, and protagonists of political theatre — regardless of whether the performances themselves were in rural or urban spaces. Additionally, political theatre in the countryside might as well be invisible since theorisation relies largely on metropolitan political theatre to which most scholars have convenient access.

JS too has significant urban middle-class presence, role, and leadership within it. Nonetheless, the long-term work of creating theatre teams in villages has provided a regular space for nourishing talent, having fun, debating, and protesting for landless labourers, agricultural workers, and farmers. JS's work makes village theatre teams the centre of political action and theatre. As such, despite middle-class privilege and persona within JS, the structure of the organisation insists on the recognition that agricultural workers are subjects and spect-actors of history, rather than objects of historical inevitability. For this reason, labelling their work 'street theatre' is a predictable but unacceptable misrepresentation because it imposes political and aesthetic criteria of judgment which neglect the particular processes through which JS's work is produced and consumed. Given these representational and epistemic exclusions, the anomalous existence and practice of JS sheds light on what I call 'development dramas' (see Introduction), which signify the ongoing drama of scripting and accomplishing hegemonic processes of 'development'.

JS's political theatre is rare. But invoking its rarity to justify its insignificance leaves intact conventional definitions of political theatre, action and struggle, as well as conventional understandings of rural citizens and their ability to script power and the future. In this chapter I consider how 'rural' is represented and placed in imagining, constructing, and disseminating modes of being and becoming in India. In the next chapter, which is a companion to this one, I examine how theoretical debates — on class struggle, productive work, and state formation — constitute rural political theatre as anomaly. Needless to say, these modes of representation are mutually constitutive but nonetheless contribute to different modes of thinking and acting. Together, these two chapters construct the layers of this historical and theoretical anomaly to problematise the politics of represent-ing 'development'.

I begin this chapter by moving back in time to consider theatre's evolving relationship from colonial capitalist development towards national liberation, post-colonial development, and neoliberal globalisation. I focus on the way in which rural culture is constructed, the degree of acting and scripting power rural citizens are accorded, and what counts as political theatre. I then move on to describing the context of group theatres in West Bengal, focusing specifically on the work of Utpal Dutt and Badal Sircar because both these ground-breaking directors took on specific and innovative relations to theatre traditions and performances in rural spaces.

The IPTA, post-colonial patronage for regional folk forms, and group theatres in West Bengal each facilitated particular modes of being and becoming citizens of and in India. Each also offered a pedagogic and performative intervention in the ongoing making and unmaking of rural citizenship and identity. In so doing, they also helped demarcate the meaning, limits, and space of progressive, political theatre in West Bengal. JS emerges within the terrain of possibilities and limitations demarcated by this history of using theatre for political action in contemporary West Bengal.

Bhadralok 'Engineers of the Soul'

> For the Kolkata middle class of the late nineteenth century, political and economic domination by a British colonial elite was a fact. The class was created in a relation of subordination. But its contestation was to be premised upon its cultural leadership of the indigenous colonised people. (P. Chatterjee 1993: 36)

As colonial capitalism intersected with feudal systems of power, cultural practices patronised by princes and feudal landlords saw shifts in sources of financial support. The British elite contributed financially and aesthetically, constructing a theatre attached to a proscenium stage, enacting classic dramatic texts, theatre repertories, and commercial success. Yet, unlike Partha Chatterjee's (1993) narrative of subordination of native by colonial elite, Sudipto Chatterjee has argued in his book *The Colonial Staged* (2007) that the Bengali theatre canon must be understood as a hybrid one — neither purely native nor purely a mimicry of colonial masters. Experiments with demarcating the boundaries of appropriate content, form, and able actors characterised the Bengali canon as a hybrid construction in the late eighteenth and the nineteenth centuries.

The Hybrid Bengali Canon

The early colonial stage in Bengal tried and failed to capture the distinctive characteristics of 'native'. During the Bengal Renaissance, colonial rule was staged through the plays by Michael Madhusudan Dutta and others. Dutta's writings, ideological goals, and innovations insisted on liberating Indian theatrical traditions from the past judged against the standards of classics in European theatre (S. Chatterjee 2007: 69). In so doing, theatre of the Bengal Renaissance simultaneously claimed and renounced cultural sovereignty by recuperating from 'traditions' of Sanskrit and Bengali those elements that could, by European judgement, bring native traditions into a political modernity that would make them fit for self-representation.

Despite the experimentations with melding European and native, as Sudipto Chatterjee (2007) shows, racism, sexism, and classism indelibly shaped the hybrid creations of the Bengali stage. The exclusions central to liberal modernity were internalised by the Bengali intelligentsia's notions of culture. For example, although Sanskrit theatre and folk theatre such as *jatra* had common origins, the cultural intelligentsia of the Bengal Renaissance distanced itself from popular forms, seeing them as vulgar and tied to urban working classes (S. Banerjee 1989). By the last quarter of the nineteenth century however, a regional expression of Bengali nationalism was emerging through the valourisation (rather than outright rejection) of popular theatrical forms imbuing them with techniques, frames, and cathartic goals of European theatre. In some ways, this meant the racist and Orientalist project of European political modernity was being contested even while seeking inclusion within an exclusionary discourse of modernity.

While theatre was a mode of defining an emerging sense of nation under colonialism, it was equally an object for colonial control. This was as true in Bengal and India more generally as it was in other parts of the colonial world. The censorship of drama through the Dramatic Performances Control Bill of 1876 was the legislative outcome of nervous rulers.[2] One official, Sir Richard Temple, was convinced that plays were means of presenting events from the perspective of the natives with the aim of swaying public opinion. In his words, '[t]here is I think an obvious necessity for some power to prevent the acting of political plays. I can think of nothing more calculated to do serious harm than the acting of such plays at a time of political excitement' (quoted in Bhatia 2004: 38).

Not surprisingly, censorship affirmed the power of theatre for the Bengali elite who searched for and found safe genres and spaces of cultural practice to articulate their anti-colonial protest. In this search, the Bengali elite identified plays of religious content, which were exempt from censorship laws, as productive sites for appropriation, thus moving into the classical past and inventing a tradition of mythological plays set to contemporary themes. In this context of Orientalist rejection of *jatra* by Bengali intelligentsia and colonial censorship, Girish Chandra Ghosh (after whom JS named their organisational centre Girish Bhaban) offered an exemplary intervention for the Bengali theatre. In Sudipto Chatterjee's words, he tried to 'strike a mean between the somewhat realistic style of acting he saw at the British theatres and read about and the 'alienation' technique the *jatra* tradition had taught him' (2007: 160). Ghosh was also singular in taking Binodini Dasi on as a student despite her background in the red-light districts of Kolkata, training her to become one of the most famous actors of her time. JS's round performance stage at its organisational centre is called Binodini Manch.[3]

Ghosh's mythological plays had numerous characters that had access to divine truth for having shunned the materiality of bourgeois life. The historical plays of Ghosh and D. L. Roy in the late nineteenth and early twentieth centuries used heroic characters from Indian history to construct nationalist messages through critiques of Hindu orthodoxy, bourgeois, and colonial rule. Roy's *Neel Darpan* (The Indigo Mirror) broke new ground as a historical play that made the Indigo Rebellion of 1860 its subject.[4] It depicted work and life in the countryside for the first time, going against the grain of the urban bias of subject matter of plays at the time. The play vividly represented the inhuman treatment of the peasant. In response the colonial authorities censored the play and the Bengali intelligentsia promptly issued its apologies. Although the peasant voice was finally heard on-stage, as Ranajit Guha (1974) has argued, the problem was the profiteering European planters who did not embody the essentially good intentions of the colonial rulers. Despite its obvious protest of the peasant condition, this play ultimately expressed reverence for the rulers and viewed the planter's atrocities through a liberal lens (Guha 1974).

Bengali playwrights of this time critiqued colonial capitalism and colonial rule, but this critique helped constitute the hybrid Bengali theatre canon, contributed to giving shape to liberalism through the colonial encounter, and invented 'tradition' for these purposes. Sudipto Chatterjee argues that in these plays, 'the traces of sedition are counteracted with proper homage to the imperial seat of power' (2007: 234). While they inserted protest into drama and selectively critiqued authorities, these plays were not arguing for transformation of colonial capitalist rule. Not surprisingly, the plot and actors were essentially disconnected from peasant audiences and popular lived experiences.

Quest for Economic and Cultural Sovereignty

Much of this changed with the revolutionary theatre of the IPTA — the cultural wing of the Communist Party — in the 1940s. Genre and subject shifted again to reconnect with people and expressive traditions in the countryside. At this time, the Communist Party of India (CPI) which was formed in the 1920s, was the primary faction against the Congress Party. The Meerut Conspiracy Case of 1929 — when the British held a trial and accused communists of conspiring to overthrow the Raj with the help of the Soviets — played a significant role in briefly uniting the Congress together with the Communists.[5] This unity was short-lived because the Communists contradicted the Civil Disobedience Movement by supporting the Allies in the war against fascism. The united front of Indian resistance to colonial rule was torn asunder.

In this context, when the prisons in India were flooded with political prisoners of the Civil Disobedience Movement, middle-class theatre turned explicitly to the task of constructing a role for the masses in the fight for freedom. In 1936, the International Association of Writers held a conference for the Defence of Culture (against Fascism) in London where they devised a plan to write an encyclopedia on world cultures (Pradhan 1979: 13). Members of the Progressive Writers Association who became leaders of IPTA attended this conference in London and were enthused to write the entry for Indian culture (*ibid.*). IPTA's project of constructing Indian culture was not just a product of a nationalist movement's need to define national culture to ignite mass participation, it was also a response to an international struggle located in Europe that was battling the rise of fascist rule. IPTA reworked the existing valence and efficacy of theatre as entertainment with its aspirations of high culture into a political weapon for anti-colonial consciousness-raising and critique of colonial capitalism in a combined battle to achieve sovereignty and equality.

In this construction — drawing inspiration from international struggles — rural masses and their culture became particularly ripe grounds for a legitimate cultural claim to sovereignty because rural culture had a historic, and therefore 'authentic', rather than colonial, tie to land. IPTA's larger aim was to 'mobilise a people's theatre movement throughout the whole of India as a means of revitalising the stage and the traditional arts and making them at once the expression and organiser of our people's struggle for freedom, cultural progress and economic justice' (Pradhan 1979: 129). In its Draft Resolution the leaders claimed that this was not 'a movement imposed from above but one which has its roots deep down in the cultural awakening of the masses of India' (*ibid.*). Bringing together diverse languages, cultural practices and forms within the Indian subcontinent was an essential component of the project of collective consolidation against hegemonic colonial rule.

Although 'masses' connoted workers and peasants, the search for tradition was initiated with special focus on rural India because of assumed ties between culture and agriculture, land and past in the claim to national territory and cultural sovereignty. Despite pre-colonial trade and global flows during colonialism, representations by Indian economists and nationalist leaders mapped a 'national' space onto a 'national' economy (Goswami 2004; Trivedi 2003). The drain of the wealth from cotton farmers to Manchester was represented as a straightforward choice between British metropole and Indian hinterland: 'To whom will you give? To foreign mills or to our poor cultivators' (Trivedi 2003: 18). The Bengal Famine of 1943 highlighted on the eve of Independence that peasants bore the burden of colonial territorial conquest, capital accumulation, and imperialism. And the play *Nabanna* (New Harvest) captured the Bengal famine as an outcome of these world-historical relations. The longue durée[6] of accomplishing capitalism through a combination of territorial conquest and metropolitan industrialisation had produced a *similarly* longue durée of 'authenticating' a specific historical place for the rural subject in modernist, nationalist, and socialist narratives of struggle and social change.

Folk or rural indigenous culture arguably became particularly significant to the *bhadralok* because *rural folk* helped reconcile the socialist and nationalist projects of the twentieth century (Wallerstein 1989).[7] In IPTA's construction, the rural subject would simultaneously be the site of authentic tradition justifying a claim to sovereignty *and* the ultimate expression of disenfranchisement and exploitation in colonial capitalism. The first sees the rural subject as a cultural difference and repository of static past traditions and therefore the grounds for demanding territorial sovereignty. The second view suggests that raising rural consciousness regarding current exploitation within a global economy would be a means for claiming economic sovereignty and equality within a new nation.

IPTA's deployment of culture for political transformation demonstrates Partha Chatterjee's (1993) argument about nation-building being a middle-class phenomenon — a phenomenon which enabled the *bhadralok* to negotiate their position as rulers and ruled. IPTA leaders wrote plays representing the 'lived experience' of colonial exploitation and took these to non-metropolitan sites and villages to mobilise masses into consciousness and the fight for freedom (Pradhan 1979, 1982, 1985). The leaders had distinct ideas about how to make the lost cultural heritage 'progressive'. IPTA representatives also believed that this would make rural culture contemporary, 'revive the lost in that heritage by interpreting, adopting, and integrating it with the most significant facts of the people's lives and aspirations in the people's epoch' (Pradhan 1979: 129). As an anonymous critic argued,

> Progressive theatre cannot be suspected of anything but its inherent character: its clear-cut determination to be progressive. It is not, for instance, interested in who goes to bed with whom, or boy meets girl, boy gets girl. True, these developments are a part of life. True, the theatre's task is to entertain. But progressive theatre believes in projecting, examining, recreating or baring the ideologies of our day. It does not look away. And it also contrives to keep an expert eye on its ability to entertain its audience. (Pradhan 1982: 64)

In the process of naturalising the aim of political theatre, IPTA leaders also naturalised the subjects of transformation. After all, its project of repoliticising rural folk culture to fit nation-building aims for socialist futures needed stable subjects *to* transform:

> Now, those who wish to help this blossoming of the masses through the stage, will have to be aware of the real character and natural form of the flower, as well as keep in view the task of removing the dross. Hence their plays must not only be poetic, mystic, romantic, but pure realism must also be made spiritual. (Pradhan 1982: 121)

The question for a critical narrative of development dramas is of course what is the natural form of the flower, who gets to aid its blossoming, and how?

In time, IPTA's work increasingly became an effort of cleaning folk culture of its 'unhealthy' aspects. *Apasanskriti* (unhealthy culture) within rural culture, in its view, was disabling rural subjects from overcoming their condition. Predictably, it was definitions of *apasanskriti* guided by modernisation ideals and *bhadra* (literally: decent, genteel) mainly Hindu culture that directed projects of cleaning folk culture. Moreover, despite the above reference to giving pure realism spiritual form, as Rustom Bharucha has argued, IPTA understood spiritualism in secular terms because of the *bhadralok* agenda of reconciling nationalism with socialism (1999: 33–39). To these middle-class leaders, the contexts of producing and consuming folk culture mattered little. As a result, they led a struggle against colonial rule by defining rather than decolonising the place of rural citizens in the path to modernity and freedom.

This is not to say there was no internal criticism within the IPTA. Sachin Sengupta noted at an IPTA meeting in December 1952 that it embodied the limits of a *bhadralok*-dominated people's theatre where actors were ultimately urban middle-class citizens:

> in the dramas produced by them [the middle class], just as the rural liveliness of the village people or the *gana* becomes either artificial or stiff, or exaggerated, so also they cannot everywhere satisfy the *gana* or the masses either. The second weakness that is noticed is that characters are not taken forward to a logical development, through their own environments, but are dragged forcibly towards a pre-meditated development along a single track. (Sengupta in Pradhan 1982: 113)

In a profoundly contradictory essay, Sengupta argues that *a priori* definitions of 'people's culture' and ideology be removed because 'transformation of man is a historical truth' while insisting that 'darkness that spreads up to the horizon has to be removed with the lights of innumerable factory chimneys' (1982: 120–21). The outcome of industrial development will be the emergence of the 'natural form of the flower' (*ibid*). His writing highlights the problem of representing rural culture in the first decade after Independence when the *bhadralok* middle-class took on the reigns of rule. The track of nation-building, equality, and industrial development thus guided *bhadralok* representations of the rural subject and the task of social and cultural engineering. The documents on the Marxist cultural movement compiled by Sudhi Pradhan bear the traces of such contradiction in the project of social engineering over and over again.

Conflict within the IPTA eventually led to its dissolution. Artists within IPTA who agreed with its larger goals nevertheless challenged its mode of work. Some within it refused to see it as the subordinate cultural wing of the CPI and conceived the power of culture in its own terms. These artists saw the need for a cultural front led first and foremost by artists rather than politicians. These members eventually left to begin the Group Theatre movement in West Bengal. What brought IPTA members together for the best years of its work was the belief in the role of the middle class '[...] in mobilising and guiding the masses [...] who will also be engineers of their souls' (Ghatak 2000: 24).

For IPTA's early years, rural Bengalis were key people in an ideology about social transformation. G.P. Deshpande (1985) has described the IPTA's work as 'fetishising folk' by an alienated middle-class. Without the 'folk', the sincere commitments of the progressive elite's connection to soil and indigeneity had shaky material foundations. Yet there is scant information on what the audience actually made of such interventions. A rare reference to audience reception illuminates the problem of IPTA's performances: '[...] in the 24-Parganas district, a peasant leader (Khoka Roy) had rushed backstage to persuade performers to supply a commentary since the peasants could not understand anything' (cited in Bhattacharya 1989: 17).

The issue of who failed to understand what remains a challenging question. What we do know is that the IPTA represented the reconciliation between tradition and modernity, between socialism and nationalism for middle-class cultural and political activists in its grassroots politicisation of indigenous cultures for anti-colonial resistance. The need to define rather than decolonise 'rural' character and soul reveals an attempt at decolonisation abstracted from the lives of subjects. Political theatre incorporated rural culture without giving citizens control over means of representation. Indeed, because rural culture was the authentic tie to land and tradition for the *bhadralok* to mobilise in rhetoric and en masse for anti-colonial revolution, after Independence, rural citizens continued to be seen largely as occupying the space of tradition and past. They did not share one of the spoils of Independence that accrued to urban citizens — their recognition as coeval producers of the future and critics of Indian modernity.

From Revolutionary Theatre to Postmodern Despair

Post-Independence national policy scripted the role of culture in distinctively Nehruvian terms which emphasised regional diversity of traditional cultures united into a national identity, a trend which lasted till the late 1980s. True of most of Jawaharlal Nehru's nation-building ideas, in the realm of culture too, a spectacular effort was made to consolidate creative forces under one centralised rubric. Nehru himself became President of the three cultural institutions inaugurated in New Delhi — the Sangeet Natak Akademi, the Lalit Kala Akademi, and the Sahitya Akademi. These institutions took on the form and content of the Nehruvian ideology especially under the directorship of Ebrahim Alkazi (Das Sharma 1995: 9).

Post-colonial development harboured a profoundly ambiguous relation to rural space and culture. On the one hand, the Indian theatre canon was reinvented in classical terms, and on the other hand, rural cultural practices so key to the anti-colonial rhetoric and revolution were incorporated into a narrative of national unity in diversity. If the core of IPTA's ideology focused on rural masses and the progressive transformation of their culture, the core of constructing a national culture in the post-Independence period focused on the traditional and classical. This shift represented a move back to elite traditions as the core of an Indian performance aesthetic. Notwithstanding anthropological and linguistic evidence that the classical and folk were constructed in dialectical relation (Marriott 1990), there was a shift from folk to classical as central markers of cultural policy and the exclusion of rural cultural practices from definitions of 'indigenous' traditions for a national culture. The heritage that mattered to nation-building now still belonged to the past, but the complex work that 'rural culture' had done under colonial rule as rooted in the past, tied to land, *and* exploited in the present was dispossessed of valence in the dominant imaginary. As Aparna Dharwadker (2005) has shown, in *Theatres of Independence*, the defining feature of national culture was an invented heritage of cultural glory.

At the same time, the decades after Independence witnessed intense periods of creative experimentation with 'theatre of roots' through which urban playwrights erased the present and the modern in a cultural nationalism that relied on reinventing classical literary theatre traditions and idioms as national theatre

(Dharwadker 2005). The marginalisation and ambiguous appreciation for rural culture was apparent in 'folk' performances which viewed living traditions of the village as resilient markers of material survival in the face of urban drain on resources and the unified pursuit of development (*ibid.*: 311). Regional folk traditions were celebrated in festivals organised with central government funding as rich, vibrant, varied markers of India's diversity within an assumed unity in the 1950s and 1960s. The centralisation produced a 'race for recognition and integration into the mainstream' which in turn divided and conquered regional theatre workers among themselves (Arambam 2008: 5). But in folk festivals, rural cultural practice and citizen no longer featured as rationale and subjects of an imagined future of equality and sovereignty.

As in other post-colonial contexts such as Kenya, so in India, folk theatre was recognised as a powerful site, and historically inherited styles of indigenous cultural struggle animated by land struggles, agricultural rhythms, open air performances, and accessible expressive traditions in oral cultures (for Kenya, see Kidd 1983; wa Thiong'o 1998). For a national cultural intelligentsia, 'folk' represented a dynamic and profoundly promising counterpoint to the colonial segregations of urban theatrical spaces and styles. This view of 'folk' systematically neglected to see it as equally a construct of post-colonial segregations and representational inequality.

Aparna Dharwadker canonises four categories of post-colonial experimentations with folk theatre: those playwrights who study and draw on folk material as resources in their plays; those who go beyond 'add and stir' of folk materials to weaving folk narratives and conventions in specific plays; those who rescript and present well-known older folk plays; and those who represent classical and European plays in folk idioms (Dharwadker 2005: 313–14). Each of these trends in experimentation can be canonised as India's na-tional theatre because they generated an explosion of recognition and interest in folk, as well as a fascinating corpus of plays and conventions.[8] A stagist narrative of history and development marked the rationales of those who experimented with *folk forms* and wanted to give them contemporary relevance, and those who refused such experimentation arguing that the context supporting these forms had been left behind. Dharwadker finds that contemporary playwrights had a diversity of rationales for experimenting with folk — its emancipatory potential, its relation to myth and religious consciousness, its ability to combine various arts into a single performance, and its reliance on text and performance. Ultimately she sees these experimentations as a syncretic contemporary form representing urban folk theatre rather than rural theatre. After all, barring two experiments — Habib Tanvir's Naya Theatre and Subanna's Ninasam — none of the experiments with folk theatre has rural actors nor performs in rural locations (*ibid*.: 323).

The particular invocations and use of folk form in West Bengal reveals continuities and differences with this agenda of experimenting with and institutionalising 'folk'. Here, Utpal Dutt, an erstwhile member of IPTA, was renowned for taking plays to rural audiences, performing revolutionary plays in the *jatra* style. His aim was to politicise rural indigenous forms by modernising them in a socialist narrative. Giving new direction to IPTA's legacy, Dutt's socialist revolution showed the continuities between events in classical mythology, colonial history, contemporary imperialism, and the current predicaments of Bengali citizens. Yet, he was beholden to a binary representation of class struggle where the exploited were presented in stark opposition to exploiters. Dutt's deployment of folk form for Brechtian political effect placed inordinate faith in the possibility of showing the path of grand historical change on the Bengali stage. His progressive aesthetic using satire and humour revealed the embodied and historical oppositions of oppressed and oppressor (Bharucha 1984).

In a style significantly contradicting Dutt's theatre for revolution in West Bengal, Badal Sircar's Third Theatre focused on the alienated post-colonial middle-class and its incarceration within a historical subjectivity that disabled it from leading or participating in revolution with the masses. Rustom Bharucha (1984) has analysed contributions made to the post-colonial stage by Sircar's innovations. Bharucha argues that although Sircar's original vision made powerful contributions by revealing the poverty of the middle-class imagination and commitment, his plays themselves became increasingly stylised and abstract rather than contextualised and relevant to the problems of marginality and exploitation. Sircar was among few playwrights of the time who bothered to adapt and perform his plays in rural spaces. Yet, epitomising the post-modern dilemma of critiquing authority without envisioning an alternative political vision for the future, he represents a stage in West Bengal's development dramas that was at once refreshing and debilitating. Refreshing, because his plays did not search for a consciousness and 'culture of the oppressed' that would resolve a national and socialist future. And debilitating, because there was no alternative vision at hand — just new experiences of colonialism, capitalist exploitation, and alienating rule.

By the mid-1980s, Partha Chatterjee (1997) argued that political theatre had lost its relevance in West Bengal because its dominant envisioning is by middle-class playwrights patronised by the Leftist government. He counters the widespread claim in these group theatre circles that people in Bengal are sick of politics and thus prefer the tinsel of commercial productions to political theatre.

> It is far more likely that the audience is tired of the *kind* of theatre served up to them in the name of political theatre. What was new in the late 1960s and early 1970s is now hackneyed. The plain fact is that the practitioners of political theatre in West Bengal have nothing new to say. They are unable to talk about politics as something that is immediate, relevant, and lively. (Chatterjee 1997:114)

And this he goes on to say is despite the inducements from the Left Front Government (LFG), more than any previous government, to group theatres in West Bengal. Chatterjee suggests that this is less of a paradox than an illustration of the designs, censorship, and even violence of the state which ruled out forms of struggle and political interpretations that were outside its ideological order.

> The artistic crisis is more the result of constraints created by the very fact of the existence of a Left establishment in power. Just as workers' or peasants' or students' movements have lost their militant edge, in much the same way political theatre has lost its bite, the sharpness of its critical gaze, its precision in identifying targets, its capacity for satire and irony, and the nobility of anger. The subjects today are abstract, general, not too immediate: the treatment vague, cautious, blasé. If people seem tired of political theatre, it is not because they have suddenly forgotten their politics. It is because the practitioners of political theatre lack the artistic courage to talk about the politics of the day. (Chatterjee 1997: 114–5)

Narratives of this kind describing the end of political theatre in West Bengal are not isolated claims. Darren Zook (2001)makes a similar argument about political theatre in Kerala which competes to out-farce the farcical and increasingly complacent Leftist politics. About political theatre in the British context, Baz Kershaw (1999) argues that theatricality has so permeated everyday life that live political theatre performances no longer embody an alternative space. In a counterclaim, Randy Martin (2006) argues that to declare political theatre dead is akin to declaring the state dead. The pervasiveness of theatricality makes it all the more important to study live performance and political theatre *in relation to* the theatricality of power, rule, and domination. With this view of the contemporary historical conjuncture and its relationship to political theatre, I turn now to JS.

Jana Sanskriti

Practicing in West Bengal but excluded from LFG patronage and attention, JS is a singular and anomalous political theatre group. JS's Director Sanjoy Ganguly told me that they are rendered marginal because they are invariably judged against existing reputable, progressive forms in West Bengal. He said,

> The story is that JS is non-Marxist and against Brechtian epic. In West Bengal when you say non-Marxist that means non-progressive. Now if you say this in progressive circles the idea is that we are not progressive. And yet I know Left politics, I was a part of it in the past. Just because Badal Sircar is more extreme Left and CPM is considered revisionist this is the story that is spread. How is it that the only group in West Bengal that has worked in villages consistently does not get attention or funds from the state government? The Academy never requests a workshop. If this was any other state, our work would be much more well-known. (11 April 2001)

Part of the reason for the lack of recognition is that few commentators on JS's theatre have actually witnessed their rural theatre teams at work. On occasions when JS has performed for urban audiences, they are mistakenly labelled 'street theatre' by the cultural intelligentsia as in the opening anecdote to this chapter.

When viewed as street theatre, rural Bengali actors and activists are judged as more or less 'progressive' versions of the existing street and group theatre traditions patronised by the ruling Left and professionalised by the urban middle class. This label is a predictable but unacceptable misrepresentation because it neglects the particular processes through which JS's work is produced and consumed in the countryside. Excluded from institutional modes of recognition and representation, their work represents a fight against the de-politicisation of both rural citizens and political theatre in West Bengal. The symbolic value of the organisation interrupts and intervenes in a narrative of development that excludes some citizens/actors from the creative work of scripting power and political plays. I turn now to some of the basic characteristics of this organisation.

JS was started by an urban middle-class Bengali man — Sanjoy Ganguly. He worked as factory middle-management and was involved in trade union politics till the early 1980s, when he quit union politics and his job to begin life as a full-time political activist and social worker in urban slums. The search for an adequate political practice to fight his disillusionment led him to explore rural issues, which slum inhabitants described as the source of their urban problems. Ganguly spent two years travelling extensively in rural Bengal trying to understand life in villages. He also exposed himself to various political philosophies and ideologies from popular figures of Bengali spirituality — Lalan Fakir and Ramakrishna — to the revolutionary writings of Marx.

In 1985, JS was formed as a cultural organisation that addressed specific issues faced by agricultural workers and women through theatre. Today this organisation is composed of three urban, middle-class members, and over 750 agricultural and wage labourers in West Bengal. JS's rural members come from landless to middle class and low-(or Scheduled Caste) to middle-caste families. Three out of 10 people in the central coordinating committee of JS are from non-agricultural backgrounds. All these central committee members have had affiliations with a range of regional political parties. Five out of 10 coordinating team members are women. Like the historic actress Binodini Dasi who struggled with great difficulty to reconcile her aspirations of an acting career with aspirations for marriage to nurture multiple modes of belonging in the early twentieth century, four out of the five JS women actors and leaders remain single. Beyond the coordinating team itself, it is constituted by an approximately equal number of (predominantly but not exclusively Hindu) men and women. With the exception of coordinating team members who work as full time actors and activists for a modest monthly salary, all JS workers have livelihoods dependent on agriculture, and approximately three-fourths of JS members are dependent on selling their labour for subsistence needs. Most JS members do not do theatre or political work for a living. At the same time, JS's theatre does provide employment and supplementary income for some of its activists and actors.

After a relatively itinerant existence, in 2000, JS built its organisational centre in a suburb of Kolkata called Badu. There are two integral *practices* to JS's work: performances and fieldwork. Together with theatre team members of villages of South 24 Parganas district (primarily Mathurapur, Kulpi and Pathar Pratima Blocks), JS's coordinating team of leading actors and activists share the tasks of scripting plays and challenging power relations off-stage so that political and cultural activism feed each other.

The first practice involves rehearsals, theatre workshops, enactment of plays, engagement in Forum Theatre (explained below), and organising religious/cultural festivals.

The second practice, fieldwork, involves calling meetings, debating and brainstorming sessions, and 'ideological training' aimed at building coherence and continuity across seasons and disparate village communities. Village theatre teams are also engaged in political campaigns and bargaining with *panchayats* for the right to

Figure 1.1: Rehearsals in Tarinipur village in the community performance space built in 1997 through JS mobilisations

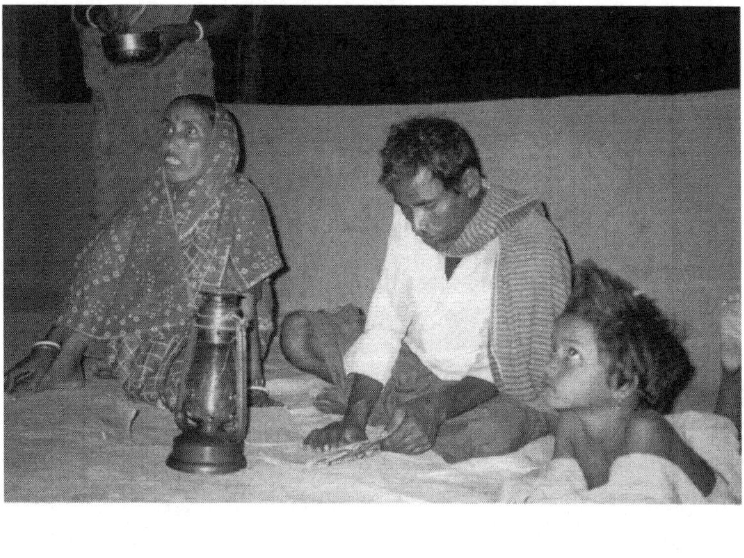

Figure 1.2: Strategising political action across villages at Sriramkrishnapur

cultural spaces, fighting dowry and domestic violence, mobilising anti-liquor agitations, employing local artists to perform in *jatra* and *gaajan* (folk theatre forms) festivals, and demanding the right to work in their villages.[9]

It is noteworthy that JS has never received institutional funds as an organisation for its theatre work. It has thus far run on donations from friends, door-to-door resource-raising, and a one-time MacArthur fellowship to Sanjoy Ganguly as an individual practitioner. Their funding for building the JS centre in Badu came from the Human Resources Ministry of the central government of India.

In 2001, JS began to receive funding to institute and manage pre-primary schools. Although this is clearly in the model of providing a development good, JS views schooling in continuity with its theatrical work, joined as they are by pedagogical goals. Money for these schools has come from corporations such as ICICI bank and Tata, a domestic conglomerate. JS coordinates approximately 150 'learning centres' which are basically pre-primary schools servicing approximately 3,750 children from 150 villages and giving employment to 150 women in the age group of 20–35 years. It views its work in pre-primary schooling as a temporary intervention, as long as the funding lasts. They are not willing to continue their work in the education sector at the cost of their theatre work. Rather, they are working towards making them complementary by bringing the issue of public education on-stage. Their commitment to education is first and foremost to 'make education people's agenda' in Ganguly's words, rather than allowing the rampant privatisation of education while public school teachers neglect their commitment to quality education.

Tata funding for JS work no doubt raises questions because Tata is the very domestic corporate group that they critique in their play *Unnayan* and a key beneficiary of the ruling Left's coordinated expropriation of agricultural land.[10] Does the funding for pre-primary schools allow JS to be incorporated into Tata's public display of corporate social responsibility? This funding has not stopped JS from being on the public frontlines of protest against land expropriation in Singur and Nandigram. Their play *Unnayan* makes no secret of who is to blame in the expropriation of agricultural land. Indeed, Tata is depicted as controlling the West Bengal finance minister and chief minister (see Figure 1). The JS public protest against their own funders is plain for all to see. Moreover, for JS, Tata and the LFG only happen to be the object of recent protests. The larger critique is of the kind of aggressive capitalism that requires the government to succumb to undemocratic practices.

Still, JS leaves itself open to critique for accepting funding from a sullied source. But rather than pretend that they are not tied to circuits of capitalist development, their dramatic protests on- and off-stage are a refusal to temper critique and maintain some control over the terms of their funding. Ganguly is at pains to establish that Tata has never intervened in the JS agenda. This enables JS to use their insertion into circuits of capital for rural employment and for enhancing the quality of rural schooling in West Bengal, while critiquing the insertion of Tata's capital when it dispossesses agrarian *futures* and peasant livelihood. Either way, the analysis of their cultural work shows that processes of production and rule hardly bear stark oppositions to the processes of resistance.

JS cultural festivals typically involve performances of their plays, which are a mélange of forms ranging from the 'local' to the 'global'. In the late 1980s, Sanjoy Ganguly came across Augusto

Boal's 'theatre of the oppressed'. Among the various methods that constitute Boal's theatre, 'forum theatre' refers to the process of scripting plays by weaving together images portraying daily experiences enacted by participants in theatre workshops. Often Ganguly, and increasingly non-urban middle-class actors, weave these stories told in kinetic form during workshops into a short play on given social issues. The themes of plays build upon the political campaigns at any given time.

The play is performed for an audience. A second enactment of the play uses a 'joker' who prompts the audience to rescript the play at any given stage of its telling. In the Forum Theatre format, audience members are encouraged to step on-stage to rescript roles, norms, and taken-for-granted interactions of daily life that lead to the extraordinary social issues being discussed. Boal's term for an audience member who intervenes in the play is spect-actor. I have on occasion witnessed ten-minute first enactments turn into three hours of discussion with scores of interventions from the audience. With these routine, kinetic debates witnessed publicly, JS aims to educate alternate social norms and possibilities and make imagined possibilities daily material realities.

Since 1985, JS has grown in other districts in West Bengal and built alliances with people's movements elsewhere in India. They now have theatre teams in the states of Delhi, Gujarat, Tripura, Uttarakhand, Maharashtra, Goa, Jharkhand, Madhya Pradesh, and Orissa. Each of these theatre teams are an outcome of an initial request for a theatre workshop by a mass organisation to Sanjoy Ganguly. He and other coordinating theatre team members travel to conduct these workshops in various parts of India, and increasingly abroad, teaching people the embodied vocabulary of 'theatre of the oppressed'.

At a JS Festival in 2004, the team from Gujarat performed a chilling play called *Danga* on the post-Godhra carnage, the Tripura team performed on the challenges of daily life in the midst of the insurgency, the Maharashtra team comprised of Katkari tribals performed a play on the challenges at the ration shop, with the local political leader and at the landlord's fields and so forth.[11] At another Festival in October 2006, a Federation of Theatre of the Oppressed was formally constituted as a collective of cultural groups and people's movements from 12 states in India.

These festivals allow JS to experience itself as a collective of locally grounded struggles that share their critiques and imagined strategies with each other. They have also brought to India scores of practitioners and performers of 'theatre of the oppressed' from Pakistan, Palestine, Brazil, Spain, France, the United States, and Great Britain. While there continue to be very real hindrances of language at these festivals, a shared vocabulary of theatre that insists on spectator participation helps generate the collaborations among cultural workers across borders and inequalities of post-colonial development. The effectiveness of JS's growing international network is beyond the scope of analysis here. As JS's work expands in scale and reach, can it replicate the depth and strength of its work in the rural Bengal context? As they grow, how vigilant can they be regarding the problematic use and abuse of 'theatre for development' (Plastow 1998)? This remains to be seen and studied taking into account the different contexts within which the use of theatre is incorporated into political struggle.

There are significant differences and continuities in the context within which Boal's theory emerged and the ones in which theatre of the oppressed is practiced worldwide, impacting characterisations and critiques of the theatrical form. These evolving differences and continuities reveal the degree to which this theatre technique is constituted by the histories of power in a particular place. Boal's 'theatre of the oppressed' is of course based on Paulo Freire's ideas on 'pedagogy of the oppressed' (Freire 2000). Writing in the context of military dictatorships and post-colonial inequalities in Brazil, Freire drew on liberation theology to develop a pedagogy that would actively fight the banking concept of education where students are conceived as passive receptacles of information servicing a capitalist society. He redefined literacy as acquiring the critical capacity to read the world. Like some popular religious movements in India and liberation theology in Brazil which gave humans direct access to god, this educational theory allowed all humans direct access to the process of constructing knowledge. Augusto Boal wrote *Theatre of the Oppressed* in the 1970s, also combating military dictatorship and neocolonialism in Brazil. Boal articulated a poetics that responded to authoritative structures by translating into a theatrical process Freire's commitment to the praxis of reading the world and con-structing knowledge-systems collectively.

Boal was part of the Workers' Party in Brazil when he developed *Theatre of the Oppressed* and continued to be committed to this party and further developed direct political intervention through his Legislative Theatre (Boal 1998).[12] He drew on Brecht's understanding of the purpose of theatre for bringing socialist revolution but went beyond Brechtian techniques of encouraging audience response. His theory took the ideals of socialism and inserted democratic participation into aesthetic form. Boal's signal contribution — the spect-actor — nurtures and brings the creative powers and critical thinking of audience members onstage into a process of rescripting a play. In principle, it insisted on multiple possibilities generated in particular contexts through modes of reflection upon social and historical location — or praxis. Boal constructed a model of aesthetic practice committed to constructing collectivity, which did not assume a prescripted future for all.

This theatre, especially Forum Theatre, became increasingly popular through the 1980s and 1990s in disparate contexts all over the world.[13] The last two decades have witnessed a dramatic increase in funding for those who use theatre for development. In each context, different traditions of existing political theatre combine Boalian method with interactive indigenous forms of cultural practice thus producing community theatre, theatre for development, and grassroots subaltern theatre, as the case may be. Ironically, a democratic mode of political education and action can also become a 'democratic' tool for delivering development messages. In certain contexts theatre has become an effective communication mechanism for delivering prescripted visions of development and liberation where theatre fits neatly into a 'service-delivery' model of development (Ahmed 2002; Kerr 2003; Plastow 1998).

This is the danger of a form of politics that emphasises a humanist position which 'assumes a type of equality that is obviously not there' (Taussig and Schechner 1994: 30). Problematic incorporation of 'theatre of the oppressed' into circuits of international capital apart, more importantly, the content of 'development' as scripted into theatre for development is not always subject to *in situ* definition. In this kind of use of theatre for implementing prescripted definitions of development, some of the basic methodological principles of Boalian theatre are violated. Rather than encouraging contingent construction of people's problems as they see it, theatre becomes one cog in an 'anti-politics machine' — James Ferguson's (1994) term for the depoliticising institutional and discursive apparatus of development policy and practice.

The comfortable collaboration between theatre and depoliticised notions of development have encouraged theatre scholars and practitioners to document its 'uses and abuses' in Ethiopia and Eritrea while scholars in Bangladesh have 'wish[ed] we could have a world without Theatre for Development' (Ahmed 2002: 208; Plastow 1998: 97–113).[14] The co-operation between political activism and neoliberal development through a decentralised state contributes to 'unstated contradictions' (Feldman 1997: 46–65) and more specifically a rationale that declares political theatre dead. The challenge, as I see it, is to rethink how we know political theatre and political action when we see it. We cannot deny the politicising possibilities that can and do exist within cultural practices in an increasing commodified world. Nor can we assume that a cultural practice is progressive by dint of theoretical or ideological claim. Indeed, a depoliticised veneer can accomplish political representation in practice, notwithstanding dilemmas and contradictions.

Power does not somehow disappear on the Boalian stage. The 'structured unpredictability' of the Forum Theatre ritual is situated within power relations (Forester 1996: 323). On JS's stage, as some constraints are relaxed to enable the process of imagination and stepping out of oneself, other hierarchies and histories of power are given dramatic public force. The process of transformation that it initiates must therefore be studied by looking at on-stage in relation to off-stage in order to capture and specify 'who comes to create new relationships and act on new commitments in actual practice' and how they do it (*ibid.*). Precisely because categories of liberalism and humanism mark this theatre, I go beyond the claims and principles of progressive theories to study its meanings in the lives of people. Ethnographic analysis, attention to spectators and spect-actors, the relation between off-stage and on-stage practices become key methodological devices to accomplish such a task. I say more on the ambiguity and complexity of JS's practice in chapter four.

Conclusion

I have tried to show in this chapter that theatre has been reorganised and used, from a variety of perspectives, as a tool for constructing resistance, empowerment, and development in colonial and post-colonial India. In its capacity to imagine, construct, and disseminate modes of being and becoming, theatre is formative. It has helped shape and rework colonialism and national liberation, post-colonial citizenship and subjectivities, nationalism and neoliberal globalisation. Through these transformations, I have argued that 'rural culture' gets written into and out of colonial and post-colonial cultural and political representations in ways that ultimately deny rural actors a dialogical place and coeval presence in development dramas. Evolving categories of analysis and processes of representation render rural political theatre anomalous and anachronistic.

Tracing the history of these development dramas provides an explanation for why JS's theatre comes to be misrepresented and misunderstood in contemporary West Bengal. This anomaly suggests that a 'surplus of meanings and practices is always available for articulation' even though they are dispossessed of meaning through representational inequality (Sivaramakrishnan 1999: 7). We must understand this surplus of meanings *in relation to* state power rather than as external to it. JS's anomalous theatre is not always a site of resistance that stands apart from forces of rule and dispossession. Rather, as an anomaly, their theatre draws on multiple cultural forms, histories of power and relations of rule even as they reveal that dominance and hegemony is tentative and constantly compromised in contemporary West Bengal.

Seeing the Bengali state as 'a unified symbol of an actual disunity' (Abrams 1988: 79) suggests that political theatre and political economic processes of development both produce and disrupt ongoing development dramas and processes of rule. JS's existence and growing strength despite ruling discourses to the contrary establish this anomaly and the dominant terms of using theatre to politicise rural culture as mutually constituted and mutually thwarted outcomes of Bengali political society and development dramas (Sivaramakrishnan 1999: 30).

✷

Notes

1. National cultural policies in India, as elsewhere, invariably combined inclusions with exclusions, incorporation and folklorisation, centralisation and marginalisation as they imagined national culture (For excellent studies of the dialogic production of emergent national culture and canons see Dharwadker 2005 and Dalmia 2006, for India; for Tanzania, Askew 2002; for Brazil, Williams 2001; and for Venezuela, Guss 2000).

2. Nandi Bhatia has shown in her book *Acts of Authority/Acts of Resistance* that the consolidation of British colonial powers came to be, at least in part, formed as a direct reaction to the emergence of political theatre as a weapon in the hands of the Bengali elite (2004). This weapon was perceived by the British to have perilous, and not entirely predictable power.
3. Despite her fame, Binodini suffered great humiliation and disappointment both from audiences as well as her closest mentors. The act of bringing women on-stage could just about be tolerated for prostitutes, but it could not co-exist with the normative prescriptions of marriage and motherhood for women. Thus, a woman such as Binodini who had aspirations of being actress and wife faced censure and humiliation.
4. Indigo plantations were a significant source of commercial agricultural profit in colonial Bengal in the early nineteenth century. The plant was grown for its blue dye used in the textile industry. The tenant cultivators were forced to grow this cash crop in adverse conditions while the surplus was appropriated by Europeans planters. When indigo prices fell in the mid-nineteenth century, the misery of the tenants increased further prompting revolts in nine districts of Bengal.
5. Jawaharlal Nehru, the President of the All-India Trade Union of Congress, accused the British government of using the communist threat as a way of stymieing the labour movement in India.
6. Longue durée refers to the school of historical analysis that stresses long-term historical structures rather than historical events. This school of thought, particularly the work of Fernand Braudel, influenced the world systems approach to capitalism and development.
7. Literally *bhadralok* means genteel folk. They are neither an industrial nor (any longer or necessarily) a landed elite, but rather a cultural and intellectual one. *Bhadralok* were created as a result of the limited rights over property that Bengali landlords could have under the British Permanent Settlement Act of 1793. This Act gave landlords the right to collect revenue but in fact projected wrongly that this would encourage landlords to improve production along the lines of estates in England. In the absence of full and secure rights, over time, landowners either sold their land or retained absentee control over it. Moving to the urban areas of the then undivided Bengal, they nurtured instead their status and value as an educated and cultured class of people that came to be called *bhadralok.* They were simultaneously the most educated into European ideologies and practices and its harshest critics. They were thus historically poised to occupy both hegemonic and counter-hegemonic spaces in cultural and political life in Bengal.
8. Dharwadker's analysis of contemporary plays and their experimentations with folk by playwrights addresses 'why serious urban playwrights have turned to folk materials, and what effects and meanings the indigenous forms communicate' (Deshpande quoted in

Dharwadker 318). Some playwrights refuse to dabble in folk because they argue that the context which supported 'song, dance, and color in folk drama' and rural culture has passed (Elkunchwar quoted in Dharwadker 325).

9. Panchayats are local institutions of self-government that are conduits for development funds and projects.
10. After raging struggles and countermovements over two years, on 5 October 2008, the Tata car factory was moved from West Bengal and welcomed by Chief Minister Narendra Modi and farmers in Gujarat. Tata's departure reinforces the terms of the ideological battle: the choice is to want 'development' as capital will have it, or not.
11. The massacre of Muslims as revenge for a train of Hindu pilgrims burned in Godhra, Gujarat happened with the supportive leadership of a right-wing majoritarian provincial government in Gujarat. This event prompted widespread protest and human rights enquiries across India. JS's play represents the deliberate political making of a riot. Tripura is a state in the north-east of India almost entirely surrounded by Bangladesh except on its eastern portion. After the Indo-Pakistan war of 1971, Bengali refugees from Bangladesh flooded Tripura. Since the 1970s, insurgent groups have attempted to expel the Bengali population. Bengali ethnic hegemony in eastern India as well as the Indian government's problematic merger agreements with various independent kingdoms in the north-east in 1949 contribute to numerous secessionist wars in this region. The atmosphere of daily distrust and militancy in Tripura is the subject of the JS play. Katkari tribals from Maharashtra work as bonded labourers and continue to be treated as 'criminal tribes' in post-colonial India despite the de-notification of their administrative categorisation as criminal during colonial rule. Ration shops are nodes of the government public food distribution system, which store and sell subsidised provisions. As politically and economically disadvantaged groups in precarious conditions of survival, the Katkari experience at the ration shop plays a significant role in their plays. In each case, hegemonic relations of rule and normative political culture were combated through the plays which emerged out of workshops with members of mass organisations.
12. Significantly, the Workers' Party of Brazil for example had a number of liberation theologists in it including Paulo Freire who was Education Minister in the late 1980s (Taussig and Schechner 1994: 19).
13. In North American and European contexts, Boal's Theatre of the Oppressed has typically been a powerful mode of addressing personal oppression but not always extending to understanding connections between internal oppression as it echoes political and economic structures of oppression.

14. This ironic result of the use and abuse of theatre for development parallels trends in other realms of development practice captured by critical development theory as the 'tyranny of participation' (Cook and Kothari 2001).

Chapter Two

The Work of Political Theatre in a Democratic Place

Political theatre is undervalued in sociology and development studies literature which resists seeing performance as political action, indicative and constitutive of material realities, democracy, citizenship, or historical change. In chapter one, I established that rural political theatre is an anomaly that exists despite the fact that rural culture is tied to past and tradition. In this chapter, I argue that scholarly conceptualisation treats political theatre as safety-valves in contexts of political repression. For example, notwithstanding recent debates within agrarian studies scholarship (Brass 2002; Beverly 2004), agrarian studies tends to frame the agrarian question by focusing on land and resource struggles (Bernstein 2006; Cowen and Shenton 1998). Increasingly, this scholarship has incorporated the promise of post-colonial, subaltern, and cultural studies for understanding agrarian developments (McMichael 2006, 2008; Wolford 2007). Yet, it is still far from the norm to analyse rural cultural practices in general, and political theatre in particular, to understand political action and resource struggles in the countryside. In fact, the suggestion of studying political theatre to study agrarian political economy will strike the reader as a suggestion to focus on superstructural expression as opposed to the political–economic base.

Rather than treat political theatre as safety-valve political action, I analyse it as 'normal' political action to ask: What is the work of political theatre in a democratic place? In this book *Illuminations*, Walter Benjamin argued that while in the feudal world art had ritualistic and spiritual value, 'the work of art in an age of mechanical reproduction' had acquired a secular purpose and political function. Invoking Walter Benjamin's phrase for the present I ask, what does political theatre *as* daily political action accomplish in contexts where electoral success has sacred value and fetishises legitimisation of democracy and development policy? Rather than view parliamentary Communism as *the* viable and valuable material and epistemic space for political action and policy-making, I argue that Jana Sanskriti's political theatre attempts to rescript the hypothesis of social equality by taking the question of value out of the crucible of reductivism that is exchange value.

In the first section of this chapter, I argue that political theatre addresses material and representational inequality beyond the impasse of parliamentary Communism and agrarian reform in contemporary West Bengal. Secondary sources show that the Communist Party of India-Marxist (CPM) has addressed the needs of the dispossessed under massive national and global constraints. At the same time, it has settled for building alliances that secure electoral success rather than choosing a confrontational politics of transformation. In this context, Jana Sanskriti (JS) has built networks and translocal connections among various mass organisations within India and beyond. Their transnational ties are not so much with funding organisations as translocal struggles across South America, Western and Eastern Europe, and South Asia which combat collaborative relations of exploitation, rule, and domination by imperial capital and nation–state. JS is one part of the transnational 'social Left' to use Gerardo Otero's terms (2008: 163–77), constituting 'transnational governmentality' (Ferguson and Gupta 2005: 981–1002). They combat the governmentality of the Left Front Government (LFG) in West Bengal which, as the 'party of the poor', is enabling growth and job creation by normalising the paradigm of procuring capital investment through an aggressive capitalism that accumulates by dispossessing.

In the second section of this chapter, I argue that political theatre must be recognised as the productive labour of meaning-making, refusing epistemic closure, and making particular historically available meanings and practices count in public, institutionally-valued, and normative ways. Rather than defining productive labour solely as generative of exchange value, I argue for recognising that discursive struggles are not *solely* traced and sourced through the history of capitalism. We ought to also recognise where and when productive labour may contribute to the reproduction of capital accumulation, but does not *necessarily* do so. That is to say, labour can also be considered productive because it constitutes and fortifies histories of power, practices of living, and social formations that are devalued or dispossessed of significance and legitimacy within capitalist history. This has indirect implications on the construction of productive labour in the economic sense. However, the point is that the mechanisms, processes, and judgements that separate economic from non-economic precede the separations themselves (Mitchell 2002).

In the final section of this chapter, I argue that insofar as political theatre does the work of reinforcing dispossessed meanings, practices, and possibilities, this kind of theatre ought not to be viewed as a safety-valve ritual of resistance to repression. Within area studies literature, studies of political theatre in South Asia have typically concerned themselves with how theatre emerges as mode of political expression and bastion of struggle under conditions of severe repression. JS's political theatre and activism is no more theatrical and no less 'normal' than the political actions more readily characterised as 'state' action. This kind of theatre should not be relegated to liminal time and fictional form which assumes that theatre ultimately reinforces structure. Rather, I argue that studying political theatre in normal times, as a daily means of political action in a democracy, among the prized constituencies and beneficiaries of a government, lifts the veil off state power. Studying political theatre in relation to off-stage political action reveals the ways in which the promise of representational equality can constitute 'state' conceptualised as 'politically organised subjection' (Abrams 1988: 58–59). At the same time, my argument is that political theatre is distinct for presenting 'state' as malleable process because as kinetic, staged, and live performance power is subject to improvisations and transgressions. To recognise this is to acknowledge that disrupting subjective and structural closure is accomplished by 'everyday forms of resistance' (J. C. Scott 1987) as well as collaboration (White 1986: 56).

Class-Struggle

Reflecting on Nikolas Sarkozy's victory in 2007 and its disorienting effects on the French Left, Alain Badiou insists on a new Left agenda that recognises a distinction between empirical Communism or real experiments of Communist governments, and the Communist hypothesis which is 'the proposition that the subordination of labour to the dominant class is not inevitable' (Badiou 2008: 37). As Badiou reads the conspicuous consumption and accumulation of Sarkozy's politics, he interprets them as evidence that the failure of 'empirical communism' is inadequate comfort for capitalist state systems today (*ibid.*: 34). The likes of Sarkozy, Thatcher, and Reagan have tried to extinguish the validity of the Communist hypothesis itself. The very talk of any alternatives must be ruled out, projecting capitalist modernity as the only mode of ensuring victory in the war on poverty previously, and on terror presently. Given such ideological extermination of alternatives and the epistemological incorporation of alternatives into the market episteme (Da Costa and McMichael 2007), Badiou insists that the agenda of the Left is to rejuvenate the conditions of existence of the Communist hypothesis. He divides history into two stages of attempts at realising the Communist hypothesis. The first phase is characterised by the preliminary enunciation of the hypothesis in the French Revolution and the Paris Commune; the second is marked by examples of hypercommitment to accomplishing the hypothesis in practice through inordinate discipline starting from the Bolshevik Revolution to the end of the Cultural Revolution.

Badiou claims that both phases of experiments were ultimately ineffective for different reasons. Because the party-state refused to wither away and instead turned into authoritarianism, the current historical conjuncture poses two reified and impoverished ideological alternatives: Communist practice, strongly associated with corrupt and ineffective party-states, and imperialism, legitimised as *the* only available defense against terror. In the face of these two problematic options, he argues that the agenda for the Left is to 're-install the communist hypothesis — the proposition that the subordination of labour to the dominant class is not inevitable — *within the ideological sphere*' (2008: 37, emphasis mine). Arguably this perspective is Eurocentric and neglects the recent history of Latin America which turned to the political Left in the second-half of the twentieth century precisely at the moment when the political Left became discredited in Europe and America (Ballvé and Prashad 2006). At the same time, the failure of the European experience of empirical Communism and its capacity to move imagination and practice of the social Left towards NGO-isation and depoliticisation of politics and poverty is striking evidence of the hegemonic efficacy of 1989. Thus, there is some truth to Badiou's claim that there is significant work to be done to reignite the promise and possibility embedded in the communist hypothesis.

Badiou argues that reinstalling the Communist hypothesis in the ideological sphere can only be done by beginning with a simple axiomatic principle — 'there is only one world' — which he views not as an objective description but a performative claim (2008: 38). Although Badiou does not indicate how this performative claim might be accomplished in practice, he concludes his essay like this:

> This is our task, during the reactionary interlude that now prevails: through the combination of thought processes — always global, or universal, in character — and political experience, always local or singular, yet transmissible, to renew the existence of the communist hypothesis, in our consciousness and on the ground. (2008: 42)

Although post-colonial theory has warned against assuming unmediated access to 'thought processes — always global, or universal, in character', (Badiou 2008: 42) as I view it, JS's contribution to class struggle is precisely at this level of performing the ideological strength of a hypothesis that representational and material inequality is not inevitable. In terms of imagining and materialising alternatives, their theatre addresses the alienation of the 'social Left' from the 'political Left' in India (Otero 2008). Because they focus on redistributing means of representation, JS is as insistent on reimagining Communist ideals in the West Bengal context as they are on representing historical difference in practice. In some ways, their theoretical commitment to representational equality nurtures their attention to historical difference and ambiguity in practice, as I show in chapter four. Through their various practices, they attempt to perform the ideology of representational equality and historical difference into reality, to produce an internal and collective recognition of its value and meaning, and to build a moral economy and polity on this basis. Since 1985, they have struggled to redistribute the means of representation as a constitutive force of *their* struggle.

In light of this claim about JS's theatre, it is worth asking what it means to address representational inequality in a regional context where relatively progressive redistributive policies and democracy is the source of governmental legitimacy. Against historical odds, the CPM in West Bengal implemented land reform as soon as it came into power, securing tenancy rights for sharecroppers

(Operation Barga), distributing land over the legal ceiling to marginal and peasant holders, improving food security, irrigation reform, and increasing agricultural productivity and purchasing power in rural areas (D. Bhattacharyya 1999; Harris 1993; Lieten 1990, 2003; Rawal 2001). In 1978, well before the rest of India, the Party implemented panchayati raj which decentralised political representation and governance to institutions for local government elected by villages (approximately 10 villages make one panchayat).

These local institutions of rural political representation and development have been called 'red panchayats' where 'red' signals the singular political economy of panchayats in West Bengal where economic redistribution through land reform strengthens the institutional efforts towards political decentralisation for the poor. However, as Glyn Williams has argued, while the CPM intended panchayats to be nodes of consciousness raising, panchayat politics remains a matter of building and maintaining dominant factions 'rather than the party- or issue-based politics the CPM's leadership would have hoped for' (Williams 1999: 240). Notwithstanding countless public and academic debates about the effectiveness and practice of LFG policies, the government's consecutive electoral success since 1977 has been the final measure of the voice of the rural poor, to a large degree quelling doubts or criticisms of the policies and the red panchayats. Some critics of the CPM argue that the militant politics of anti-nationalist and post-colonial Leftist struggle turned to reform almost as soon as the party came into power in 1977 (Menon and Nigam 2007). As another scholar puts it, CPM reforms 'benefitted the dispossessed but simultaneously created durable conditions for electoral support for the LFG from a broad alliance of classes' (D. Bhattacharyya 1999: 281).

The CPM mode of waging class struggle (see chapter three) administers rule and conduct by directing welfare towards the poor as in a social democracy while remaining parliamentary Communists who nurture the ideological expectation that socialism will come when the moment of capitalist development is right. This is the way in which the party has affirmed the Communist hypothesis in the realms of ideology and political action. Although the recent turn to capital insertion seems new in West Bengal, the CPM self-projection on their website asserts that bringing capitalist development into fruition was always their goal since capitalism is more progressive than the pre-capitalist system, and because capitalism must come before socialism can come:

> It must be kept in mind that the struggle for industrialisation is the struggle against the pre-capitalist system. The land reform agenda taken by the LF government in the last 30 years is nothing but another step forward to capitalism. It will be a mistake to find socialism in it. Emphasising on industry in recent days is also capitalistic in character. The intermediate era between feudalism and socialism is capitalism. Therefore, in this socio-economic system, capitalism is one step forward to socialism. By countering the negative areas of capitalism and with a struggle to eliminate this system at the end, we must utilise the scope of industrialisation at this moment. Development in agriculture and industry by maintaining the self sufficiency of food actually indicates an overall development.[1]

However, while the CPM insists on countering 'negative areas of capitalism', valid questions remain about their claims that *this* industrialisation (rather than the kind governed by any other party) is the kind of capitalism that takes us 'one step forward to socialism'. Is socialism hastened or delayed by putting a welfare band-aid on capitalism's 'negative areas'? The political Left also selectively applies principles of identifying 'negative areas of capitalism' in different contexts. For example, Aditya Nigam has shown through a study of left-wing trade union's refusal to ratify the World Trade Organisation's social clause[2] that the political Left in India chose to give unconditional support to the central government as the latter resisted the imperialist capitalist machine of the WTO. In this case, the 'negative areas of capitalism' — imperialist rule and exploitative working conditions within India — battled against each other for attention by the political Left. Parliamentary Communism's need to secure state power and procure capital investment produces a contradiction within its logic of class struggle.

At the same time, it has to be recognised that no other political party in India has even admitted land reform into its manifesto. Within the contexts of world-historical and central government constraints and emboldened by regional electoral success, the standard refrain of the CPM itself has become: How much can a regional government do in the context of global capitalism and a bourgeois central government? Yet, in 1996, the CPM central committee prevented the Party from joining the central government and allowing politbureau member and then Chief Minister of West Bengal Jyoti Basu to take the invitation as Prime Minister of India because the extant central government was considered bourgeois. Basu called this a 'historic blunder' and a missed opportunity to a play a part in reshaping politics at the centre.

A final area of complexity lies in the relations between the political and social Left. They converge against land acquisition for capital investment in contexts where the political Left does not control regional governmental power. However, where it does so such as in West Bengal, the CPM has caricatured its opposition (including the social Left) as 'outsiders', Narodniks, Naxalites, anti-progressive, and even right-wing for opposing its policies of state-led investment and industrialisation. Rather than see its opposition in differentiated terms, the party chooses to view them as a monolithic, anti-progressive force. On the whole, the class struggle logic of the CPM has managed these internal and external complexities by subjecting its decisions to a stagist narrative of development and relegating the primary location of politics to the developmental state within a parliamentary system.

As beneficiaries of LFG policies through the conduit of red panchayats, the rural poor in Bengal are not supposed to be engaged in critical representations such as political theatre. Although JS is the theatre of the agricultural labourer, the farmer, and the daily wage-labourer in rural Bengal, it is also open to all regardless of political affiliation. Their theatrical work onstage and political work off-stage dramatises the ways in which some rural Bengalis have refused LFG, and especially CPM monopoly over political representation and the normative closure on the very meaning of development, class struggle, and political collectivity in West Bengal. Yet, far from bypassing the state in order to roll back its relevance and power, JS builds translocal alliances to pressure the 'state' and reignite the possibility of revaluing dispossessed meanings and rural futures by reorganising social relations among the poor as the *condition* for capital insertion. Their approach to class struggle is in part to build translocal alliances, strengthen popular demands that will help governments procure capital not on the backs of working class citizens, by subordinating labour to the dominant class and the terms of capital, but based on renewed social relations among working classes. But most of JS's work within the class struggle is to dramatise, publicise, and refuse closure on debate in a world of shrinking possibilities where competition, violence, and racing to the bottom are normalised as the dominant relations among the poor.

JS envisions its work of combating representational inequality as complementing land and labour struggles so that the needs and terms of rural work and social life are subject to public debate. At a spect-actor rally on 22 October 2006 in Kolkata, approximately 10,000 people who are active participants in JS theatre teams, workshops, and Forum Theatre performances in villages, rallied in silence. They carried posters with slogans: 'Working class cultures have been removed from the altar of intellectual society' (*Chintar jogot theke shromojeebi shilper angan theke shorano hoyeche*); 'Creativity is a symbol of society' (*Shilpo samajer upoma*); 'We want the right to creative debate in society' (*Amra shilpo charchar adhikar chai*). These statements about the exclusion of working-class representation from intellectual and creative debate are glimpses into the kind of political action that constitutes JS's focus. In claiming intellectual debate as a right, they refuse the stagist narratives of pre-capitalism, industrial capitalism, and socialism, and claim recognition for the role rural citizens have played in constructing development.

This does not explicitly preclude respect for the accomplishments of the CPM and the LFG. In fact, there are questions among JS members who wonder whether they and other groups will mobilise the redistribution of *khas jomi* (vested land appropriated by the state during Operation Barga) to pressurise completion of CPM's work. In recognition of CPM reform, Sanjoy Ganguly argues, 'economism has contributed much to the labour movement in the past. I do not deny the need for that even today' (Ganguly 2004: 230). But for him, economics and parliamentary politics simply do not empower people to recognise hidden talents *and* their own capacity for oppression (*ibid.*: 255). In JS's work, the 'Communist' hypothesis will be reinserted into the ideological sphere when political action and democracy are founded upon a lived political process that recognises every person's capacity to oppress *and* be oppressed. This is the primary JS ideological conviction and source of ethical political action.

Their conviction is founded in the understanding that while capitalism is an aggressive source of domination and dispossession in the present, it is not the only history of power (Chakrabarty 2000) that shapes daily life and structures of oppression, sources of ethics, justice, politics, and injustice. As such, to reinvigorate the hypothesis of equality in the ideological sphere, we have to attend to historical difference through redistributing the means of representation. While I articulate this theoretical conviction in this chapter, the argument is fleshed out in the ethnographic chapters (chapters 4, 5, 6 and 7) of this book.

Ganguly's critique of the economism embedded in West Bengal government policy echoes recent debates in agrarian studies which have also begun to chip away at the epistemic assumptions about the place of agrarian livelihood and future within narratives of development and social change. These debates have moved past an idea of the homogeneous, undifferentiated peasantry out there, waiting en masse for transformation or preservation (Bernstein 2006, 2008; Cowen and Shenton 1998; McMichael 2006, 2008; Hart 1998; Brass 2002). Today the central agrarian question has arguably shifted to understanding the relationship between specific conditions and processes of peasant livelihood, mobility, and agrarian industrialisation on the one hand, and the struggles against dispossession on the other (Araghi 2000; de Haan and Rogaly 2002; Hart 1998; McMichael 2008). Philip McMichael (2008) has discussed the dispossession of meaning embedded in a 'world agriculture' organised around solving the problem of 'food security' which is a partial, even politically motivated, response within the history of capitalism. He analyses peasant mobilisations of the transnational organisation Via Campesina which reveals that food sovereignty involves a struggle for a 'complex of rights'.

> Put simply, rights struggles include workplace conditions, civil/social rights in the state, and human rights in/for representation in global society. [...] Thus 'food sovereignty' combines a formal politics of citizenship and the social contract, with a substantive politics of rights expressed through a reformulation of multilateralism combined with a revaluing of agrarian relationships. (McMichael 2008: 289–90)

The sovereignty of meaning, nation-state, and ecological wisdom are various levels of peasant mobilisation in this vision of agrarian development. Here, a richer palette of social relationships inform the political history of capitalism so that the agrarian question is neither reduced to a 'back to the future' logic characteristic of agrarian populism, nor exclusively the redistribution of welfare by the nation-state, nor to the unassailable 'death of the peasantry' through capitalist transformation.

Moreover, the focus is on understanding an agrarian economy as a mode of social reproduction which includes but is not reducible to 'economic' terms. The multidisciplinary approach in this literature may take land as a clear starting point but views it as node and expression of diverse relationships: 'Land is sustenance, territory, culture, ecosystem, possession, power, and profit' (Wolford and Tewari 2008).[3] This literature subjects the materiality of the most basic natural resource — land — to denaturalisation by unravelling the many historically and politically unequal meanings and uses of land reform depending on who initiates such reform, to what end, and how (Wolford 2007).

Far from studying the subaltern peasant as embodying 'alternative culture', agrarian subsistence and resistance are shown to have multiple relations to power, 'development', and 'modernity'. Peasant mobilisation can contribute at once to agrarian populism in a post-colonial state-making project while enhancing global governmentality through environmentalism *apart from* practicing and giving meaning to 'indigenous' ecology and agronomy (Gupta 1998). Yet, peasant struggles today also insist on the possibility of incorporating exemplary values and relations of reciprocity and ecology within and despite a world agriculture and economy. Drawing on the lessons of the Subaltern Studies project while rejecting its essentialisms, these perspectives recognise that peasant resistance occurs within political relations and inequalities of capitalist history, but attempts to transform the terms of these relations of subjection (Beverly cited in McMichael 2008).

These debates help overcome an implicit base/superstructure division, as well as a spatial organisation of a state 'up there' and a civil society or grassroots 'down below' (Ferguson and Gupta 2005; Ferguson 2006) that continues to pervade analyses of struggle and structure. Following Philip Abrams notion of 'structuring' and sociology of process — 'an alternate to our tried, worn and inadequate sociologies of action and system' — allows us to reject such a heuristic division (Abrams 1982: xv). In this vision, the study of class struggle and political action refuses to characterise representational process as less effective sites of social transformation and constructing collectivity — a position that implicitly assumes that these are somehow secondary to or autonomous from the political–economic history of capitalism. Rather, these epistemic struggles are understood as constitutive of 'class' struggle in this book.

Studying theatre invariably led me to rural perceptions on- and off-stage that highlighted people's anger and despair at definitions of 'progressive' collectivity, the 'value' of schooling for girls and boys, 'cheap' labour, and 'material' distress. JS's work of rethinking how we know cheapness, progressiveness, productivity, and materiality when we see them may not produce lasting and large collectivities for class struggle, but it certainly critically rethinks and fortifies social projects that construct collectivities committed to class struggle. Rather than treat state power as the sole locus of consolidating class struggle, JS's political action builds a translocal collectivity that nurtures debates over similar and dissimilar experiences of dispossession, rule, and struggle. Far from disregarding the importance of state power, JS's work begs for an audience among the political Left, hoping to challenge and push them, for as Badiou puts it, 'there is only one world' (2008: 38).

Productive Work

As described earlier, JS's political and cultural work focuses on redistributing the means of representation rather than the means of production. As such, a significant question is how to conceptualise cultural work as work. Is cultural work any different from any other form of work? Critical social theory has questioned the tendency to place art in a stratified realm by recognising the world of production and power relations that produce, receive, and glorify a work of art or help sell it (Horkheimer and Adorno 1944; Becker 1982; Griswold 1987; Radway 1991). Walter Benjamin wrote in the first-half of the twentieth century that '[f]or the first time in world history, mechanical reproduction emancipates the work of art from its parasitical dependence on ritual' (1968: 224). That is, for the first time in history, the work of art could have a demystifying and therefore transformative rather than a mystifying role in society. In the contemporary conjuncture however, cultural work has come to be seen in terms of the culture industries, expressing what Anthony Giddens (1998) has called the 'Third Way'. Situating culture industries in a global context, they are seen as a 'substantial sector of the economy, a sizeable mode of production, and also a field of employment, increasingly of self-employment' (McRobbie 1999: 26).

This world-historical conjuncture is relevant to rural West Bengal where the biographies of JS actors took form. JS's core coordinating political actors and activists chose cultural work in response to a combination of factors such as disillusionment with jobs, unemployment, inadequate education, politics of the times, seeking creativity and fun, landlessness, debt, and/or abandonment by husbands. These rationales speak volubly of the impossibility of unified subjectivities among 'the oppressed' even as these biographies tie JS actors to common legacies of colonialism, post-colonial development, the current conjuncture of neoliberal dispossessions, and diversified livelihoods in rural contexts.

The culture industries' literature of the 1990s conceptualised a 'new materialism' which connected these historical 'large scale changes with the small scale cultural economies and livelihoods upon which so many people now depend for a living' (McRobbie 1999: x). However, more recently Angela McRobbie (2000) has specified her position to show that there is a striking contradiction within New Labour and the Third Way which tries to recognise the policy challenge to poverty while depoliticising poverty itself. Played out graphically in welfare politics and women's work, she highlights the problematic 'gender mainstreaming' within the Third Way which incorporates 'women without feminism' (*ibid.*). Thus, as culture industries offer new opportunities for employment, they are also emblematic of the uncertainty and fragility of work, the commodification of creativity, and myriad exclusionary practices of global capitalism (Beck 2003).

These debates around cultural work in the history of capitalism make it imperative to investigate the details, possibilities, and limits of given cases of cultural work and pedagogical alternatives. However, I argue that this literature could also conceptualise the productivity of cultural work beyond seeing labour as oriented towards generating exchange value. A focus on defining culture industry and cultural work in terms of exchange value neglects the analysis of cultural work such as JS's which is situated in circuits of capital but whose primary productive outcome is not exchange value. Can we tell the history of this work of meaning-making as socio-historical change? How should cultural work be conceptualised if and when it disrupts the privileged place of the market episteme? Is such cultural work productive labour? More specifically, is cultural work productive labour and part of the economy when it does not generate exchange value but rather struggles against epistemic dispossessions and closures on the social relations that constitute 'economy'?

In the *Grundrisse*, Marx says that a product of labour only becomes a product when it is consumed by an active subject. Use gives a product its productivity, and productivity gives consumption its purpose (Marx 1857). Despite this masterful appreciation for the inter-relationship between consumption and production, subject and object, he also suggests that while a piano-maker is engaged in productive labour, a pianist cannot be considered a productive worker. The latter 'only exchanges his labour for revenue', and therefore does not reproduce capital (Marx quoted in Chakrabarty 2000: 68). Pre-empting critics of such logic, Marx says,

> But doesn't the pianist produce music and satisfy our musical ear, does he not even to a certain extent produce the latter? He does indeed: his labour produces something; but that does not make it *productive labour* in the *economic sense*; no more than the labour of the mad man who produces delusions is productive.

In Marx's discussion of the labour process and process of valourisation he claims, that 'A *use value* for capital, labour is a *mere exchange value* for the worker' (Marx 1857: 305). Marx's theory of value no doubt provides powerful commentary on capitalist history being minutely attentive to the politics of representation. Nonetheless, perhaps it is worth revisiting what we miss when we understand labour as mere exchange value for the worker and make this the starting point for understanding the worker in the political history of capitalism. Perhaps this is a necessary exercise for going beyond the economism of 'development'.

I understand JS's work as productive labour not just in terms of the exchange value of their creative labour but because their cultural work dramatises and historicises alienation, delusions, and anomalies. As Marx asserted in relation to the fetish of the commodity, alienation and delusions have world-historical meaning. Similarly, as mentioned in the last chapter, anomalies and anachronisms such as JS's work have world-historical meaning. These meanings and their value might be occluded from our vision because of social conventions in a given historical conjuncture. But this does not mean that anomalies contribute nothing to historical formations and social relations, or, that they do not express epistemes which struggle against the ongoing naturalisation of conventions that render labour as 'mere exchange value for the worker' (Marx 1857: 305). JS's cultural work is productive labour because it refuses normative and structural closure on the meaning, use, and out-come of labour.

Cultural work, as I conceptualise it, expresses and transforms the relationship between processes of meaning-making and multiple histories of power. Meaning-making is necessarily a political (even instrumental) endeavour — to the extent that all action is political, claims for legitimising certain meanings over others are no different. While all work invites questions of culture, cultural work at once recognises capitalism as cultural, while rendering capitalism one of many histories of power engaged in meaning-making struggles that play a constructive role in making social formations. JS is engaged in cultural work not just because they do theatre but also in the sense that they script power, represent social problems publicly, and struggle to make certain meanings count in contexts where they are marginal.[4] Thus, this kind of work can reproduce capital, but it can also result in practices that produce certain modes of living and learning as authoritative, moral, and legitimate — in a sense producing history itself (Bennett 2007; Corrigan and Sayer 1985).

By focusing on JS's cultural work, I do not mean to suggest that the CPM has only focused on redistributing the means of production to the neglect of a cultural programme. As others have argued before, the CPM has a differentiated and complex cultural programme (Bannerji 1998; D. Bhattacharyya 1999; M. Bhattacharya 2004; Chatterjee 1997; Ruud 2003). Its cultural project, as Himani Bannerji has described it, is to bring about a 'coincidence of liberal democracy with class struggle' (Bannerji 1998: 86). Or, put differently, 'the culmination of the incomplete revolution — the genuine independence that bypassed India' which will combine the gains made by the bourgeois democratic revolutions in European history and subsequently the task of the proletariat who will democratise India to usher a socialist revolution (*ibid.*: 86–87).

The CPM addresses this project through multiple means. Its cultural wing draws and develops the legacy of the anti-colonial Indian People's Theatre Association (IPTA) taking plays to rural areas and organising cultural festivals. The IPTA continues to have a branch in West Bengal which performs plays such as Brecht's *Mother Courage* in cultural festivals in rural areas. In the early 1980s, the West Bengal government took the initiative of protecting some of the 'dying' cultural forms. Malini Bhattacharya (2004) argues that women's songs sung in marriage rituals, for example, were being lost as a result of the increasing feminisation of labour and reduction of women's leisure time due to forces of globalisation. She thus documents the role that the state government has played in recuperating and protecting rural artists by using its Information Department to organise district festivals of 'folk and tribal culture' (*ibid.*: 162).

The work of protecting and recuperating cultural practices is also governed by a secular–modernist commitment demonstrating continuity with IPTA's principles outlined in chapter one. For example, the cultural festivals organised by the Information Department specifically encouraged women artists 'some of them married, [to give] a performance of Muslim marriage songs on that stage. They were mostly from families of landless labourers and small peasants' (M. Bhattacharya 2004: 162). She tells us that bringing songs that are typically sung during marriages in exclusive spaces for women to a public stage comes with its share of battles between progressives and conservatives in the area (*ibid.*: 161). The goal of the government was to simultaneously save a cultural form, while bringing its artistic agent and practice out of the private sphere of the family so that it would no longer be considered 'a "sin" for a Muslim woman to sing in public' (*ibid.*: 161). In Bhattacharya's words, 'it makes the exercise of a preeminently secular creativity possible for them' (*ibid.*: 163).

Clearly the CPM government has given rural subjects access to cultural spaces, saving culture from the forces of capital, and making public performance legitimate for rural women. Other forms of state patronage for cultural work include support for the group theatre movement in West Bengal. As mentioned in the previous chapter, playwrights like Utpal Dutt attempted to modernise performance traditions such as *jatra* by broadening core plots on religious mythology and instilling them with contemporary anti-imperial significance. Indeed, as Arild Engelsen Ruud (1997) has shown, novels and dramatic performances have been key rites of passage and modes of politicising rural Bengalis. Participating in reading and performing plays have helped modernise tradition and rural backwardness, offered rural youth an opportunity to transcend structural divisions off-stage to glimpse a better, more moral society in stories and heroes (*ibid.*). As Ruud puts it, these stories have educated villagers into the ideologies and values of the middle-class educated elite who scripted the plays (*ibid.*).

Apart from these efforts at cultural construction and modernisation, one of the most effective spaces of cultural work in the countryside is the formation of rural Communism through political representation. Ruud (1999) has also attended to cultural politics in the making of rural Communism in West Bengal by examining the status of a previously 'untouchable' caste called the Bagdis of Bardhaman district. He has shown that the Bagdis have aligned themselves with the CPM and been an important constituency in rural party politics. In doing so, the Bagdis have been able to shed some of the ritual impurity and marginalisation that has historically marked their caste status. However, as Ruud has argued, this must be understood as not just a Bagdi strategy but also as a CPM cultural programme: 'Bagdis are tied to the party by being given representation in, but not necessarily control over, public positions' (*ibid.*: 268). This suggests that while 'representation entails status', for the CPM, giving this caste access to representation is a demonstration of citizenship for a party that needs to survive in a parliamentary democracy. This is not to say that it does not enable Bagdi social mobility, but that the terms of such mobility are constrained by the terms of parliamentary Communism.

Taking into account the CPM cultural programme, my aim is to recognise the similarities in the kind of work that JS and the CPM do while identifying differences. In their engagement with JS or CPM's cultural work, rural Bengalis are variously mobilised to 'compete and struggle both *for* such goods [resources and imagination], that is compete for things which are agreed to be worthwhile, and over the definition of what is valuable or worthwhile' (Sayer 2005: 3). Both JS activists and CPM cadres use their bodies and give labour time to work that lies within circuits of capital and contributes to the formation of state power. In JS's case, their work of democratising representation cannot be understood 'purely as a Hobbesian pursuit of advantage in terms of economic, cultural and social capital' (*ibid.*: 3). Their work should count as productive work because they also question the assumed calibrations between subaltern ideologies, capabilities, and structural positions common to Marxism and neoliberalism (Sen 1999; Marx 1852; Marx and Engels 1848).

They dramatise publicly and kinetically the ambiguities and complexities within subaltern capacity, structural positions, and ideology as constitutive effects of power. At the same time, theatrical labour produces kinetic representations of social hierarchies, normative assumptions, and structures *as malleable,* acknowledging that the coercions of dominant history dispossess certain representations more than others. To use Jill Dolan's terms, in this political theatre, questions of 'as *is*' are posed in order to reopen questions of 'what *if*' (Dolan 2005: 141). The tensions between constructing an 'empowerment' agenda and revealing onstage the ambiguities of subaltern power as the complex nature of power itself, helps generate and socialise an 'alternative' sociality which refuses the normative closure and structural binaries assumed in ruling epistemes of politics and struggle. This brings me to the possibility of addressing representation as means and engine of social and state-formation in a world of entrenched inequalities.

State-Formation

Despite the cultural turn in sociology, compared with bureaucracies and electoral politics, political theatre is placed low on the hierarchy of what really counts as politics (Steinmetz 1999). Although this literature is beginning to analyse the theatricality, spectacle, and ritual of state power, it is a long way from viewing political theatre as formative of state and society. Even among sociologists who recognise theatricality as engine of political life and constitutive of repression and democracy, theatre is of interest when conceptualised as *metaphor* for understanding social relationships, electoral politics, nation, and political struggle.[5] Rather than treat culture as autonomous in explanatory frameworks of social action, I argue that we shift focus to take *forms* of theatrical action as seriously as other forms of social action, which are more readily assumed to constitute the 'political' or 'economic' (Alexander and Smith 1993; Swidler 1986). This is not so much a question of autonomy as it is a question of the efficacy of cultural actions such as theatre in re-vealing and reconfiguring ideological distinctions among various forms of social action.

Conceptualising political theatre as productive work must reconcile the problem of whether this theatre invariably serves as an ephemeral, fictional, and imaginative ritual with safety valve function. The functionalist interlude within social theory conceptualised ritual as momentary inversion and society's mechanism for containing conflict. In this view, rituals ultimately reinforced structural power, consensus, and hierarchy through cyclical experiences of ritual catharsis (Durkheim 1912 (1995); Gluckman 1963; Turner 1975, 1995). Here, catharsis is understood as purging emotional suffering in an unequal society rather than as emotional route to intellectual clarification (Ford 1995). Seeing theatre as essentially ephemeral rests on narrow definitions of what counts as social action, change, engines of social transformation, and how we know the state when we see it.

What does count as legitimate political action? Electoral democracy is an increasingly contested sign of political representation in West Bengal and elsewhere in the world (Otero 2008; Zalik 2007), and often the terms of contestation focus on its ritual dimension (S. Banerjee 2006; M. Bannerjee 2007). As Alain Badiou put it in the aftermath of the French elections in 2007, 'It is good to vote, to give a form to my fears; but it is hard to believe that what I am voting *for* is a good thing in itself' (Badiou 2008: 31). While theatre is readily perceived to have genealogical links to ritual, electoral politics when perceived as ritualistic, is a means of challenging its legitimacy. As I view it, in West Bengal, elections are, no more or less than political theatre, involved in producing a series of normative assumptions about what effective political action and collectivity is all about. Perhaps more than political theatre though, elections are site for ritualised legitimising of the status quo of 'capitalo-parliamentarism', even if this by no means makes electoral-democracy in itself repressive (*ibid.*).

Within structures of 'capitalo-parliamentarism', political theatre is largely celebrated as resistance to domination and hegemony. Much of the appreciative literature on the role of political theatre in South Asia views it as extraordinary political action (see Nagar 2000, 2002; Ruud 1997 for exceptions). Theorising political theatre as flourishing in contexts facing colonial censorship (Bhatia 2004; Chatterjee 2007), governmental repression (Afzal-Khan 2001; Mangai 2000; van Erven 1992), terror and anomie (Obeyesekere 1999) marks much of the scholarship on the role of political theatre in South Asia for example.[6] In these narratives, political theatre is born and flourishes in moments when legitimate forms of political action lose transparency, or their commitment to democratic representation, or undermine systems of accountability. To greater or lesser degrees, these studies view performance as extraordinary, creative action that emerges in conditions of repression and censorship — extraordinary not just in the sense of spectacular, but also in the sense that there is an assumed normality and ordinariness to legitimate political action, governmental, or state action.

Victor Turner's (1995) social drama model of ritual plays a subconscious role in these analyses. His ritual process transports participants in ritual through liminal time and space where people of varied rank can experience 'communitas' by glimpsing the vulnerability and malleability of social power. The conception of political theatre as resistance against repression helps understand historical moments of rupture when theatre becomes a visible, dramatic, even desperate mode of assertion and protest. Like all stories, this view is partial appreciation of the power of theatre because it does not capture political theatre itself as ordinary political action, in ordinary times, as an everyday engagement, a 'normal' practice in democratic contexts. Rather, it conceptualises political theatre as liminal and sees it as rites of passage that exist outside of social time, structure, and space. But as Susan Seizer puts it about the category of off-stage in her study of the social life of Special Drama, 'Is there ever, in any firm sense, a truly "off" for anyone in life?' (Seizer 2005: 298). Ultimately, seeing theatre as an ephemeral act of resistance requires that the proof of *theatre's* social effectiveness be demonstrated in evidence of structural domination overcome. It also generates problematic expectations that subjects of domination and repression act in unified, productive ways towards singular ends with radical outcomes (O' Hanlon 2001).

What remains useful about Turner's model is that it is applicable to actors *and* audiences who might be drawn to performance to release themselves from the 'inhibiting restraints of the "as is" for the more liberatory possibilities of the "what if"; that is a common human need for hope' (Dolan 2005:21). Jill Dolan explores the political possibilities in Turner's communitas by suggesting that our activism should therefore turn towards encouraging theatre-going so that more people can experience the 'utopian performative' in staged performance since this can nurture the curiosity and possibility of finding and making a better world elsewhere, in another time. Her suggestion is to take seriously the transformative and affective power of the performative moment during a staged performance rather than deferring judgement and making the power of performance dependent on its social effect in the off-stage afterlife of performance.

Dolan's perspective is significant and I admire her analysis of the utopian performative in staged performances. However, to the extent that her theory follows Turner's conception of communitas, she constructs the utopian performative *in* performance, felt in the fleeting moment of witnessing staged fiction. Seeing theatre as nurturing possibility when it reveals the 'utopian performative' in staged performance relegates the time and space of utopian performatives to staged fiction. Or, to put it differently, surely there is no such thing as normal political action. After all, what political action does not embed within it utopian performatives? JS's theatre requires a theory of political action that works with a more porous understanding of staged and off-stage political action and imagination.

This is because 'theatre is always in the world' (Taylor 1991: 19). Diana Taylor has rejected the Geertzian dichotomy of those societies where 'power served pomp, not pomp power' (Geertz 1981: 13) to show that the modern Argentinian state, not unlike Geertz's nineteenth century Bali, accomplishes rule through theatricality and spectacle (Taylor 1997). The ephemerality of performance injects vulnerability into any (always more or less theatrical) claim to power while inserting the possibility of bringing multiple repertoires of embodied knowledge into the archives of legitimate history (Taylor 2003). In this view, ritual is hardly momentary reversal, but the very means of effecting power, an ongoing 'historical practice' (Comaroff and Comaroff 1993: xxiii). Here, political theatre is just as ordinary and theatrical as the political action of state rule. Staged and everyday performativity as defined by Judith Butler can be equally effective in refusing to play normative scripts loyally (Butler 1990). My point is that it is not always clear whether utopia is nurtured in ritual and imagination to be realised off-stage or whether off-stage spectacles of power generate alternative scripts.

My study of JS's theatre pushes me therefore to study the utopian performative in staged performance *in relation to* the utopian performative in everyday life. After all, the whole point of 'theatre of the oppressed' is to generate discrepancy between fiction and reality, stage and off-stage, actor and audience. For example, the 'stage' in their practice is space that is both demarcated as fictional as well as deliberately 'everyday' as in a village square, a school courtyard, bus stop, or beside the public tube well. In JS's practice, actors and audiences are seen as social actors even as they perform on-stage precisely because the distinction between actors and audience, actors and social actors are deliberately disrupted in 'theatre of the oppressed'. Representing the ideological boundary between real world and fictional world as an utterly unstable one is *the* utopian performative that sustains the 'theatre of the oppressed' performance.

Constructing the ideological boundary between fiction and reality as a nebulous one is a significant productive engine which helps refuse normative closure and socialise alternative norms and relationships. This is why JS members attribute power to their theatrical action without specifying direct causal connections between moments on-stage and transformation off-stage. Such connections remain nebulous so that it is not so clear whether the engine of change was off-stage political mobilisation or on-stage political representation. The analysis of what actors who encounter and live an 'alternate' reality, framed as fictional on-stage, do in their off-stage lives with this fleeting experience, knowledge, and rehearsal of alternatives is therefore worth examining. Not in order to determine whether an idea for transformation was first conceived on- or off-stage, but rather precisely to understand and dramatise the blurred nature of that ideological boundary and dialectically fed relation between staged performance and everyday performance, fiction and reality, staged political action and everyday political action.

The blurred boundary between staged performance and everyday performance has implications for conceptual formation of domination, liberation, and state-formation. There is no 'pure' and bounded space of political theatre separate from state processes. After all, political theatre has a shared history with state power and state processes co-opt theatrical resistance (Taylor 1997; Zook 2001). For this reason, we ought not to reify political theatre as an autonomous historical force. At the same time, this theatre can be a vehicle for state-formation because even though theatricality invades everyday life and politics, the live performance of theatre 'displays more of the process of constructing representation than do other cultural artifacts' (Martin 1994: 23).[7] As such, political theatre can be a mode of learning and displaying what it means to be a 'good' citizen, 'progressive' leader, and what makes a 'healthy' society.

Invariably, such definitions construct imagined communities of struggle with boundaries of inclusion and exclusion.

This conceptualisation of theatre as formative of society and state runs counter to the pessimistic view that the post-modern world (saturated with spectacles and everyday performances) renders political theatre useless. Against this perspective, Randy Martin argues that 'The disavowal that live theatrical performance retains relevance is not unlike the dismissal of the ongoing importance of the state' (2006: 25). That is, not unlike other spheres where the rolled-back state coexists with the continued relevance of the state, in conceptions of 'political' theatre too, the state participates in its own rolling back and transnationalisation as well as in the hegemonic control over political theatre itself. At the same time, political theatre and activism such as JS's attempts to pressure the formation of the state by building transnational alliances and audiences presenting alternative trajectories. This is the sense in which political theatre can be viewed as one practice of political action and 'politically organised subjection' through which to understand state-formation (Abrams 1988: 58–89). Seen this way, beneficiaries of popular electoral vote and those engaged in JS's political theatre are part of a continuum of translocal political action that constitutes the 'conduct of conduct' and state-formation.

JS's long-term engagement through its village theatre teams, with their regular 'forum theatre' events which perform the same plays over and over again in agricultural communities, constitutes a governmental regime of practice whereby they socialise, *regulate*, and problematise conduct of self and other. Their theatre does this by regularly generating collective reflection on representations of oppression publicised and enacted by JS leaders and spectators alike. Other than a core team of activists who receive a modest salary and act as leaders within JS as organisation, participation in its theatre does not have an exchange value nor does it come with political privilege for JS members. Engagement with JS has not been a conduit to normative definitions of material power or positions within village politics. To some extent, this nurtures engagement on-stage, freeing audiences to question representations by its leaders and spect-actors alike.

In JS's work, jokers and the spect-actors are theatrical figures on-stage *and* types of political actors off-stage. The function of the joker on-stage is to break audience silence and upset the constructed distinction between the fictional stage and real life off-stage. The spect-actor on-stage symbolises the possibility of redistributing and democratising public and political representation. JS activists are required to repeat and transpose these on-stage goals and practices in their activism off-stage. At the same time, even when the joker approximates the Gramscian 'organic intellectual', he or she represents the structure of power and ideological relations within which democratisation of representation takes place. Rather than acting as if the stage is unstructured by power relations, or an autonomous force of history, it is used as safe space where some power relations and real hindrances are relaxed while other kinds of imaginative powers and possibilities are collectively nourished in public space.

The ultimate goal of the spect-actor, as JS activists see it, is to intervene in a pre-scripted representation of a social problem and rescript it in ways that produce an alternate ending or alternate norms of behaviour. Through their engagement in forum theatre, spect-actors enact, embody, and stage the fact that social relations are malleable — a dramatic representation of that which makes performance 'a paradigm of process' (Schechner 1986: 8), and illuminates the power of performance to reveal 'structuring' publicly (Abrams 1982). Although Augusto Boal does not ascribe theoretical debt to Gramsci, his goals for what Forum Theatre can accomplish approximate Gramsci's 'philosophy of praxis'. This is Gramsci's term for the process through which humans acquire a 'critical and coherent conception of the world, [with]. [...] a consciousness of its historicity' (1971: 324). Yet, as I have come to understand 'theatre of the oppressed' in JS's practice (and mentioned in subsequent chapters), the principle characters — the joker and spect-actor — bring not just new political forms and initiatives, alert audiences to multiple possibilities and outcomes, but also dramatise the fact that there is no straightforward and determined path to liberation. This is a theme to which I return more fully in chapter four.

Within the commonsense of West Bengal's political Leftism, this is a significant contribution to de-centring 'liberation' and the ideological space of progressive politics. Thus, attending to the tensions, contradictions, and heterogenous nature of their practice, I view JS's everyday political activism and theatre as 'less about giving voice to shared values than about opening fields of argument; about providing the terms and tropes, that is, through which people caught in changing worlds may vex each other, question definitions of value, form alliances, and mobilise oppositions' (Comaroff and Comaroff 1993: xxiii). This very process of nurturing the capacity to represent oneself and opening fields of argument approximates the Foucauldian notion of government which 'extends to cover the way in which an individual questions his or her own conduct (or *problematises* it) so that he or she may be better able to govern it' (Dean 1999: 12).

JS's political theatre stages the state — or politically organised subjection — in action. They bring recognition by low-caste, landless labourers such as Prasad Sardar who have historically voted for the government that 'You don't have to obey people like the blind. You don't have to suffer from inferiority. You don't have to think that you are capable of nothing'. These may seem like personal realisations, far too distant from the outcome of large-scale electoral politics. But, after years of engagement in political theatre with JS, members have become central nodes of political leadership and activism, refusing the terms of Party political activism, giving advice and strategising collective action in the village. In other words, although engagement with JS comes with no promise of political–economic benefit, long-term work with it often produces the outcome of enhanced political position for activists who not only develop a sense of self-confidence, but also get exposure to translocal politics and a reputation for being able to command attention with public officials. Thus, on the one hand JS attempts to regulate and discipline the boundary between social movement and state and claims that they are not themselves a part of state or providers of welfare and service. On the other hand, there are numerous JS activists who have become prominent political figures in their own right in their village contexts. This is most apparent in the recent election of three JS members who became officials as they won in the panchayat elections of 2008. While these members had to leave the group in order to retain its non-partisan profile, the point I wish to make is that despite the ongoing attempt to discipline a boundary between state and social movement as well as between theatre group and state politics, events and processes in JS history are testimony to the bleeding and blurring that marks the relationship between political theatre and state in West Bengal. The state is malleable in deed, at least in part, because JS activists have imagined it as malleable in on-stage action.

Conclusion

My research contributes the study of cultural work itself to the rich and rapidly proliferating body of innovative literature on agrarian developments. It asks what we can learn about agrarian class struggles, materiality, collectivity, and dispossession when we are not looking directly at land struggles. Emergent on-stage are significant cues about dispossessed meanings and alternate collectivities which prompt theorisation of rural political theatre as a telling case of class struggle, productive work, and political action.

Political theatre has been considered insignificant in conceptions of development because rituals and cultural critiques are generally assumed to perform momentary safety-valve functions while ultimately reinforcing existing structures of inequality and hierarchy. Against these views, I have argued that political theatre embodies, expresses, conducts, and problematises relations of rule and inequality. It is not by default less 'productive' than capital accumulation, less 'transformative' than the policies of a newly elected leader, and less 'equalising' than land reform. A significant part of our ability to understand the work of political theatre depends on reimagining of productive labour, political action, and struggle.

✷

Notes

1. *People's Democracy*, 4 February 2008, http://pd.cpim.org/2008/0204_pd/02042008_agriculture.htm (accessed on 8 August 2008).
2. The social clause of the WTO would bring a minimum of work place standards into effect.
3. http://gi.unc.edu/programs/mellon/about_us.html (accessed on 28 January 2008).
4. To say that theatre is work is hardly an original statement. The theories of Bertolt Brecht, Ervin Piscator, and Augusto Boal are founded on the recognition that 'people produce it; others consume it; it serves specific aims within or against specific institutions' (Taylor 1991: 20). Yet, although this is understood well in performance studies, the implications of this, for understanding development deserves attention.
5. Yet, although this is understood well in performance studies the implications of this for understanding development deserves attention.
6. Here my comments are focused on the literature on political theatre in particular rather than indigenous forms more generally or the debates on intercultural performance (Bharucha 1996; Chauduri 1998). In the

study of indigenous forms in India particularly, scholars are much more attuned to the broad environment, time, and space of performance, its everyday presence in lives, its ability to question local modes of power, and its interaction with and sometimes displacement from changing modes of performance (Gupt and Hansen 2005; Hansen 1991; Kapur 2006; Schechner 1983; Seizer 2000). Recently scholars have focused much more on showing that that 'folk,' 'indigenous' and 'national' are hardly a priori reflections of theatrical tradition – little or great (Bhattacharya 2006; Deshpande 1985). Rather they are in constant transformation, appropriation and evolution into ever hybrid form as 'folk' is drawn into contexts and discourses such as nation, colonialism, and a 'theatre of roots'. Bringing together the complex trends and types of Indian theatre – classical, indigenous, 'foreign', and professional — at long last, the canon of Indian theatre is being consolidated with increasing sophistication (Chatterjee 2007; Dalmia 2006; Dharwadker 2005). Yet political theatre of the kind documented in this book is marginally placed or absent in these accounts. My effort is to insist on the theatricality of everyday life and political action in all forms, while understanding the distinctiveness of live performance as a mode of political and cultural action. In so doing, I believe we broaden what counts as the canon of modern Indian theatre. In my view, Rustom Bharucha has consistently struck this balance between theatricality and theatre in his work. See especially *Theatre and the World*, *In the Name of the Secular* and *The Politics of Cultural Practice: Thinking Through Theatre in the Age of Globalization*.

7. Studying live performances in Cuba and Nicaragua, allowed Martin to de-center state-centred views of socialism as well as an a priori notion of what socialism is by studying 'socialist ensembles' as they emerge in the civil societies of Cuba and Nicaragua, negotiating state and market (1994).

Chapter Three

Political Society in Formation: Staging Early Critiques

The CPM has built its organisational strength and hegemony in West Bengal through institutions such as the trade union, the panchayat, and women's association, among others. These institutions were meant to be grounded modes for constructing collectivity among the working class, of village society, and among women respectively.[1] Recent scholarship suggests that these are also institutions of governance that serve to decentralise development and distribute welfare. Through the trade union, panchayat, and women's association, in West Bengal state agents reproduce the terms of exercising power, citizens in distress in turn make claims on welfare provisioning, and government representatives distribute or withhold welfare as one means of securing votes from citizens (Chatterjee 1997; Corbridge 2005; Rogaly et al. 1999; Ruud 2003). In effect, through these institutions, the Left Front Government (LFG) has bartered votes for welfare, normalising paternalistic, often compromised, and mercy politics — the hallmark of Partha Chatterjee's concept of political society.

For Chatterjee, Indian bourgeois democracy is distinguished from its European counterpart because in addition to civil society peopled by the urban middle class who are under the 'moral–political sway of the bourgeoisie', there is a political society peopled by the rural and urban poor (2008a: 57). His account of democracy is animated by a Gramscian distinction between civil society and political society operationalised through a Foucauldian lens of governmentality. In post-colonial societies where socio-economic policies of the developmental state combat poverty and 'backwardness', citizens are first and foremost enumerated as various population groups on governmental surveys (landless, squatters, jobless, refugees, below-the-poverty-line card-holders, and so forth). Civil society, founded on ideas of 'popular sovereignty', equality, free entrance and exit, contract, deliberative procedures, rights and duties, is limited to those 'culturally equipped citizens' who have the privilege to realise idealised equal citizenship (Chatterjee 2004: 41). The rest of the population are only 'tenuously, and even then ambiguously and contextually, rights-bearing citizens' (*ibid.*: 38). Outside civil society proper, yet enumerated and living within national territory, these populations are both subject to control and potential claimants on state welfare and rights. These citizens are routinely pushed towards criminal and illegal action as a result of government inability to reconcile private property rights with the mandate of welfare for all citizens.[2]

These tensions of realising liberal democracies in post-colonial societies are particularly problematic in the neoliberal conjuncture. The state faces an exacerbated tension as it has to invite capital investment by constructing a receptive environment for privatisation of various publics while providing citizen welfare from shrinking public coffers and resources. Chatterjee's examples of 'politics of the governed' show how illegal action (such as squatting on public land, stealing electricity, travelling on public transportation without tickets) enables citizens to win government attention and collaborate with officials to form 'political society'. Two related processes constitute political society: first, a mutual recognition between populations and governmental officials of the instrumental power of the vote (Chatterjee 2004: 41); second, giving the 'empirical form of a [given] population group the moral attributes of a community' (*ibid.*: 57). Thus, the governed reduced to enumerated categories resuscitate democracy in Chatterjee's terms, by making claims on the developmental state's grammars of welfare distribution. Articulating illegal action as necessary for survival incorporates 'illegality' and 'immorality' into a moral claim to governmental care. This is how marginalised citizens with or without the collaboration of 'parties, movements, and non-party political formations' carve out political society in the face of historically entrenched odds (*ibid.*: 46).

In this chapter, I describe the textual content of three early Jana Sanskriti (JS) plays to show that JS members and leaders were representing and critiquing the formation of 'political society' in Bengal in their dramatic texts in the late 1980s and early 1990s.[3] Through an analysis of these plays, I argue for the reconceptualisation of political society in three distinct ways. First, the conceptualisation of political society must address explicitly the tension between providing a critique of civil society politics and normalising criminality and violence as the 'politics of the governed' (Chatterjee 2004). This conceptualisation is comfortable with a realist presentation of this incorporation of illegality, criminality, and violence into the fold of democratic politics. Prompted by the work and plays of JS, I make a distinction between the kinds of criminality that prompt stealing electricity or squatting on state land, and the kinds of criminality where politicians and corporations hire mercenaries, participants in riots, and so forth. While acknowledging that these are different kinds of 'criminality' of the poor by recognising the 'dark side of political society', Chatterjee claims that he cannot commit to a full explanation of 'how criminality and violence are tied to the ways in which various deprived population groups must struggle to make their claims to governmental care' (2004: 75). In this chapter, I show that JS's early plays stage critiques of the insidious formation of the 'dark side of political society' as the normative social relation among the poor as well as between government and the poor in West Bengal.

JS leaders are all too aware of the material distress and constraints that push people towards such politics of criminality and violence. Arguably, theatre is JS's means of constructing an alternate political society — one that refuses the subjective and structural closure that assumes that the rural poor have no choice but reproduce violent and competitive social relations. As Sanjoy Ganguly puts it, 'Theatre is just a weapon for me to do my politics'. In this politics, JS finds itself negotiating existing hierarchies and powers. As a result, they sometimes work parallel to, sometimes in negotiation with, and sometimes combat panchayat activities, the *morol* (village moral and political adjudicator), religious groups, and party politics. Yet, in contrast to the academic literature on political society, the protagonist characters in JS plays (and JS activism as mentioned in later chapters) represent the complex collusions and formation of political society, but they refuse to resign themselves to a democracy held captive by government through political society. By his own admission, Chatterjee leaves unexplored the 'dark side of political society' through which 'criminality and violence are tied to the ways in which deprived populations must struggle to make their claims to governmental care' (2004: 75). JS plays point to the imperative of contesting political society because the formation of political society attempts to normalise criminality and violence as the inevitable core of social relations among the poor. As such, these plays dramatise and question the insidious formation of political society as criminal and violent social relations among the poor, and between the government and the poor, in order to rescript political action and representation.

The second contribution I make to the reconceptualisation of political society is to refuse the separation of government and market-based welfare. Significantly, for Chatterjee political society means that 'the vast bulk of democratic politics in India is not under the moral–political leadership of the capitalist class' (2008a: 57). That is to say, for him, government, not the capitalist class, rules the terms of democratic political action in contexts of material deprivation and electoral dependence. In this chapter, I contest this separation arguing that perpetuating the idea that the poor have no choice but illegal, violent, and criminal modes of association and political action works in conjunction with the idea of a 'race to the bottom' and the market episteme of competing for individual self-interest. This extension of the legacy of liberal capitalist and imperial rule is represented and critiqued in JS's work which shows that political society functions on the principle of distributing welfare for those who demand governmental care. However, apart from constructing welfare as the right to governmental care, the formation of political society also naturalises welfare as scarce resources to be acquired through competitive individual pursuit of political favour and negotiation. This normalises governmental duty of welfare distribution as a political exchange for the vote. Political society in formation expresses the inextricably linked processes through which the political authority and rule of a market episteme comes to be accomplished, normalising the 'social' of social relations.

The third conceptual development I make is to suggest that patriarchy is a constitutive mode of forming political society in rural Bengal. Here, the violence and criminality that help the poor secure benefits for and from government are played out on the bodies and lives of women in distinct ways. Extracting governmental care through violence counts on the political–economic insecurity women face in questions of land and legal rights, and reproduces rationales for regulatory norms that ostensibly protect women by placing severe controls on women's everyday actions. The JS play *Sarama* shows how patriarchal rule in Bengal — within the household and within state institutions — helps construct political society and normalise a market episteme. In the sixth chapter, I show how patriarchal rule and political society are revealed and challenged in political action off-stage.

The next three sections of this chapter analyse three early JS plays — *Where We Stand, Song of the Village, Sarama* — juxtaposing textual critiques with secondary sources that situates the plays within the context of LFG policies and institutions of governance and academic analysis that debate these policies and collectivities as Leftist compromise or alternatively as Leftist progressivism (Bagchi 2005; A. Basu 1992; Chatterjee 1997; Fernandes 1997; Kohli 1987, 2006; Lieten 1990, 1994, 2003; Mallick 1993; Rogaly et al. 1999). In the context of three decades of LFG interventions in the industrial and agrarian sectors, as well as in the sphere of gender equality, these three plays present critical perceptions of and negotiations with LFG policies and institutions of governance and forms of political collectivity. Within the polarising terms of the debate empirically demonstrating Communist Party of India-Marxist (CPM) success (Lieten 2003) or failure (Mallick 1993), the complex relation rural Bengalis bear to the party's policy and discourse gets buried.

The Limits of Trade Union Collectivity: Amra Jeikhane Dariye

Amra Jeikhane Dariye, meaning 'Where We Stand', written in 1993, is Sanjoy Ganguly's second play. Unlike the characteristic focus of JS plays on experiences in villages, this play is an expression of Ganguly's own disaffection with trade union politics. He described why he Left trade union politics with which he had been involved since the 1970s:

> **Ganguly**: I got involved in the trade union and that's when I realised that trade union leaders conducted politics to their own end. They will keep you satisfied, incite you to say things and then go behind your back when it comes to facing the violence. I spoke against them, they claimed to trace me to Naxal activity and out I went. [...] I left the party in 1981. I left my job in 1984. I started JS in 1985. [...] CPM politics was the same, leaders inciting people to say things and then taking the backseat when trouble came.
>
> **Researcher**: When did the party become like this?

> **Ganguly**: From the very beginning. But there was good work that the party did. Yes there was. But the day the party divided CPI into CPM, and CPI (M-L) (*he pauses*) my father joined CPM because at that time what you did was affiliate yourself to leaders and you would go where your leader went.

Ganguly has a particularly critical view of CPM leadership from its very inception, decrying its veneer of collective politics for what quickly became individual political and economic aggrandisement.

What are the political–economic features of the moment within which Ganguly's disaffection from trade union politics can be situated? In 1981, there were 9.6 million cases of labour dispute in West Bengal (Kohli 2006: 1367). By the late 1980s and as a result of capital flight, the fatigue had spread — within the CPM and with the CPM — not just among the urban middle class but even among the industrial working classes. In the 1980s, West Bengal had the highest percentage of chronically loss-incurring industries (Pedersen 2001: 656), vociferous labour militancy and high unemployment (Kohli 2006: 1367). The Party could blame capital flight on discriminatory central government licensing policies and budget allocation, and found reason to turn centre–state ideological differences into a strategy for unifying all classes within Bengal into a 'partisan and confrontational subnationalism' (Sinha 2005: 196). Iconic representations like 'unruly business climate', 'sick industry', and Kolkata as a 'dying city' signalled accumulating industrial decay and inordinate rural unemployment. Despite moves to combat this reputation as a politically irascible and economically moribund state through joint sector industrial development in the mid-1980s, internal dissension in the Party did not allow such efforts to achieve fruition for another 10 years (Sinha 2005: 125).

In the campaign leading up to the 1987 elections, the Party sought to buttress its youth membership, diversified its campaign techniques from large political rallies to political plays, door-to-door campaigning, and opted to stress on LFG's position on issues such as minimum wages rather than dwell on abstract esoteric theories (Sen Gupta 1989: 886). In the 1987 election, the Congress Party had the largest percentage of votes in West Bengal, with 41.4 per cent of total votes compared with 39.3 per cent for CPM (*ibid.*). Because the Left Front had a coalition of parties, the CPM continued in power. However, the problem of declining support among industrial working classes manifest in the 1987 election (Pedersen 2001: 656) continued through the 1990s (Das Gupta 1998).

Sen Gupta attributes the heavy losses for the CPM in the 'popular vote in urban-industrial districts' in the 1987 elections to a 'feeling of despair that prevailed in the industrial belt close to Kolkata' (Sen Gupta 1989: 888). In one such industrial belt close to Kolkata, Ganguly experienced his political coming of age, gave up his involvement in the political Left, to construct a version of the social Left. *Amra Jeikhane Dariye* was written at a time when urban, middle-class Bengalis believed that labour unrest had become an end in itself. This class of urban citizens may have participated in affirming Leftist politics bringing the CPM to power, but they also harboured the expectations of rationalised government, modern life, and urban conveniences. On the one hand, this is the time and place of Sanjoy Ganguly's politics; on the other, Ganguly's reasons for searching a new path had to do with alienation from a political collectivity that was engaging in individualist, duplicitous politics of private benefit gained by those who supposedly led on the strength of public trust.

Ganguly wrote *Amra Jeikhane Dariye* reflecting on the early days of this disillusionment with organised Left politics in the industrial sector. Ganguly highlights the divisive effects of self-serving politics in a supposedly collective political organisation. He also depicts the collusion of trade union leadership with police violence, compromised Leftism, and coalitions for electoral gain. Ultimately, these factors combine to explain the betrayal of 'development' in West Bengal. The opening song of the play goes as follows:

> Your address and mine — Padma, Meghna, Yamuna
> Turning the bend around Mekong and Volga,
> I found my direction in Ganga's flow.
> Song doesn't worry about language differences
> The language of the heart takes care of thirst
> We cross seven seas
> To stand where we stand
> To find our limit.[4]

While recalling relevant international histories and transnational flows, the play announces a commitment to a politics of 'where we stand' to 'find our limit'. The song is followed immediately by actors recalling revolutions and wars, beginning with the Russian Revolution and ending with the fall of the Soviet Union. This historical timeline is the backdrop for analysing the organised Left, and their construction of 'development' in India.

In the very next scene, Comrade Bikash is discovered dead by his trade union friends. Bikash is a common Bengali name meaning arising, awakening, or development. His death, then, is a more or less straightforward metaphor for the death of development in the context of post-colonial Bengal. His comrades mourn his death without knowing how he died. The play is constructed around the awakening of Bikash's soul to tell the true story of his killing to his friends who are unable, from their location, to see his death as a sign of collective betrayal. The grand outcome of historical revolutions and the subsequent fall of the Soviet Union in the metaphor of Bikash's death unambiguously present the betrayal of post-colonial development.

His death, we subsequently find out, is a result of the actions of his corrupt and self-serving trade union leader Tarit, who used Bikash as bait for an avowedly 'people's' cause. Bikash's friends ask Tarit how the criminals can be brought to justice.

> **Workers**: But will there be no justice for this murder? Will the guilty not be punished?
>
> **Tarit**: We will have to try. It is so easy to murder [...] if you understood this. Because of the lack of adequate evidence, most cases 'Not Guilty'. Finished! And that's why, well never mind, all these things [...] All of you now settle down. There is much work ahead. I should probably go see wicked Maganlal [factory owner].

The portrayal of Tarit as self-consciously relying on a corrupt justice system shows a trade union leader actively manoeuvring between those seeking justice and those perpetrating it by externalising blame on a corrupt 'system'. The audience then witnesses Tarit's corrupt relations with another trade union leader — Maganlal — who ordered Bikash's killing. Maganlal buys Tarit's silence and justifies his actions on the basis of Bikash's disloyal and 'disruptive' actions within the factory. In Maganlal's words, there is no injustice in killing Bikash because 'that bastard, son of a bitch, works in my factory, gets after me [for a job], eats my salt, and then bites the hand that feeds him. So I removed him [...] You tell me, where is the injustice in this?' Bikash violated the rules of negotiation and exchange germane to maintaining the equilibrium of political society and for this he had to die.

Coyly but surely, Tarit extracts a fat bribe from Maganlal in return for quelling calls for justice by Bikash's friends. Bikash rises

Figure 3.1: Coyly but surely, Tarit (right) extracts a fat bribe from Maganlal (left)

from the dead to tell the audience how he was shot outside the factory gates and left by the railway tracks to make it appear as though he had been killed in an accident. 'Does the truth remain suppressed?' he asks the audience implicating them in the ongoing normalisation of violence. Bikash appears to Tarit as his conscience to remind him that Comrade Lenin's freedom fighters are alive in every village and city. His voice after death questions the nature of the organised politics of the time, and its collective betrayal of both development and anti-capitalist struggle. However, Tarit dismisses his conscience as inconsequential. Instead, he tells his friends who await justice, 'They don't know that if you murder one Bikas, thousands are reborn. Comrade Bikas, we have not forgotten you, and we will not forget you.' The scene ends with actors begging around for a conscience: 'Where can I find some conscience? Can I find some conscience here?' Actors in turn address the audience directly:

First person: One day they used to have a conscience. In these few years, they lost it somewhere.
Second person: They have become animals without their conscience.

Third person: All around just deals (*aposh*).
Fourth person: Politicians with the police.
Fifth person: Ministers and Business.
Sixth person: For this, you are responsible. I am responsible. We are all responsible.
Seventh person: We are the ones who give birth to them.
Eight person: We are the ones who nurture them.
Ninth person: And they are the ones who cheat us.
Chorus: Yes, they are the ones who cheat us.

Again, highlighting the formation of political society based on 'deals' without a conscience, actors challenge audience members to recognise their own participation in making political society. This is consciousness-raising aimed at a Gramscian recognition that the power of hegemony relies on consent. The rest of the play shows how people are scared into conformity, including the rape of women at police stations, how Party politics divide and allocate people to Party leaders rather than encourage debate on principles, and how development projects help discipline citizens into submission. The play expresses disillusionment with experiences of socialism since the historic revolutions that had flowed from the Mekong to the Ganga. Yet, the complaint is patently not with Leftist political philosophy, but with its practice in West Bengal. Trade union members and naïve party cadres are portrayed as fools of leaders only engaged in the pursuit of redistribution and anti-capitalist struggle in a cynical rhetoric, while reducing democratic politics and welfare provisions to an instrumental game about votes. This is the dialogue between two politicians seeking votes:

Politician One: Friends! Election is coming up. That's why I am here. To beg for votes from you. I couldn't imagine that you would show up in such numbers on my call. Now it makes me realise that you all have deep love for me. After all, I have constantly failed to do things for you. So, help me with your votes, so I may serve you again.
Politician One's followers turn into little goats that bend to the right.

Politician Two: Friends! We have done a lot for you. And we have not been able to do a lot. They have hindered every effort of ours, put a spoke in every wheel. Therefore, to overcome these hindrances we have to destroy them. We have to turn this state into a golden state. Just give us one chance. I will be able to serve your interests with your vote.

Politician Two's followers turn into little goats that bend to the left. The two politicians shake hands as the goats are in opposing images to the right and left.

Here, political society is an outcome of dividing the poor against each other, while politicians conspire to accrue the financial and electoral benefit from violence between the poor. This is also explicit translation of JS's position that their representations question the limits of the party system itself rather than any particular political party.

In this play, corruption is a mode of highlighting that while trade unions battle capital publicly, its leaders appropriate public money privately. In Ganguly's play, the weakness of the trade unions as organisational collectivities is not anti-capitalist theory, but rather the blatant pursuit of monetary and political advantage by its leaders, and the threat of violence to curb dissent within. This representation on-stage is echoed in the work of some scholars who have recently argued that political violence has helped manage labour relations, constituted decentralised democracy, and furthered short-term electoral gains in West Bengal (Corbridge et al. 2005: 210; Rogaly 1998; Ruud 1999).

Ganguly's play on trade unions as one significant collectivity in West Bengal takes up a relatively narrow set of complaints with trade union politics, ignoring its largely masculine and patriarchal practices (Fernandes 1997).[5] Moreover, despite initial references to world-historical events such as the fall of the Soviet Union, his play does not relate the failure of collective politics in West Bengal to global dilemmas of decolonisation, the ongoing 'assassination of the Third World' (Prashad 2005: 117–27), and the 'extremely unfavourable material conditions under which socialism's battles had to be fought, both internally and externally' (Ahmad 1992: 23). Some argue that if 'unfavourable conditions' constrained what the Soviet Union could do — a superpower in the Cold War — then the West Bengal government can hardly overcome capitalist forces within a corner of the Indian polity. Recognising the state government's weaknesses — illiteracy, corruption among lower and middle cadres, an industrial policy that approximates that of the bourgeois centre — Aijaz Ahmad asks, '*Can* the states go against the Centre in some basic way?'[6] (Ahmad 2000: 234). Seen through the lens of this JS play, the question to be raised in response is this: if state governments cannot 'go against the Centre in some basic way', then what ideological interest can people have to vote for a Party that claims to be a regional anti-capitalist force (*ibid.*)? In a similar vein, I ask below how 'red' a red panchayat really is. As local institutions of decentralised development, even they seem to be mainly of instrumental rather than ideological interest to voters, perpetuating division and competition among the poor for welfare distribution.

How Red is a Red Panchayat? Gayer Panchali

If urban–industrial voters are the CPM's Achilles heel in West Bengal, then what of its celebrated beneficiaries — rural citizens? The situation in the rural areas is different from the problems that afflicted West Bengal industry in the 1980s. Against historical odds, the CPM implemented land reform, securing tenancy rights for sharecroppers, distributing land over the legal ceiling to marginal and peasant holders, improving food security, irrigation reform, and increasing purchasing power and agricultural productivity in rural areas (D. Bhattacharyya 1999; Harris 1993; Lieten 2003; Rawal 2001). In 1978, well before such initiatives took root in the rest of India and the broader neoliberal turn to 'good governance', the CPM implemented *panchayati raj* which decentralised political representation and governance to institutions for local government elected by villages (approximately 10 villages make one panchayat).

Some scholars argue for direct causal connections between agrarian reforms and agricultural growth in West Bengal (Lieten 1990, 1994) while others mock such reforms for their inadequacy (Mallick 1993). I draw on sources that celebrate the developments to understand a positive view of the CPM (Lieten 1990, 1994) and combine this with competing analyses of rural development in the state (Chatterjee 1997; Corbridge et al. 2005; Rogaly et al. 1999). Analysing a play on agrarian social life, and assuming that rural citizens are not just farmers and labourers, I try to reveal what we can learn about agrarian society when we are not looking directly at agriculture or land rights.

Sanjoy Ganguly's play *Gayer Panchali* meaning 'Song of the Village' was first performed in 1987 in Mathurapur block of South 24 Parganas. This play was scripted through a process of engagement and involvement in peasant life and politics. The play evolved over time through performances and post-performance interactions with audiences. The play made a consolidated case against the compulsions of seasonal migration for employment, the right to work and live in the village right through the year, and the lack of rural populations' access to healthcare, either in rural spaces or in urban spaces when they travelled for dangerous work in the construction industry. This play has been performed by agricultural and wage labourers at least hundred times a year, mostly in the 1980s and 1990s, across West Bengal, in select states in India, and internationally as well.

Unlike the CPM in Kerala where the Party led land struggles and lost in parliament, in West Bengal, the Party chose a compromised tenancy reform and won electorally by maintaining citizens' administrative dependence on the Leftist government (Herring 1983). Prioritising democracy rather than class confrontation, the Party redefined exploitation not as surplus appropriation but as fighting the parasitic lifestyles of big, absentee landlords (Kohli 1987: 100). Atul Kohli argues that the CPM has shown considerable ideological discipline, unity through democratic centralist organisational structure, and incorporated 'the lower classes to buttress state power as a tool of social reform' (*ibid.*: 96). The CPM regime moved from class confrontation to 'development and a democratic–socialist ideology' (*ibid.*: 99). The Party leadership of upper-caste absentee landlords had the difficult task of neutralising the *jotedars* who were the rich peasantry belonging to intermediate castes while pursuing an agrarian reform agenda without opening the floodgates for reactionary violence and central government intervention (Mitra 2001: 112–13).

CPM land reform has primarily benefited sharecroppers by registering them under Operation Barga[7] giving them security as tenants and entitlement to 75 per cent of crop share to the cultivator.[8] Unlike registration of sharecropper rights, locating and redistributing land held above the maximum ceiling (surplus or *benami* land) has proved trickier. Instead of pursuing this policy adequately, the Party has shifted its agenda using its 'red panchayats' to provide supportive development programmes that benefit sharecroppers and landless labourers (Kohli 1987: 117–42). There are multiple and diverse implications of transferring institutional power through red panchayats and tenancy reform from 'dominant propertied groups to a politicised lower-middle'

(Kohli 1987: 113) section of rural society (Rogaly et al. 1999). Dipankar Basu (2001) has argued that agrarian reform initiatives of the CPM substituted the rule of the rich peasantry with the rule of middle peasantry evident in its policies of tax relief for landlords, high procurement prices, and limited distribution of state-held land to the landless, and by increasing the dependency of farming on inputs which only the rich or middle peasantry could afford.

While high procurement prices should be beneficial to cultivators, this is the case only when they are net-sellers of grain. In the Kulpi, Pathar Pratima, and Mathurapur blocks of South 24 Parganas district where JS does its work, villagers depend on a combination of agricultural and non-agricultural sources of income. The majority of the population here constitutes net-buyers rather than sellers of rice. As such, any additional means of providing welfare such as inputs for farming, loans for starting small businesses, and subsidised access to education and health through the red panchayats became significant sources of support for households, especially during seasonal scarcities.

Although the panchayats are meant to serve as conduits of development programmes to support the poorest section of rural society, there is a common perception that they are in fact instruments of maintaining loyalty to the ruling political Party within the panchayat's jurisdiction. No doubt the landless and the poor typically gave the Party their support. What Kohli provided as justification two decades ago remains the dominant perception on the ground today, 'the CPM favors its political sympathisers and gains electoral popularity by channeling resources to select groups. The CPM is, after all, a political Party and not a charitable organisation' (Kohli 1987: 139).

Song of the Village brings together stories of people's experiences of coalition politics among CPM leaders, panchayat corruption, and class disadvantage in the Bengal countryside. This play begins with a song written by Digendralal Roy. Roy's song describes the uniqueness of 'my land of birth' (*amar jonmo bhumi*). The lyrics suggest 'my land of birth' is the best among all nations in the world, full of flowers, created from blood, woven through memories and dreams. There is no other country quite like it — 'I was born in this place, may I die right here in this place' (*amar eyi deshe te jonmo jeno eyi deshe te mori*). In the JS play however, this song has satirical purpose followed as it is by this exchange between the *sutradhar* or the mediator and the characters on-stage:

Mediator: Who are you all?
All: We don't know.
Mediator: Are you history sculpted into stone?
All: We exist at the mouth of death.
Mediator: Why? What do you do?
All: We work in factories and fields. We are labourers. We keep the wheels of civilisation moving. Our blood, sweat, and labour produces new creations. We want to build our lives in new ways.
Mediator: What do you want at this moment?
All: To stay in the village, to work in the village, to cultivate crops, from village to village we want work right through the year.

Agricultural labourers, this beginning suggests, live at the mouth of death even as they develop the nation. Although labouring classes construct a nation's future, their position remains a marginalised one with little power to craft the terms of their life. The new life labourers want allows them to live and work in rural communities. In a context where migration is disrupting relationships between men and women, feminising agricultural work, and rendering 'community' increasingly fragile, the right to work is, in a significant sense, a demand for recognising the right to work *in the village* (Bagchi 2005; Roy 2007; UNDP 2004).

Struggling with the challenge of living and working in the village, this play rages against the assumption that agriculture is no longer productive enough, that the village is vanishing, and aspirations have incontrovertibly shifted outwards towards the challenge and promise of urban life (Rogaly et al. 1999; D. Gupta 2005). Even though the framing statement of the play suggests peasant solidarity and identity 'To stay in the village, to work in the village, to cultivate crops, from village to village we want work right through the year', the actual problems depicted in it have little to do with the glories of peasant life, work, or identity. Indeed, a significant vignette in the play focuses on the death and insecurity that befalls migrants to cities and their families. Rather this popular JS play focuses on corrupt governmental practice in the distribution and allocation of development goods and benefits to depict the political economic forces that have helped push aspirations towards a future beyond the field.

Those who question the viability of rural futures give inadequate attention to the fact that viability, belonging, and sense of place are outcomes of regional interactions, multiple processes, and movement (de Haan and Rogaly 2002; Gidwani and

Sivaramakrishnan 2003; Hart 1998). Agrarian studies have recently begun to theorise peasant struggles as efforts to accomplish multi-layered sovereignty negotiating local, national, and transnational politics (Desmarais 2007; McMichael 2008). Suggestions of agrarian non-viability also ignore the fact that the structure of redistribution through the rural developmental state continues to make rural livelihoods viable by piecemeal reversals of the effects of primitive accumulation (Corbridge et al. 2005; Chatterjee 2008a).

The second scene of the play begins with a song. The Integrated Rural Development Programme (IRDP) loans were launched in 1980 by the central government of India which identified rural poor and gave them various inputs and assets to enable them to cross the poverty line. The song in the JS play mocks the IRDP plan by highlighting its real beneficiaries.

> The IRDP came to reduce poverty,
> And IRDP loans went straight to the big farmers.
> The poor farmer begged their leaders for IRDP loans,
> And they got the IRDP loans.
> But the very next day the money went straight to the money lender.

The 'cost' of the loans for the poor farmer is a paternalistic bond with particular local politicians while the ultimate beneficiaries of the IRDP 'non-corporate capital' or 'noncapital' (to use terms recently coined by Chatterjee 2008a and Sanyal 2007 respectively) are village money-lenders. However, whether this is state capital or non-capital, it is still money. As such, individuals competing for scarce monetary gains reproduce the market episteme and commodify democratic politics.

In another scene early on in the play, a poor farmer taking his goat for sale to the market is accosted by a politician. This politician demands that the farmer sell the goat through him since he got the farmer the loan through which the latter bought the goat in the first place. The farmer first pleads with the politician begging to let him proceed unhindered. He calculates aloud how much of the loan repaid previous debts, how he already gave five of the fattened goats to the politician, and asks why the politician insists on setting his sights on this last goat. 'Sir, you are kind, you are my mother and father, please let me go so I can sell this goat in the market myself and get the right price for it.' His plea falls on deaf ears.

The farmer (who wants to sell his goat) recognises the legitimacy of the politician's authority insofar as he had claimed his right to a loan through this politician in the past. He enacts the 'sincere fiction' of a leader's legitimacy by addressing the politician as a parentlike authority (Bourdieu 1977: 171). This is a classic example of performing deference in peasant societies where villagers avoid confrontation with local authorities by enacting subtle arts of resistance instead (J.C. Scott 1987, 1990; see Hart 1991 for a critique). The enactment of a sincere fiction simultaneously preserves and produces the reality of a politician's paternalistic authority and embodies the recognition that his authority depends on legitimacy granted in moments of interaction. In this case, the interaction produces the politician as (fictive) parent. When the villager's attempt at resistance fails, the limits of this fictional parent's care and the performed deference become clear. The play thus stages in public space the limits of 'hidden transcripts', making the play itself a public confrontation with political authority and publicising (the limits of) 'everyday forms of collaboration' (White 1986). They also question the strategy of 'everyday forms of resistance' which are hidden to no one but nonetheless serve to protect the unequal terms of villagers' relationships to local authority (J. C. Scott 1987, 1990).

The politician insists slyly, 'It is because I think of your welfare that I am in politics today, right?' This is a critique of the CPM practice of invoking high politics as a way of explaining and disregarding 'unsavoury features of local politics' (Chatterjee 1997: 166). On-stage, the politician continues:

> **Politician**: Where did you get the goat?
> **Farmer**: IRDP loan.
> **Politician**: Where did you get the IRDP loan?
> **Farmer**: You had it arranged for me.
> **Politician**: Listen all! Did you hear him? This here, me, *I* arranged it for him.
> **Farmer**: It is true you arranged it for me, but is IRDP your father's property?
> **Politician**: Son of a sow! You bring my father into this? I will not let you take this goat to the market!

When the farmer resists the politician's designs of siphoning a profit, he is beaten up by his lackeys.

The politician smiling deviously then dances with his stick singing: 'In my hand I carry democracy's stick. Look at the authority of its walk. This stick has such qualities, it is bathed in blood.' Note that

Figure 3.2: 'In my hand, I carry democracy's stick'

Ganguly did not script this song to read the bloody stick of development. His satirical focus on the bloody stick of democracy is a reference to the 'red panchayats' and the ways in which the institutions and 'activities of the developmental state [...] [are] brought under the management of the Party' through it (Corbridge et al. 2005: 207). The corruption of development speaks of the corruption of local institutions of governance and democracy, where rural development is a problem of rule that links 'discipline and development' (Chatterjee 1997: 141–71). This combination of discipline and development is vividly apparent when we step offstage and consider the debates around what these institutions have accomplished.

When in 1978 the CPM instituted panchayats as institutions for local governance, the big farmers and supporters of the Congress Party who lost their land through Operation Barga changed their Party political affiliation to the former. In 1999, Prasad Sardar, a key activist and actor with JS, pointed to a tube well in his village and said, 'This is not a tube-well.' This was not an absurd statement. He was getting at the fact that the CPM panchayat installed the pump of the tube well after one set of elections, dug 30 feet into the ground after another set of elections, and the villagers were still waiting for the tube well to be dug down till the pipe reached the water table so that the tube well could actually pump water to the surface. This was an everyday expression of how the panchayat disciplines Party loyalty for the long-term which is incrementally prolonged through the piecemeal delivery of development goods. This is not to say that the CPM has not made significant improvements in irrigation in West Bengal, but that the gains accrue in spaces of and in pace with ongoing Party loyalty.

Some researchers have suggested that Operation Barga changed the power structure in rural countryside so that implementation of the local government system could become meaningful (Ghatak and Ghatak 2002). Indeed, 'In all the last five elections, the CPI (M) led Left Front and its constituents have retained their overall hold over the panchayat system at all levels' (Ghatak and Ghatak 2002: 47) sometimes estimated at a 'share of Village Council seats ranging between 60–70%' (*ibid.* 2000). While elections ensure some anti-incumbency voting, since key administrative services and poverty alleviation programmes are carried out through these institutions, the benefits of voting for the ruling Party of the region is high which encourages incumbency votes. Masterfully, the CPM secured support from the powerful in the countryside while constructing a counter-hegemonic agenda of making small-peasant cultivation viable through decentralised governance and land reform. The Party and the local governance institution became inextricably linked as the red panchayat's development work aided in legitimising and constructing CPM as the hegemonic political collectivity in rural Bengal.

Over time, the number of very poor panchayat representatives did increase (Lieten 1994). But studies also show that while panchayat elections of the late 1980s and 1990s brought peasantry and agricultural labourers to power in high percentages, over time, Party politics has come to dominate institutional action. As another set of institutions of state power rather than people's power (H. Bhattacharya 1998), they render people disinterested in constructing decentralised democracy (M. Bhattacharya 2002), and make citizens unwilling to invest in re-envisioning the terms of local development projects (Williams 1999). More recently, with the reservation of 33.3 per cent seats for women (Munshi 2005), studies find that women panchayat leaders are able to prioritise their welfare needs such as drinking water and roads, (Chattopadhyay and Duflo 2004) income opportunities and nutrition programmes

(Ghatak and Ghatak 2000). These studies show that the marginalised are far from neglected in rural development in West Bengal. My point rather is that the CPM remains the chief conduit through which power is accessed, and hence it defines the terms of gaining access to resources and representation.

A debate amongst various members of the panchayat in the JS play highlights the grounds for red panchayat legitimacy. While constructing a list of beneficiaries of IRDP loans, the local leaders argue that as big and middle farmers occupying the seats of the panchayat it is their duty to ensure that the bulk of the loans go to rich and middle farmers. The sole politician who argues against this scheme is keen that small farmers who voted for the local officials continue to have cause to support their leadership. This panchayat representative suggests that if leaders failed to give small farmers loans proportionate to their presence in the village, how can leaders expect the vote in future panchayat elections? In response to this intervention, the leader says, 'Oh shut up mister! You can't do politics with all these principles in mind. We give promises knowing that we won't keep them. Do you understand? So keep your principles to yourself.' The leader supports his statement with the logic that he for one has to recover the 50,000 rupees (approximately $1,200) he spent to secure his position of panchayat leader.

These might seem like exaggerated accounts to those who believe in the promise of red panchayats, but the cost of getting schoolteachers' jobs and local leadership positions were part of daily conversation, not really the surreptitious activity of a few. Government schoolteacher jobs are particularly coveted for they are a source of relatively high and secure income in rural areas as well as an important conduit of gaining a foothold into CPM power structures (D. Bhattacharyya 2000). Notwithstanding the blurred boundaries between panchayat and ruling Party authority, as Arild Ruud has shown, the local governance institution has limited power because the power of the ruling Party and its daily presence in village life far exceeds the power of the panchayat (2003: 160–64 for findings in Burdwan district). To occupy the few political positions or get the few jobs available in villages, you had to either be able to buy access or be granted one through a political favour.

In the play, panchayat leaders are constructed as differentiated with some more willing than others to build a local governance institution along corrupt lines, rather than on the principle of proportionate representation, i.e., some more than others believe in the rhetoric of the CPM as *the* collectivity for the poor with the practice of giving proportionately to them. Other leaders believe that elected leaders compromise on their duties of political representation seeing this compromise as the cost of orchestrating peace with dominant classes in rural society. Some scholars have argued that through its land and political decentralisation reforms, the CPM has lived up to its historically middle-class character and *bhadralok* structural location. Middleness has allowed them to construct class alliance among a highly differentiated peasantry and rural populace in political–economic terms (Bhattacharyya 1999, 2001). Moreover, their mode of incorporating lower classes relies on a pedagogical process that constructs a middle-class and caste out of the lower classes in agrarian society (Ruud 1999). Together these leaders of various class and caste backgrounds construct a political society that offers little room for deprived populations to manoeuvre except through Party loyalty.

Corruption of red panchayats becomes particularly significant in light of the memory of the Tebhaga movement in 1946 in the South 24 Parganas region which was initiated by the Krishak Sabha (the peasant front of the Communist Party). This movement mobilised for the reduction of the landlord's share of harvest from half to a third of the produce. The success and spread of land struggles in Bengal hold iconic value for the material situation of the contemporary peasantry. This is in part because the memory of this movement survives in bodies, stories, and songs. In part, this is also because the CPM continued land campaigns in the 1960s and 1970s with significant effects on agricultural growth (Lieten 1990). At political meetings and cultural events, the Party reinforces this history of rule, land campaigns and rural development (Chatterjee 1997; Corbridge et al. 2005: 208). These historic land campaigns are modes of affirming collectivity and explaining food security in the present. While villagers recalled the land campaigns, they also speak critically of the limits to the 'progressive' local system tied as it was to Party politics. As one JS activist put it, even where there is a will to fight corrupt and illegal means of livelihood, the panchayat can only do so much because 'the Party holds the reins behind them' (*lagaam dhore aache*).

In a few other rapid scenes, this JS play covers disparate issues like a defunct health system where rural clinics don't have antidotes for snakebites while these in the city do have them, doctors don't attend to poorer patients, poor women aren't educated enough to know that they need to vaccinate their infants against diseases like polio. The final story, adapted from the life of one of JS's members, is about a man who leaves for the city to earn an income from the construction industry. On the day that he is expected back, an eager wife cooks his favourite meal. Instead of his return, the family receives news of his death and how he fell from the flimsy scaffold of a construction site. All the hospitals turn the injured man's friends away presuming their inability to pay for treatment from their visible class position and rural origins. When finally they find a willing hospital, the man succumbs to his injuries.

In these scenes, we see the tyranny of state officials unperturbed by their audience *and* an appeasing state official attempting to secure his future, legitimacy, and instrumental gain by providing for small farmers. We see a violated and exploited farmer who *nonetheless* strategically enacts what Bourdieu has called the 'sincere fiction' of calling a politician his mother and father. In the playful representation of tyrannical politicians, the differentiated depiction of farmers themselves, and the alliance between state officials and rural ruling classes, this play shows that the state is not an external entity to villagers since its status as authority is produced through relations of rule and experiences of disadvantage. Although red panchayats are one example of an institution that realises 'development' through the participation of villagers, this does not mean that most villagers choose, far less determine, the purposes and projects to which they are given access. Many can access income, secure livelihoods, generate capital, or participate in political representation to the extent that they do not violate Party objectives, criteria, and goals. *Song of the Village* shows that development and decentralised democracy secure the future legitimacy of CPM hegemony in particular, and practices of political Party rule in general, placing this goal above the future of Bengal's marginalised and insecure citizens.

The panchayat elections of May 2008 came in the aftermath of conflict over land expropriation in Singur and Nandigram. In these elections, reports of CPM violence against Revolutionary Socialist Party members suggest that the Party is willing to quash local leadership even when held by coalition partners within the LFG (P.S. Banerjee 2008). Recent elections reveal more than ever that far from constructing collectivity and an ideology that confronts capitalist ideologies and forces, red panchayats are modes of 'pitting poor against the poor in a society where poor people had a long legacy of united struggles on the basis of the class line' (*ibid.*: 17). If CPM leadership and reforms are makers of a panchayat that counts, then the panchayat mode of rule is accomplished through the distribution of development 'goods' and formal representation by the poor rather than constituting a substantive mode of decentralising power, redefining the terms of government, or confronting class.

Decades of on-stage JS representation has shown that panchayats are modes of rule through which the market episteme of private economic gain is materialised, among state politicians *and* villagers — vote for me and I will give you a loan to rear some goats. As the play shows, the ultimate capital gain hardly accrues to villagers where moneylenders and politicians siphon profit on the backs of the poor. However, through this veritable race to secure the few available loans, villagers and state officials combine to nurture a definition of 'social' where competitive individual pursuit of monetary gain and electoral supremacy rules the formation of social relationships. Legitimising a paternalistic state leaves insecure villagers thoroughly vulnerable to violence and extortion. Rhetorical grammars of distribution attach to poor farmers and low-caste villagers, but are insistent first on loyalty to a hegemonic political collectivity and sometimes reproduce a sense of being subaltern.

For example, Arild Engelsen Ruud has speculated that 'very poor Panchayat representatives can have a detrimental effect on representative democracy' because they have less time for politics (Ruud 2003: 163). Similarly, Dayabati Roy (2008) has recently quoted Scheduled Caste leader Khagen Malik to show that given CPM Party control over panchayats, despite and indeed *through* decentralised governance, leadership can serve to reproduce rather than challenge class and caste subjectivity. In Malik's words, 'Only economically solvent people can devote sufficient time for the Party and assume leadership position. One needs money to be involved in politics. Politics is based on economy' (*ibid.*: 32). This is a far cry from the red panchayat defined as a collectivity representing decentralised development and mode of class struggle. In light of caste, class, religious, and gender inequalities in India, constructing an inclusive yet equitable 'collectivity' is no small feat. Yet, to privilege Party loyalty as conduit of all progressive goals masks the hierarchies and histories of power within political parties and the multiple ways in which agrarian reforms and political decentralisation subject villagers to rule just as much as it creates opportunities for voice. In the final section, I consider gender hierarchies by studying the accomplishments and perceptions of CPM-affiliated gendered political action in West Bengal.

Protecting a Patriarchal State: Sarama

The JS play *Sarama* is named after the protagonist, raped by Party thugs, who punish Sarama for the 'crime' of mobilising support against their rule in the neighbourhood. Written in 1992, this play shows who in Bengal's political society (including but not exclusively Party personnel) collaborate to cover up and condone Sarama's rape. This is the only play analysed in this book that I have not seen performed. *Sarama* reveals the making of political society, but focuses on how a patriarchal Party system relies on and reproduces gender inequality and regulatory norms. Sarama's rape is a 'gender' question because of multiple and intersecting considerations since patriarchy within the family is held in place by unequal property relations, lack of women's control over income, household assets, as well as their limited movement and sexuality. This play focuses on the Party system's role in perpetuating violence against women. In a crucial scene depicting interactions among representatives of the Democratic Women's Association (DWA), the CPM-affiliated women's collectivity, the play reveals the contradictions at the heart of the dominant women's collectivity in West Bengal. In passing, the play also suggests a distinct absence of male family and friendship supports for women like Sarama who are violated for acting against authoritative male violence. Before I come to the specifics of the play, certain historic trends of gendered action as well as the particularities of allocations for gender provisioning and reform must be considered.

Several tensions and paradoxes characterise the incorporation of gendered action and presence in the construction of collective political action. Family and household, in their heteronormative form, have been historically significant idioms and vehicles of social, political and cultural life in colonial Bengal and anti-colonial imaginaries (Bannerji 2002; Chatterjee 1993; Sarkar 1984). Despite the fact that middle- and upper-caste women were not supposed to leave their homes (the more respectable you are, the less need for you to leave your home), during the anti-colonial Civil Disobedience Movement led by Gandhi, women's presence in political activism rose significantly. Tanika Sarkar (1989) has explained this paradox by showing that during the nationalist movement, women's participation in political action was seen not as an infringement on caste rules but as servicing caste-based norms. Middle-class nationalist leaders tied the value of women's political activism to the respectable and often, religious vocabulary of *shakti* (female power) and women's nurturing roles thus encouraging low-caste groups to enlist their women into political action. In other words, increasing women's presence in collective politics was rewritten as a symbol and norm of high caste practice (*ibid.*).

How is this legacy in gendered political action in Bengal manifest in post-colonial developments? In an analysis of political activism and state–society relations in the late 1970's and early 1980's, Amrita Basu (1992) has shown how the CPM strategy of parliamentary communism realises the democratic centralism of its Party structure in part by nurturing the democratic centralism of the patriarchal Bengali Hindu family. The ultimate expression of having accomplished this are embodied in the words of Purna Das, the executive member of the West Bengal DWA who said, 'We see the CPI(M) as our family. Like our family it protects us' (quoted in A. Basu 1992: 54). Recent data suggests that the DWA has a membership of 3,821,946 women (Munshi 2005: 89). The CPM clearly escaped problems of bringing women out of homes for action because they were not seen to be questioning 'home' or working against it. Today, there is a celebrated camaraderie among the Leftist government and a variety of affiliated women's organisations such as the DWA, West Bengal Women's Commission and All India Democratic Women's Association. These organisations have much to celebrate and have justifiable pride over their accomplishments.

However, since the 1980s there has also been a growing field of violence produced through the combined nexus of Party, panchayat, and women's associations. Though there is ample evidence of strong membership, active participation in DWA meetings, CPM rallies, and election days, Amrita Basu (1992) has argued that the CPM has neglected to challenge gender, ethnic, and caste inequalities. Recent studies have updated and affirmed her claims. Since 1992 when the central government formally liberalised the Indian economy, the trends of shrinking employment opportunities, feminisation of poverty, unemployment, and reduced public provisioning have affected numerous regions in India. West Bengal is no exception. The state government leaders have justifiable pride in claiming that land reforms protected small-peasant agriculture from the predatory corporate agriculture that afflicts regions such as Vidarbha in western India where farmers have committed suicides in vast numbers. But there are also significant inequalities in the distribution of productive resources and public provisioning between men and women in rural Bengal.

Jayoti Gupta (2002) has argued that women have been second on the land agenda in West Bengal. Based on a survey and secondary sources, she finds that dowry payments and demands are central to differences in land ownership, alienation, and insecure futures. Informal methods of mortgaging land in order to pay dowry demands flourish in every community in rural Bengal so that dowry contributes to a 'parallel land market' and a mode through which husbands invest dowry money to start small businesses (Gupta 2002: 1747). In South 24 Parganas villages, I was always struck by the number of household conflicts that had to do with multiple marriages. Gupta's (2002) survey of Midnapore and North 24 Parganas district shows that bigamy (which I also found to be a common phenomenon in South 24 Parganas) has become a mode of multiplying capital by multiplying sources of dowry. Whoever the ultimate beneficiaries of this capital and land transactions might be, it is not women because they rarely control income and assets (Bagchi 2005).

It was not until 1992 that the LFG initiated legislation to give joint titles to wives — 14 years after the initial land reform programme. This delay complicated issues of implementing joint ownership substantially.[9] Unless women were considered to be in distress which was defined as 'widows without an adult son, or deserted and divorced' they could not be independent beneficiaries of land titles (Gupta 2002: 1748). Gupta finds that, to add to these highly restrictive rights to land title channeled through the patriarchal structures of the family, the DWA fails to take the initiative for implementing women's title to land. When the CPM-affiliated peasant unions do take up issues of land title, they do so with little specific attention to joint titles for women. The Party continues to emphasise class struggle at the expense of women's interests pitting 'women, in contradiction to the collective' rather than seeing women as integral makers of collectivities at various levels — family, Party, or state (*ibid.*: 1749). In the end, the patriarchy of the Party and its formal institutions are evident because, as land titles continue to elude rural women, women's experience of desertion, violence, and dowry demands increase as a direct consequence of the pursuit of land as productive resource (*ibid.*).

Budgetary allocations for reform and development are equally telling manifestations of marginalising the agenda of gender equality. Under the Indian constitution, state governments (rather than the central government), are in charge of many initiatives that have specific benefits for women. Nirmala Banerjee and Poulomi Roy (2004) sought to unravel the mysterious discrepancy of West Bengal's progressive reputation and yet poor performance in the public provisioning of resources and rights to women. They compared the state government's budget allocations for gender specific programmes alongside similar allocations by other state governments. This study found that the bulk of budgetary allocations that claim to accrue benefits to women are spent on equity promoting schemes (9.7 per cent) which 'offer particular services to all citizens without any effort to overcome the traditional barriers against women participating in them on an equal basis' compared with equality-promoting schemes (0.03 per cent) allocated to schemes that 'are sensitive to women's handicaps on gender grounds and try to compensate for them' (*ibid.*: 4832). Despite increasing prosperity in the state (net domestic products) in the 1990s, budgetary allocations for development projects in the social sector have stagnated placing West Bengal among the poorest rated states for allocations in the social sector. In the end, although the state government has programmes for addressing gender inequality in the social sector, it makes negligible budgetary commitments to achieve these goals (*ibid.*: 4837).

One arena that offers some hope is the arena of political representation where there has been a significant increase in women's visibility. The West Bengal Women's Commission was constituted in 1993. The CPM championed 33 per cent seats for women's leadership in panchayats in this devolution of state power and the first panchayat elections with the mandate of 33 per cent reservations for women were held in 1993 (Munshi 2005: 83–85). There is clear evidence of women's increasing presence as members, leaders, and as decision-makers who impact the flow and allocation of funds (*ibid.*; Chattopadhyay and Duflo 2004). Yet, Munshi also argues that 'restrictions imposed by male guardians on the movements and activities of women panchayat representatives who are family members is a serious impediment to the functional success of the elected women' (Munshi 2005: 85). At one end, norms of a patriarchal Hindu family system set the limits of women's equal participation; at the other end, the ideological priorities of the Party system and male leadership in it set the limits of pursuing women's interests adequately. All of this is accomplished precisely by invoking the family as the model collectivity that protects women from harm while ostensibly providing for their economic and social security.

Family is idiom and vehicle of governance for the CPM and other NGOs working in West Bengal. In part, state responsibilities are decentralised by invoking principles of reciprocity, obligation, and belonging within a Hindu *sansar* which means household in concrete terms and universe or larger household in abstract terms (Lamb 2000). The remaking of legitimate spheres of women's actions is initiated by arguing that selfless work for community (*sansar* in its abstract meaning) is the best route to alleviating poverty in the *sansar* (in its concrete and privatised meaning) (Mohan 2003: 235–40). Leaders, politicians, and NGO activists alike have used *sansar* to persuade women to work for neighbourhood, community, or country.[10] On the one hand, structures and norms of the patriarchal Bengali Hindu family contributes to normalising criminality and violence in social relations among Bengali citizens; on the other, the family provides the hierarchical terms for public and political action within the state. The JS play *Sarama* goes further to argue that the Party defines the terms of 'equality' and 'material distress' so that violence against women is not always brought to justice. As the play shows, violence against women is one mode of accomplishing governmental rule and protecting a patriarchal state.

The challenge of speaking against patriarchy and violence is not easily overcome precisely because of women's dependence on patriarchal control over economic resources. Some NGOs working in South 24 Parganas like Shramajibee Mahila Samity (henceforth SMS) specifically address the problems of domestic violence, dowry, dispute resolution, and the challenge of waging legal battles (Shramajibee Mahila Samity 2003). Among these NGOs, some favour aggressive processes of taking cases of violence against women to the police and others prefer more traditional methods like *shalishi* where informal modes of dispute resolution in the village precede recourse to courts and police (Sadasivam 2000). SMS has argued that they choose *shalishi* precisely because resolving disputes through the police, panchayats, Party system, or courts make the political stakes much higher and have greater capacity to generate violence. The report by SMS provides a vivid sense of the histories that enable and disable women's political action, the structures that constitute violence and insecurity for rural women, and the dilemmas of doing political work that connects experiences of violence in family, neighbourhood, and Party political spheres of life (SMS 2003). *Shalishi* work for SMS focuses on fighting patriarchy at the level of the regulatory norms and punitive consequences for transgressing dominant norms which become particularly vivid in cases of domestic violence and dowry.

A woman CPM panchayat leader Madhuri Das, in 2001 told me that she did not support the work of these organisations.

> I don't like how people go to the police station. Just because we are women does not mean we are saints (washed *tulsi* leaves[11]). The marital home is not always oppressive. I ask Sita why do you go to the police station just like that? The husband and wife have to live together, don't they? I have to live with people in the village, right?
>
> (8 June 2001)

Indeed, women are not always saints. JS Forum Theatre interactions have revealed all too often that mothers-in-law offer brutal support to their sons in the mental and physical abuse of wives. In certain cases, married women's families have used courts to politicise disputes, or to terrorise lower caste/class boys' families, or to exact a financial settlement through false charges — each manifesting further complications in the 'dark side of political society' (Chatterjee 2004: 75). This suggests that the terrain of seeking justice for 'private' grief is fraught with complexity and challenges. Yet, this cannot be rationale for quashing the work of public forums such as *shalishi*, police, and courts. The act of going to the public space is after all not women's first experience of conflict — typically the home is the first experience of conflict. Therefore, not going 'public' is not necessarily solace, nor any guarantee of peace and harmony in the family. NGOs are dissuaded from publicising justice and demanding Party support and some fear being driven out of LFG heartland. In this way, the Party system comes to be implicated in these forms of violence borne by women. The perpetrators of violence are not brought to justice because there is no impartial sphere of justice outside the force of patriarchal and Party rule — whether courts, Party, panchayat, or *shalishi*. The material disadvantages and distress faced by rural women slips through the cracks because of the way in which 'distress' and 'welfare' come to be negotiated in rural Bengal's political society.

In *Sarama* (written in 1992), Ganguly draws from his experience of working in the slum areas in North 24 Parganas in the early 1980s. Although the habitat in this play is a slum, the nexus of politician, women's association, and musclemen are even stronger in the rural areas where loyalty is, as we have seen, the disciplinary stick that makes 'development' and 'democracy'. The play begins with Sarama's rape. Sarama is an inhabitant in the slum. Through a combination of humour and horror, the opening statements establish three things as the thugs prepare to commit the rape.[12] First, Sarama's crime is that she was organising collective efforts to combat the reign of terror unleashed upon the slum by the hired goons of the Party. Second, the seasoned goon calms the thug-in-training who is nervous about such a brazen act though he is also excited at the prospect of the sexual encounter, 'I too fantasise about that [...]' Third, the seasoned goon is not worried since he is guaranteed a Party leader's protection and because 'No one in this slum will say a word. They have seen it all before.' When the rape is committed, despite the cry for help, not enough people protest to make a difference.

At the Worker's Party District Office a few days later, the Party goons strategise on their meeting with Alokda, the Party leader without principles, who gives these goons their immunity. The rookie is nervous again.

Rookie goon: Do you think we overdid it? All in broad daylight?
Seasoned goon: Overdid what? (*In an irritated tone*)
Rookie goon: No, I mean it is after all just before the elections. That's why I am a little concerned.

Third goon (*making fun of the rookie*): Protection! The crooked bastard is wondering whether he will get the Party's protection.
Seasoned goon: If this is wrong, then I have to say that I have done much worse than this. Yes I have done so in the interest of the Party. I have done it for the Leaders. Haven't I helped fill their pockets?
Third goon: Besides friend, the elections are ahead, they will need us

This conversation establishes the cunning of goons who have ensured Party protection for themselves, the security of their jobs and pre-empted their defense against calls for justice by committing a pre-election crime. This is criminal work institutionalised for the benefit of the political Party although it also works in favour of those strategising livelihood and job security in contexts with few options for employment.

For a minute, the audience is led to believe that this time the goons will be refused Party protection as Alok, the Party leader, refuses help regretting the day he hired the goons. Having previously justified such alliance in 'the interests of the Party', he now realises that 'supporting you has meant that we have become accomplices in your crimes.' At the same time, Alok knows that the price of alienating the goons is to lose mercenaries willing to use force on behalf of the Party if such force becomes necessary to win the election. Indeed, we have seen that this is exactly what the goons were counting on when they planned to commit rape before the elections. Forced by 'the instrumental power of the vote' (Chatterjee 2004: 41), Alok extracts election-time service and insists that they disappear from the vicinity till the criminal investigations subside.

Alok calls the Police Superintendent to buy him into disregarding the 'minor' crime, 'They did a bit of a rape. Yes, it's true that they raped a bit.' Alok assures the policeman that his 'service' during this election would guarantee a post of his choice as it did after the last elections. By the Party leader's own assessment, there is nothing wrong with such negotiations because no one's hands are clean.

Superintendent: But there are a few people in your midst who are a little too honest. What if they make trouble for us?

Alok: Oh let that go! Overdoing honesty! I have seen enough. I am not the only one eating, am I? I captured a few fisheries and give the Party about a lakh rupees a month.[13] You think the honest man is not benefiting from this? These days I see that there are a lot of people

> pretending to be Valmiki (saint). Don't worry about all that Singh-*ji*.[14] Just do things exactly as I am telling you to.

With these scenes, the play establishes the nexus that uses force with immunity and ignores crime with equal immunity. There is no force to counteract this governmental malpractice because people are hopelessly disunited. We learn of this disunity from people's responses to the news of Sarama's rape. They blame Sarama for messing with powerful forces, the Party politicians for handing society over to criminals, and themselves for not stepping in to protest the rape. In a song that follows, the play insinuates that those who were the workers, the foundation, and the future of the Party, realise today that all they can do is race to get the largest slice of the pie.

> The people who empower the Party
> You know those workers-toilers
> No matter how much they work
> They have nothing to show for it
> My ancestors were stupid
> They sacrificed their blood for the Party
> Rather than follow their footsteps of sacrifice,
> Now we take as much as we can get (*amra kore-khai*)

Along with the disunited people, the Worker's Party, the Real Worker's Party, and the True Worker's Party battle over what really happened.

At this juncture, when it is clear that there is no leadership or vision that can adequately address Sarama's situation, we encounter a day in the life of the 'Women's Organisation Worker's Party.' After all, the audience harbours hope that a women's organisation might stop the politicisation of a rape, address the question of the woman's welfare, and bring the perpetrators to justice. The three activists of the women's organisation are engaged in conversation. This exchange is interesting because there are three women belonging to different age groups (Anusuya who is 23, Bela who is middle-aged, and Deepa who is an elderly lady) which indicates varied relationships to the history of the women's organisation and the Worker's Party. Bela and Anusuya are unabashedly engaged in consumerism and enjoy all the trappings of a modern life, upscale markets in Kolkata, and chauffeur-driven cars while their husbands work as full-time Party workers. Deepa alone is troubled by the conversation.

Deepa: Oh! (in a mocking tone) You wives of jet-setting full-time Party leaders wear no less than Balucharis.[15]

Anusuya: Of course Deepa aunty! After all we do have an elite background. Why should we conceal that? In fact to not hide our background is honesty. If we begin to hide this, then we are much more likely to become hypocritical.

Anusuya misunderstands Deepa's objection to their preoccupation with consumption. Deepa is a much older lady whose husband was also from a well-educated family. Her husband gave up his job to become a full-time worker with the Party. Significantly, the only reason Deepa was able to raise a family was because of support from her brother who was a successful doctor. Deepa described this family history to highlight the middle-class sacrifices and familial support that made Party activism possible in its formative years. For the next generation such as Bela however, the lessons learned from Deepa's generation is that Party workers must avoid the economic insecurity associated with full-time Party work. Bela's children may be studying in elite boarding schools, but her sights for them are set elsewhere.

Deepa: They are doing quite well, studying in internationally-renowned boarding schools.

Bela: Yes, that's what Jojo [Bela's husband] says. But, there is no future in this country. Where are the possibilities and opportunities? Therefore, it is very important to cultivate a sensibility of independence and an aspiration to live abroad in children.

Deepa: Oh I see (*with toned down mockery*). I am certain we made a mistake somewhere down the line. Otherwise, why are our children so far from reality?

Deepa refers to the metaphoric next generation of the Party as her children, wondering where the mentoring went wrong. She regrets this species of parental aspirations for sending their children abroad, especially when voiced by leaders who are supposed to construct a progressive future of 'possibilities and opportunities' rather than write off possibilities altogether ('there is no future in this country'). Anusuya, as representative of the third generation, is even more privileged as Bela hopes her children will be in the future. Anusuya says she herself has 'studied in good English medium boarding schools. We have even been abroad. Our father has not deprived us in any way.' For Anusuya, inability to travel or study or live abroad is a sign of 'deprivation'. She looks up to her father because he was able to accomplish the balance between family well-being and Party well-being — a balance that Bela's husband has allegedly not struck. Anusuya's father did not allow deprivation to beset the family while simultaneously earning praise and respect as a leader.

As each generation provides a chronicle of its accomplishments and reveals latent anxieties, Deepa is compelled to highlight the ways in which class power combines with state power in Anusuya's family and within the CPM family itself. She tells Anusuya, 'And that's exactly why the Party is a nice cushion for you. You get to look a bit revolutionary. [...] After all, if you can get this close to state power as a revolutionary — that's pretty cushy.' Although Anusuya resents the sarcasm, Deepa continues to critique the Party's naked transition from leadership to control — 'They went to people as leaders and became the owners.' The ultimate sell-out by the women's organisation comes in the form of their refusal to support Sarama's cause.

Sutapa, another representative in the Women's Organisation Workers Party, walks in to draw attention and seek solidarity for Sarama's cause. She is stunned by Bela's refusal who says 'we cannot abandon the interests of the Party' and Anusuya who says 'As a worker's Party, shouldn't our primary concern be workers?' Sutapa is enraged, 'Unbelievable! Striking words! Look if it is workers you are concerned about, then why not let them determine their issues themselves.' Of course this gets at the heart of the issues of leadership, control, and ownership that Deepa raised just a minute before Sutapa walked in. Moreover, quite in contrast to Purna Das's[16] sentiment about the CPM 'We see the CPI (M) as our family. Like our family it protects us' (quoted in Basu 1992: 54), the CPM family refuses to protect Sarama. Perhaps the protection of Party members is restricted to those women of a particular class background. Or perhaps, it is their class that protects them from the violation of Party thugs. Or, perhaps the limits of the 'family' support are restricted to the needs of the CPM family.

Anusuya and Bela's logic for deserting Sarama has Deepa thunderstruck. Clearly holding the oppositional views of a bygone generation, she asks 'Party is just for the interest of the Party?

Then who is going to watch after the interests of people? So this state power is for the Party, not for people. The Party is not there to serve people. The people are there to serve the Party.' In a definitive statement of critique against the insidious and pervasive construction of political society, Deepa suggests that ultimately the Party of the poor is banking on people, turning Party loyalty into a hallowed and hollow end-in-itself.

Sutapa, who used to work for the women's organisation, shifts her allegiance to an organisation unaffiliated with Party work so that she can highlight the relationship between the patriarchal family, the patriarchal state, and a government that defines change according to five-year election and planning cycles. In her view, the planning model of development cannot address the nebulous and much more difficult work of addressing patriarchal norms of oppression and hierarchy within the family.

> **Sutapa**: There's no democracy in the home, how on earth can there be democracy in society? The core of patriarchy is as strong in the Party as it is in the home. Perhaps for this reason, in the course of a struggle for democracy and equality, you hide the face of familial oppression. Besides, where's the time and patience for all that? These days, all we can see is 'five years'.

In the meanwhile Sarama, the rape victim, struggles to regain her life amidst the media attention and the various forces of investigation. When the Women's Commission comes to document her case promising to take the research findings to the Human Rights Commission, they say all the right things, but Sarama is hardly fooled.

> **Sarama**: What is your Commission for? They have no independence, nor any power! The saddest part is that educated teachers speak in the name of women's independence even as they are puppets in the hands of powerful Parties. [...] You tell me why your investigation should be my headache? [...] When one of the political parties of the State declared me a tainted woman, you failed to publicly denounce such a statement. Have I not seen all these well-travelled professors who failed to get the disrespectful politician to shut up? None of them were able to say anything.

Sarama's references to institutions of investigation, documentation and academic or policy analysis suggest that institutions of learning and research are thoroughly implicated in the production of a hegemonic political society in West Bengal.

Although Sarama is clearly the victim in this story, she is far from helpless, fooled, or without options. She is also abandoned by her lover Adheer who considers her rape a 'taint'. Considering she has had three abortions because Adheer was not yet ready to marry her, it seems that he hardly needed an excuse. Sarama does not fully control her body or her sexuality, but she does make certain choices that refuse the regulatory control that patriarchal norms exercise. She chooses to have the child that results from the rape, finds a job with a social work organisation, and sends her child to school through the organisation's assistance.

There is a note of uncertainty to the play's own sense of its 'solution' knowing that not all women have access to such organisations and that laws are not enough. Although the play ends on a note of indecision and with no obvious solution, it does not generate despair. It does adhere to one unambiguous conclusion — that protecting patriarchy within households and political organisations is simply unacceptable. Assuming that 'we need to fight the war against patriarchy first and foremost today', this play ends with Ganguly's first experiment with the central principle of Forum Theatre which is to 'ask the audience what they think about all of this. Here the audience too will have to give, rather than just receive'.

Conclusion: Questioning Political Society

These three plays show the making of political society by revealing practices of rule and bring the 'dark side of political society' to the heart of their critique. They also show everyday forms of collaboration and resistance in West Bengal. That is, they show how deprived populations and marginalised citizens negotiate with agents of governmental power to move towards incremental acquisition of capital, status, and survival. The forms of corruption in the three institutions of governance and collectivity — trade union, panchayat, and women's organisation — are varied. In the trade union, money rules politics and dissent is denied space. In the panchayat, welfare is bought and votes are sold. In the women's organisation, solidarity with a woman's struggle for survival and justice is sacrificed for 'protection' from a patriarchal politics and violence against women is tolerated when electoral gain is at stake. Although these institutions compromise the promise of building working class, village, and women's collectivities in different ways, together they show that in West Bengal, as Deepa put it in one of the plays, 'The Party is not there to serve people. The people are there to serve the Party.' Here, the institutions of local governance are perhaps the most significant example because panchayats can in principle be controlled by other parties. Apparently, in West Bengal, panchayats are state institutions by definition and ruling Party institutions by default.

For those whose voices congeal in these plays, the idea that the CPM is the Party of the poor because the poor vote for them is a thorough misunderstanding of hegemony — that combination of consent and coercion through which rule is accomplished (Gramsci 1971; Li 1999a). The CPM not only provides for the poor, but rather they reproduce the terms of insecurity, distress, and vulnerability while channeling options and opportunities through itself. More significantly, they normalise the market episteme of individual pursuit of advantage for material benefits. While this competition is to gain material benefit and access to scarce resources, it is conducted through a government representative who provides access to this benefit. This turns welfare into an exchange so that democratic politics is commodified while the market episteme is normalised through welfare provisioning. These are discouraging accounts of a Party that claims to embody parliamentary Communism, and claims to be an anti-capitalist force for democracy, and class struggle.

These plays also show that CPM power may be pervasive and persuasive, but its hegemony in West Bengal is not complete. Regulatory norms of various sorts are refused: the deference that stabilises local authorities, the deceptions that corrupt unions, the patriarchal norms that refuse protection and welfare for a raped woman. What the CPM treats as hegemonic commonsense and organisational success is in fact being debated in all sorts of ways. These plays show some of the ways in which the social Left expresses its alienation from the political Left. Indeed, the recent protests in Singur and Nandigram are only the latest and most visible evidence of alienation from CPM democracy considering these plays were popular through the 1980s and 1990s. If such expressions have taken a militant form today, it is not because everyday forms of refusal and protest were absent, but rather because they were not heard.

On-stage representations are expressions of democracy, regardless of whether they are heard, valued, censored, or legitimised by state power. The stories in these plays question the seamless formation of a political society where criminal and violent behaviour is nurtured as norm in exchange for welfare and survival. Subtle use of 'sincere fictions' such as referring to panchayat leaders as mother and father perform deference momentarily. There are people like Bikash who rise from the dead to haunt their killers and inspire friends, and people like Sarama who refuse to allow Party leaders, Women's organisations, Women's Commissions, media representations, lovers, and family members to construct a total cage of political expediency. As we shall see in chapters five, six, and seven, this kind of battle against normative and structural closure in the face of mount-ing challenges to survival is as true off-stage as it is on-stage in these plays. For those who battle against the closure of possibility even as they battle against material distress and violence, Chatterjee's conception of 'political society' remains disinterested and inad-equate. These actors in rural Bengal have sought to reimagine ways that issues of justice can be addressed so that criminality and vio-lence are not normalised as social relations among the poor and acceptable exchange for a fragile and negotiated sense of welfare. JS offers its own normative judgment in suggesting that normalising criminal social relations among the poor should not constitute a democratic politics of collectivities that claims to struggle for rights and resources for the poor.

✷

Notes

1. Panchayats are institutions of local government which administer a number of different welfare and development services including public health, education, sanitation, drinking water and irrigation, disbursement of IRDP loans for housing, irrigation, and other needs, agricultural extension research and work, land reform, and rural electrification.
2. Baviskar and Sundar (2008) have recently argued that Chatterjee's discussion of democracy in India reproduces the veneer of legality assumed by civil society and state power compared with the assumed illegal action of the poor. My critique addresses the normalisation of illegal and violent social relations among the poor.

3. These plays are not performed in the Forum Theatre Format. They were scripted over time by weaving together various real life stories. Unlike Forum Theatre plays, they tend to be more direct in suggesting problems and resolution.
4. All translations from Bengali have been done by the author.
5. In a later play called *The Brick Factory*, Ganguly addresses the gender dimensions of union politics briefly.
6. 'Centre' refers here to the central Indian government which follows an explicitly bourgeois model of democracy and development.
7. Operation Barga is a sharecropper registration campaign run by the CPM in 1978 which informed sharecroppers of their rights to land that they had been cultivating. This land reform measure put the onus of proof of reason to evict tenants on the landowner.
8. With the significant Tebhaga movement of the 1940's in south-western Bengal, a policy on sharecropper rights drew on citizens' historical memory for legitimacy while deferring land struggles.
9. Despite active participation of women in the land struggles such as Tebhaga, the slogan of land campaigns in the 1960s claimed land for the one who ploughed. This excluded women because ploughing was a taboo for women even though women were seen in other forms of agricultural work (Gupta 2002: 1748).
10. I discuss implications of this invocation of *sansar* in chapters four and six.
11. She used the term *dhoya tulsi pata* which literally means washed tulsi leaves. Tulsi is a plant which is revered and worshipped for its medicinal properties. Every courtyard in a Hindu home in rural Bengal has a tulsi plant which is propitiated daily by the women of the household. To be a washed tulsi leaf symbolises the ultimate state of sanctity.
12. Thugs and goons are a commonly used force in rural Bengali politics. K. Sivaramakrishnan's (1999) study of forests in colonial eastern Bengal shows the formative presence of *paiks* who were armed watchmen for landlords of the forest in Midnapore. For contemporary politics, Ruud (2003) has discussed use of Bagdi (low-caste) *lathial* by a village leader in Burdwan district in post-colonial West Bengal.
13. Unit of measuring money. One lakh is 100,000 rupees which is equivalent to approximately $2,400.
14. *Ji* is a suffix attached to names that shows respect to the person addressed.
15. *Balucharis* are an expensive type of silk saris woven in a traditional Bengali style which are prized possessions in the wardrobes of the rich.
16. Purna Das is the executive member of the West Bengal Democratic Women's Association affiliated with the CPM which is the object of critique in this JS play where the association is labelled the 'Women's Organization Worker's Party'.

Part II

Chapter Four

Spect-actors of History

This chapter is the first in section two of this book where I demonstrate in different ways that Jana Sanskriti (JS) rescripts social relations in practice, and not just in theatre. Here, I describe the multiple sources of JS ethical political action as well as the ambiguities and complexities encountered in accomplishing principles of ethical practice and representational equality. In chapter one, I introduced Augusto Boal's Forum Theatre and its principle agents — the joker and the spect-actor. In this chapter, I also suggest that JS's use of Theatre of the Oppressed can be characterised by their distinctive materialisation of Boal's active and reflective spectator, the 'spect-actor' in staged performance. In addition to the spect-actor during performance, JS also aims to construct spect-actors of history by bringing their on-stage and off-stage political action in constant relation to each other.

In conceptualising JS actors and activists as spect-actors of history, I am addressing the off-stage component of this theatrical practice. Not to reify this component as a place, I conceptualise it as going beyond the intended goal of democratising representation on-stage to theorise off-stage as the unintended processes of acting and activism through which social relations are rescripted in practice. To see JS members as spect-actors of history requires a multilayered analysis of their daily practice and praxis. By practice, I refer to the everyday processes of realising idealised goals, and by praxis, I refer to the practices of reflection and action that inform the ongoing constitution of JS's work. In the first section, I put forth a theoretical argument that their practice embodies the tension between raising the consciousness of 'the oppressed' while 'enacting subjectivity'as complex and ambiguous rather than unified and coherent. In the second section, I study role-playing in JS Theatre workshops and performances to show that acting centralises empathy as an ethic of social interaction and political action among its members, actors, audience members, and outside observers. Against a world-historical chorus that claims that there is no alternative to development except through displacement and capitalist exploitation, JS members imagine and live social interactions and new futures that disobey segregations of class, caste, gender, and urban–rural life.

In the third section, I show how some JS members articulate this empathetic interaction as something that changed their lives. They see such social interaction as a right that should be available to all human beings so as to nurture social relationships beyond the instrumental terms of exchange value and electoral politics. In the fourth section, I show how the lessons of role-playing equality on-stage interacts with the contradictory ethics of hospitality, hierarchy, reciprocity, and deference that shapes social interaction in Bengali Hindu families. In this section, I summarise JS practice as a praxis of failure where I argue that this organisation publicly stages and analyses its own failures as mode of ethical practice, learning, and formative of democratic struggle.

In the final ethnographic section of this chapter, I draw on field notes on inauguration ceremonies, speeches during JS sessions on 'ideological training', theatre performances and workshops to argue that faith is a source of ethical and political action in JS's practice. Although I present the role of faith in this way, I conclude on a note of my own failure to access its meaning in JS's practice. This chapter thus situates JS spect-actors within larger socio-historical and life-historical contexts of multiple hierarchies of power and histories of struggle. Drawing on multiple ethics of political action and practice — from Theatre of the Oppressed, to faith, and *sansar* ethics of reciprocity and hierarchy — they act against Party political and patriarchal assumptions about what counts as progressive political action. I present these complexities to show how the goal of consciousness-raising and recovering subaltern subjectivity against epistemic binaries and representational monologues exists in tension with a daily struggle and practice that highlights the ambiguities and complexity of subjectivity.

Enacting Subjectivity

Recall the Forum Theatre format. A play scripted by people affected by a certain social problem is enacted for an audience who is equally familiar with this problem. The script shows various aspects of a given problem but resists providing a solution or resolution. In the second enactment, the joker encourages members of the audience to step on-stage to rescript roles, norms, and taken-for-granted interactions of daily life that lead to the extraordinary social issues being discussed. Boal's term for such a member who intervenes in the play is spect-actor. According to Boal, when a spectator becomes a spect-actor, victims of a social problem rehearse revolution on-stage. Rather than have solutions externally imposed on them by an authoritarian force or an ideological belief, the oppressed draw on their concrete experience of a social problem to construct change. This theatrical practice begins with the assumed stability of categories such as 'the oppressor' and 'the oppressed'.

Spect-actors are, in some senses, agents and embodiments of social change because when they step on-stage to script a solution, they have already acted against an assumed monologue of representation. They act against the assumption that power to construct solutions and script public representations is exclusively located in authoritative and legitimate embodiments of power. In this way, Forum Theatre uses the joker and spect-actor to construct spaces of lived democracy on-stage where a problem can have multiple solutions and participants encounter varied, alternative norms for living. In JS's formulation however, rural Bengalis must become not just spect-actors on-stage, but also such actors off-stage who rescript social relations. JS's organisational structure, as well as the way in which off-stage and on-stage are made to feed each other in practice, aims at connecting personal experiences of oppression with the political–economic histories of oppression so that 'Theatre of the Oppressed' can go beyond the trap of an 'individualistic emphasis' and a 'lack of political perspective' (Fisher 1994: 189). Theirs is a struggle to consider what makes spect-actors on-stage also spect-actors of history, and equally to remind each other that the latter have inner lives of oppression through which world-histories and 'outer situations echo inside' (Salverson 1994: 168). In other words, the staging of solidarity through a technique such as theatre of the oppressed is itself subject to reflection in JS's everyday practice. Their commitment to making spect-actors of history rather than spect-actors on-stage enacts subaltern subjectivity as ambiguous, contradictory, not as neatly calibrated to political–economic position, but not apart from it either.

These representational goals suggest that JS's work is another episode in the universal march of citizenship, the consolidation of nation–state, and the realisation of the liberal subject of human emancipation (Chakrabarty 2000: 39). JS does not escape this characterisation of encouraging modernisation because they explicitly aim to give a space for representation assuming the universal humanism of all. At the same time, they insist on a constant problematisation of social relations and social engineering so that ostensibly liberatory ideologies — such as socialism, development, and Theatre of the Oppressed itself — are subject to critical and public debate, and sometimes, collective thinking. They insist, for example, on multiple forms of role-playing so that the category of 'the oppressed' is publicly staged as an unstable one even as JS space is meant to give representational equality to those assumed oppressed who are denied space for speaking in dominant practices of political representation. Wrestling with the concept of spect-actors as judged through JS's work, I show that such actors are not just examples of the subaltern speaking or modes of recognising recuperated authenticity. I argue that JS's spect-actors of history inherit and grapple with, battle against, and participate in the formation of multiple hierarchies of power.

While constant problematisation is their goal, power relations, unequal histories, and ideologies of superiority and inferiority no doubt constitute their work, relationships, and representation. JS leaders and members are aware of this. As such, the construction of spect-actors of history does not amount to constructing a sovereign subject. Rather, the spect-actor of Forum Theatre can be theorised as an exemplary 'philosophy of praxis' — Antonio Gramsci's term for the process through which humans acquire a 'critical and coherent conception of the world, [with] [...] a consciousness of its historicity' (Gramsci 1971: 324). The cathartic moment for Gramsci 'is the starting point for all the philosophy of praxis' where catharsis is defined as the moment when '[s]tructures ceases to be an external force which crushes man, assimilates him to itself and makes him passive; and is transformed into a means of freedom, an instrument to create a new ethico-political form and a source of new initiatives' (*ibid.*: 367). Spect-actors on the Forum Theatre stage are meant to strive towards a Gramscian catharsis within history by refusing the completion of history's hegemonic rule. *At the same time*, JS actors stage their own participation in the making of hegemonic history by showing how they participate in silence when they see something they understand to be wrong. Rather than assume a space of ideological and ethical purity, JS practice highlights and problematises oppression by staging people's participation in relations of rule.

I argued in chapter two that political theatre stages citizen marginality and state power as malleable process. Spect-actors who step on-stage to offer a solution bring their history and power with them. In the staged juxtaposition of malleability and structural force, catharsis is bound to be complicated, far from linear. Despite the expectations embedded in Boal's (1979: 141) Forum Theatre that see it as a 'rehearsal for revolution', with its implications for eventual grand transformation, the JS practice of Forum Theatre stages 'liberation'in dialectic relation to political action and structures off-stage. In JS's practice, Forum Theatre dramatises the profound challenges of rehearsing and staging revolution, let alone accomplishing it. In this way, it is unlike a catharsis that assumes that a unitary consciousness which finds liberation through the medium of the organic intellectual and the socialist political Party. Rather, JS is committed to questioning revolution which has not transformed individual ability to fight their own capacity for oppression even when they are classified as oppressed in political economic, gender, caste or other terms.

Forum Theatre, as theory and practice, bears similarities with the historiographical interventions of the Subaltern School who wrote 'history from below' in the 1980s. The goal of writing a Gramscian history from below, without succumbing to the Eurocentrism of colonial archives and Marxist historiography, plagued the Subaltern School. Invariably they confronted the challenge of overcoming history from above without essentialising the assumed categories of 'above'and 'below'just as Forum Theatre confronts the challenge of prevailing over the monologue of superiors while reifying categories of 'the Oppressed' and 'the Oppressor'. Despite providing rich re-readings of the colonial archive, subaltern history tended to assume unitary subjectivity and an authentic voice of the oppressed in their intellectual practice. Rosalind O'Hanlon's (2001) essay offers a better strategy for the academic goal of recovering subjectivity. Here, she argues that instead of studying distinctiveness of practice, subaltern scholarship tends too easily towards insisting on a metaphysical presence for peasant consciousness and subaltern as substantive social class (O'Hanlon 2001: 146). They give subaltern consciousness 'their own history' succumbing to the notion of a self-constituting subject — an eminently liberal humanist project.

O'Hanlon objects to making the silent speak through an insistence on an originary essence that at given moments rebels against the onslaught of capitalist history's dispossessions of meaning. To her, there is no more a unitary peasant consciousness than there is a 'woman'of feminist politics defined by a shared nature and bounded essence. Her nuanced suggestion for changing scholarly strategy in recovering the subject reads as follows:

> [...] recover the presence of the subordinate without slipping into an essentialism, by revealing that presence to be one constructed and refracted through practice, but no less 'real'for our having said that it does not contain its own origins within itself. Such a strategy would not only be able to subvert the self constituting subject of idealism, but much more subtly and effectively to address the undoubted historiographical problem of determination. (O' Hanlon 2001: 153)

As I have said already, spect-actors of history are not just examples of the subaltern speaking or modes of recognising recuperated subaltern authenticity (Chatterjee 1993; Guha 1983; Spivak 1988: 271–317). This is not to say that peasant consciousness is not given metaphysical presence in JS's discourse. The tendency to see the oppressed as developing from 'less'to 'more'consciousness permeates many of JS's political and cultural practices. How could this view of consciousness-raising not guide this practice that brings together people from urban, middle-class backgrounds with middle peasants, landless tenants, landless agricultural workers, and day-labourers within the broader context of inherited inequalities of production and representation? Varied versions of 'more critical' and 'less critical'consciousness peppers daily commentary and judgment. At the same time, as I will show in this chapter, their long-term political and cultural praxis has forced recognition that every oppressed is also an oppressor, and every oppressor is also oppressed, that the intention of rehearsing revolution often amounts to rehearsing oppressive rule. With on-stage and off-stage feeding each other, they constantly learn to revalue the presence of the subordinate through practice and representation rather than seeing the oppressed as essence.

O'Hanlon argues that the focus on practice might allow us to recover subjectivity without submitting this recovery to the fiction of a unified and unitary learning process. Assumptions of unified learning processes pretend to bring liberation for all those who have been unable to speak within hegemony. My aim in this chapter is to situate spect-acting within multiple cultural registers and unequal relations of rule to show how JS's spect-actors simultaneously contribute to stagist narratives of development and history, even as they problematise its hegemony, and attempt to be conscious of their constitution of hegemony. These are enactments of subjectivity with its sources in multiple histories of power and complex forms of ethical action and struggle. In the spirit of their commitment to 'constant problematising', this chapter describes a range of JS activities and thought within their organisational practice to highlight these multiple aspects of their practice.

Changing the Subject

JS members view 'theatre of the oppressed' as a powerful tool for countering what they see as a culture of monologues in political representation and authority in West Bengal. Theatre of the Oppressed insists that the oppressed can represent themselves. As one of JS's leading activists Prasad Sardar put it, 'Unlike others who speak *for* the oppressed, JS says that it is the oppressed who know best and can speak for themselves' (28 January 2001). Ironically, through this assertion, the discourse of 'theatre of the oppressed' assumes a metaphysical presence for 'the oppressed'. Making spect-actors, on-stage and off-stage, JS's creative and political work is often constrained by just these claims of authentic subaltern standpoint, though they seek precisely to construct an alternative space for political representation where such categories can be transcended. As others have shown before, becoming liberated or developed is 'difficult work' (Klenk 2003: 99–121, 2004: 57–78).

While Prasad's statement captures JS's starting point well, it does not capture the complexity of its practice on-stage and off-stage. JS's work engages actors and members of the audience in the regular critical practice of playing with on-stage representations and off-stage reality in order to highlight the malleability of reality itself. This hinges on the central practice of role-playing on-stage, and off-stage in daily interactions. This form of theatre simultaneously relies upon people's sense of belonging to the category of the oppressed and engages them in a process of role-playing characters and situations which are not coterminous with their life experience. This kind of role-playing which can amount to stepping into your own as well as into others' shoes resists the belief or the despair that marginality is a stable place. This is an imperative first step in making spect-actors of history.

In JS's practice, role-playing entails at least three different processes. First, 'the oppressed' enact their own life experiences. Second, 'the oppressed' role-play someone else's experiences of oppression. And third, 'the oppressed' role-play becoming 'the oppressor'. Role-playing in these three ways contributes to embodied realisation of the intersectionality (Collins 1990), difference, even hierarchies among various experiences of 'oppression'. Playing someone else's oppression also has the capacity to build cross-over alliances and solidarities by recognising that despite the binary of oppressor and oppressed, no one is ever simply 'the oppressed' (Caraway 1991). Caraway highlights the limits of identity politics in constructing cross-over alliances in politics suggesting that:

> the generic 'woman of color' is no advance on the generic 'white woman'. I want to insert some tension into debates over the content of oppositional identities, to try and discern those tendencies which replicate the essentialist moves feminists of color rightly criticise in white feminism. If we can be alert to the imperialist moment of identity creation per se, we might be able to think new groups for multicultural feminist conversations. (Caraway 1991: 174)

Rejecting the notion of community based on 'a "home" for like-minded sisters', Caraway prefers a 'mediated community of feminist strangers' (*ibid.*: 199) where participants would not expect homogeneous subjectivities. Rather, this would be a community that would build a feminist political coalition among those in solidarity but not sisterhood (*ibid.*: 201).

Let me provide some examples of the three different kinds of role-playing in JS's practice to show how they might construct solidarity rather than assume 'sisterhood' and homogenous subjectivity. For example, in a Theatre workshop conducted in January 2001, I documented Prasad Sardar playing his own reality. He was known to belong to one of the poorest households that were actively engaged in JS's Theatre teams. He did whatever work he could find at any given time, from daily wage labour on shrimp farms to performing in commercial *gaajan*[1] troupes to selling plastic toys and household wares on local trains. Prasad faced routine humiliations at work which he often expressed in JS workshops. One evening in January 2001, the main theatre team (of which Prasad is a part) was engaged in one of the many theatre workshops I documented. The procedure of the Theatre exercise was such that the participants were to be assigned a number representing their sense of self on an ascending scale of 1–10. The numerical designation of people's sense of self is aimed at problematising reifications of people's sense of self-worth according to political status and economic exchange value. Participants had to imagine that the centre of the room was a space that had the designated value of 10 and enact the emotion they would feel in being in a place valued at 10, given their assigned number.

This effort, as Sanjoy Ganguly clarified, was to bring out 'the social relations at various levels. In other words you are looking at your reality through this game' (28 January 2001). The Theatre director proceeded to give examples of people or positions that could conceivably embody numbers 5, 2, and 10 — an NGO representative could be 5, a toilet cleaner could be 2, and a district magistrate could be 10. In the first round, Prasad was assigned a sense of self with the quantified value of 1. He looked despondent and inert as he walked the centre space valued at 10. When he was asked to explain what was on his mind as he mimed his sense of self, he said 'I am selling *sindur* and *alta* from house to house and thinking of the way people look at me when they see that this is what I do for a living' (28 January 2001).[2] This game made Prasad enact the story of his everyday experience. What does it mean to him to mime a sense of self that is his reality? Prasad explained:

> When I joined JS gradually my thinking began to transform — that you have a talent. You don't have to obey people like the blind. You don't have to suffer from inferiority. You don't have to think that you are capable of nothing. JS taught me that I am capable of something. That I am capable of saying something, doing something. And in this way, through the medium of Theatre, I realised I had come to do Theatre, but I was not doing Theatre. I realised I was representing my problems, my life itself. Human problems, daily problems.
>
> (Prasad, 28 January 2001)

At the same time, the director never failed to repeat that 'Your reality is not really here, you have to imagine things'. The point here was to actively generate a discrepancy between accumulated daily humiliations and the affirmation felt on-stage, and then to reassert again that reality was not on the JS stage/space but outside it, where daily humiliations and distress render on-stage imaginings mere fiction. This constant back and forth becomes a force to reckon with because it participates in the construction, regulation, and destabilisation of norms of dehumanisation and experiences of alienation.

The second type of role-playing visible on JS's stage is enacting and empathising with someone else's oppression. This is most often visible when men step on-stage as spect-actors, intervening in the role of victimised women.

This kind of intervention is far from a straightforward enactment of solidarity. Indeed, it can sometimes be a move towards reasserting domination. This form of empathising with an others' oppression is a common form of role-playing whose potential for solidarity and domination cannot be generalised. Consider this kind of role-playing and empathy in the words of long-term JS activists. In an interview in 1999, Radha Das attributed changes in

Figure 4.1: The man with his back to the photograph is a spect-actor who has intervened in the role of a wife This is in itself a source of humour for the audience and some actors on the far right

her life to the day she intervened in a JS Forum Theatre performance that had come to her village. But unlike Prasad's words, Radha empathised with oppression in the play even though it did not depict her own life. Rather, the play moved her because the play depicted others'oppression with whom she could directly identify. She said,

> Long ago, before I had even heard of JS, they had come to my village to do a performance. At the same time a women's organisation was working there. A lot of very real things were shown in the play — women's problems, the problem of excessive drinking, how families were breaking up because one member was drinking too much, how no medicines were available in the hospital, no medicines for snake bite [...] many such real things. After that the members of JS did Forum Theatre. They showed a problem of women being oppressed (*mohilader shoshon*) and asked people to intervene. I had intervened that day. As a woman, I had not faced such problems myself at that time, but I had seen my mother, aunt, sister, and neighbours in such situations. I felt this was a place where I could register my protest. I remembered the experience for a long time afterwards. Socially, politically, and economically I came from a very poor background. I probably would never have got a space where I could voice my protest. So when I found the opportunity in Forum Theatre that day I went ahead and intervened. And JS made a place in my heart. I felt, 'Really, what was I? Just an ordinary village girl, I did not know anything'. Today if I have learnt how to express myself, it is because of this JS. Through Theatre one can reach the depth of the mind of the people. I know this from my own experience. I can see the change that has come within me. I never imagined that I could reach a stage where I would be standing in front of so many people and speaking out loud.

As an 'ordinary village girl', 'socially, politically, economically [...] from a very poor background' who has worked under exploitative conditions for landowners in her village, Radha belongs to the category of landless labourers, whose predicament constitutes JS's focus concern. Nonetheless, she is not in every instance 'oppressed' and is self-conscious regarding the variation in experiences of oppression. Participation in JS work on- and off-stage over time enabled Radha to fortify her sense of power so that she stood in solidarity with her mother as her mother faced the trials of an alcoholic husband and raised four daughters midst debt and domestic violence. Radha took the lead among the four daughters in helping her family out of the cycle of liquor consumption, domestic violence, and debt. In time, this gave her a position of prominence within her household. My point is that her power is an outcome of constructing solidarity with someone else's oppression.

Finally, role-playing on-stage can entail 'the oppressed' playing the role of the oppressor. This is no innocent enactment of behaviour assumed to be someone else's capacity to victimise. The capacity for oppression and actual enjoyment from role-playing the oppressor is self-consciously treated in JS space as evidence of the oppressor in the personality of the oppressed. When 'the oppressed' role-play the oppressor, they sometimes want to become the oppressor and sometimes, they humanise the oppressor. Each of these approaches is one mode of gaining power and accomplishing control over a relationship of oppression. Consider Ganguly's words reflecting on a workshop with women in Kolkata.

> **Sanjoy Ganguly:** Have you noticed something about Mousumi? I don't know if its some kind of catharsis for her but, if you observe her, whenever there is any discussion about any problem facing anyone, Mousumi always takes an arrogant and strong [role] [...] the role of the strong oppressor that she played in the play. [...] I think that after being oppressed for so long and by observing the same oppressor, she has become a strong oppressor herself. And she is able to find release for herself through that strong feeling. This is quite common even in the villages, in others who are always being oppressed. We have seen some village women who will never replace the oppressed [as spect-actors in forum theatre]. Instead they want to become like the oppressor. Either they are not able to understand the problem and become oppressors themselves or they remove the oppressor and humanise him. Maybe they think that if we reversed roles, what good would it do? This tendency to humanise the oppressor is there in quite a number of women. They are not always like Mousumi. (Ganguly in an Interview, 1988–89: 63)

In this excerpt, Ganguly highlights two significant possibilities whereby women take on the role of the oppressor and enjoy inflicting pain and violence on others. In JS's experience, role-playing the oppressor often leads women to humanise the oppressor rather than choosing to strengthen the character of the oppressed in the play.

These are significant expressions of a relational experience of oppression. The joker in JS Forum Theatre performances will often insist that men intervene as spect-actors to role-play oppressed women in the plays. As Ganguly puts it, even the first task of facing up to internalised oppression is a difficult realisation, 'at first I don't even want to admit to myself that I am oppressed. But later, I do. That's why we often do role reversals. We ask the ones who are oppressed to do the role of the oppressor and the oppressor to do the role of the oppressed'. In this conceptualisation of role reversals, oppression is a relationship so that the oppressor is a victim of oppression even though they cause the oppression of the oppressed. Solidarity, not sisterhood, is the basis of this kind of role-playing and role reversal practice. JS's role-playing generates and dramatises multiple outcomes and possibilities rather than a linear learning process and rehearsal of revolution. This is perhaps the clearest evidence of a practice that relies on the binary categories of oppressed and oppressor as metaphysical presence in order to dramatise a play with and subversion of their stability.

The Light of the Universe is for Everyone

Role-playing on-stage encourages people to recognise the malleability and differentiation within the category of 'the oppressed'. It also permeates interactions off-stage. Prasad and Radha's words about the change in their lives are the terms in which I repeatedly heard people describe the value of JS's practice in their lives. Consider Lata Mondol's words on why she participates in JS. She told me that a lot of people in her village were suspicious of JS, largely because there did not seem to be material benefit to participating in their activities. They assumed that they were a political Party outfit masquerading as a Theatre group. Countering the normative expectations of political engagement, she said:

> Not every one need enjoy it or like it in the same way. But I like this thing. I understand that I am able to interact with people. I am able to go to people. Or, that this is a medium through which to maintain contact with human beings. A major medium. It is such a thing that now if I leave it, it will be very difficult, very sad for me. I won't be able to leave. It has reached such a stage. (Lata Mondol, 27 January, 2001)

Of course this does not mean that before JS, Lata did not know how to interact with people. However, over and over again, when I asked members what JS meant to them, they spoke in terms of JS liberating them, JS as a first in their lives, and JS as representing a 'no turning back'. No turning back from what, we must ask. What is it that JS members value in this practice especially if, as Radha's words suggest, JS plays do not always represent people's direct experiences?

Lata is a middle-aged unmarried woman who lives in a Teor (scheduled caste group) neighbourhood in a village in Kulpi block of rural West Bengal. Prior to her engagement with JS, she was already 'talking back' (Hooks 1989) to the normative expectation that women in rural India must be married — ideally by the time they are 25 years of age. Pursuing her education relentlessly, Lata contradicted her family expectations, taking on the role of a teacher in her village. JS certainly was not the first to instill in her the capacity to speak. Rather, they legitimised a social space for people like her to talk back against prevailing normative structures. Lata's words not only contest skeptics of JS's work, but also the dictum of a historical present where electoral collectivities and monetary gain are given central importance in the construction of social and political relationships.

For others such as Maya, JS's work served as a village institution that she could identify as a worthy cause, justifying her interaction with the world outside the household. While recalling her seven-year struggle to get outside her home, Maya narrated the logic of persuasion she used on her husband:

> If I don't interact with anyone outside, or if I learn nothing, I have to bear whatever is said to me, tolerate it. The light of the universe is for everyone. The way I need it, a tree needs it in the same way. If a child is born, she also needs that light. Without light and air, she will not be able to grow. That's how I used to feel . . . and then gradually I explained it to my husband. That just as you are men, you need the light and air or you need to interact with people outside, women need these things in the same way. I am also human (Maya, 2 May 2001)

She attempted to persuade her husband of an ideological equality where nature and every human being — man, woman, child, and adult — needs the light of the outside, and that this interaction with the outside makes them human.

If interaction is the mode through which we give substance to the 'social', then the possibility of overcoming regulatory norms through interaction is a significant one. It requires engaging in different forms of interaction beyond particular scripts of power marked by asymmetries in gender, caste, and class relations. The 'identity'of prime importance here is the human one even as the logic of persuasion negotiates a gendered experience. Prasad Sardar too spoke in terms of 'light'of interaction. I had asked him if he thought of himself as an artist to which he responded:

> I mean I have been able to see the light. I had never imagined that I had all this talent hidden within me. That I would be able to perform in plays like this, I would be able to talk to people. Now, if anything happens in the village, any kind of debate or decision, any prayer meeting, or festival, or problem they come to me. (Prasad, 28 January 2001)

Prasad recounts Theatre workshops and performances as a mode that nourishes the capacity to script power in a socio-historical context that systematically alienates his capacity for representation.

Interacting on- and off-stage in JS's practice, Prasad realises the value of publicly representing 'human problems, daily problems' by imagining a sense of self-confidence and self-worth that resists his everyday experience of devaluation which can, over time, materialise in a re-evaluated sense of person. Role-playing assumptions of equal representational power and worth can be a profound illustration of how experience 'changes subjects, [...] the way in which they are subject to someone else and the manner in which they come to be tied to their own identities through self-knowledge' (Gupta and Ferguson 1997: 19). This kind of shifted sense of self suggests that far from relying on essential notions of self, JS's practice aims to reveal as malleable the ideological calibrations of 'low'and 'high'persons with 'low'and 'high'places on political and economic scales. They could not have accomplished this without certain principles and ethics of interaction, and long-term engagement. I turn now to an account of these ethics of interaction.

Distance, Deference, and Reciprocity

Interaction may sound like a nebulous reason to value JS. Yet interaction is loaded with feudal, colonial, and post-colonial legacies of class, patriarchal, and caste hierarchies in daily life in India. Sharing living spaces, in addition to work ones, is a significant mode through which JS constructs and embodies its collective membership. For years, the urban, middle-class members of JS have lived and worked in villages refusing the divisions of urban and rural that separate metropolitan political activism from rural ones. More significantly, this sharing of living and working spaces is true of the semi-urban organisational centre and JS director's home in Badu, a suburb of Kolkata, in North 24 Parganas district. Here too, JS leaders share clothes, wardrobes, beds, and bathrooms with other members. This kind of interaction and sharing acts against the dominant and normative separations of caste, class and gender distinctions within the context of Indian society.[3]

As a newcomer, like other outsiders who have documented JS practice, I noticed modes of interaction that expressed the tensions of hierarchy, hospitality, and equality. Some observers documenting their work note with frustration that JS leadership is unable to discipline participants (themselves included) adequately into notions of time. This is quite simply a misinterpretation of the importance of interacting freely, outside the disciplines of clock-time and deadline which JS emphasises quite consistently. Similarly, I misread hierarchy when I cringed at the use of honorific suffixes after names. I could not understand why its members many years my senior would call me 'Dia-di' with a suffix for older sister or why women of grandmother age would refer to me as 'bon', or little sister. Here, I simply misrecognised terms of reciprocity used to address people, even though I knew from kinship terms within my own Bengali family that daughters were referred to as 'mother'by their mothers.

At the same time, those who have documented JS's Boalian workshops see lasting divisions of labour, expressions of deference and hierarchy, and their failure to equalise interaction completely (Iyengar 1999: 10–23). I have certainly seen the practice of seating or feeding men first, giving leaders and researchers chairs when everyone else sat on mats on the floor or directly on floors. When I objected to or noted such modes of interaction, those who offered such gestures always had a reason such as — 'you are our guest', 'you have just walked in from the heat', 'you are not used to this as we are' — and so forth. At the same time, members of the JS coordinating team would try to treat me 'equally'. For example, Lata tried to emphasise to her family that I was 'really a very ordinary girl' and that they should make no special provisions for me. Yet, she herself repeatedly apologised for making me sleep on the floor since I was not used to it. These interactions marked our mutual struggle in negotiating hospitality and hierarchy as we tried in our own ways to live against inherited histories of distance and deference.

Other JS leaders with whom I typically entered strangers' homes and courtyards missed no opportunity to publicly mock interactions between me and various hosts. Mahesh Pal routinely admonished hosts for treating me with too much respect 'just because she has come from the city, has a little education, and seems to have money'. Sometimes, he would put it differently, 'I have noticed when these types are around, the respect you had for me disappears' (*amar proti bhalo babohaar ta choley jaaye*). The laughter that invariably accompanied these comments only served to highlight the playfulness of tone, but they did not nullify that his humour was intended as a play with calibrations of power written into everyday interactions. Mahesh's ironic play with me routinely destroyed any misperception I might have harboured that strangers would shower me with unearned respect just because I carried the signs of privilege. In conversations with other Theatre practitioners and scholars, the criticisms of JS practice are that they are marked by the dominant persona of the director. Yet, not all of these commentators — formal and informal — are familiar with daily life in JS space and practice, and nor do they theorise the limits and accomplishments of its practice.

I am not suggesting that there is no deference and hierarchy in JS structure and practice. There certainly is. But there is no value in presenting the empirical evidence of hierarchy in its practice as ready evidence of 'failure'. I will have more to say about the presence and significance of failure in JS practice in the closing section of this chapter. Here I merely want to note that their struggle against the distance, hierarchies, and deference embedded in interactions of class, caste, and gender inequalities is just that — a struggle. They embody these hierarchical histories just as much as they attempt to overcome them. Sometimes hierarchy is a sign of respect, sometimes of reciprocal assumptions of varied authority, and sometimes simply a matter of habit. At other times, hierarchy is cut down to size with militant reprisal and devastating derision.

Moreover, not all interaction in JS is marked by a compulsion to enact a world without hierarchy. This is defining evidence of its practice being grounded in the life-worlds of its members.

Let me provide an illustration of what this means. Reciprocity in relationships is a central way in which interaction within JS is conceptualised. The notions of reciprocity and obligation that they work with bear significant parallels with ethical philosophies of interaction in Hindu households of rural West Bengal. The Bengali word *sansar* means household. There are two explicit scales of meaning to this word: (1) household and (2) the universe or wider world of people and things that a human being comes in material or spiritual contact with in a lifetime (Lamb 2000). The second scale of meaning is the larger public, community, cosmological, ecological household depending on how one imagines one's 'community'. Sarah Lamb has categorised interactions and relations within Bengali *sansars* into four types: (1) mutuality — defined by sharing goods with one another, (2) deferred reciprocity — whereby a parent who provides food and shelter for children expects children to care for them in their old age, (3) centrality and peripherality whereby adults at the donative center of the household distribute goods and services to children and peripheral elders, and (4) hierarchy — through which seniors give blessings and guidance to juniors and receive services and respect from them in return (*ibid.*: 45).

In practice, people often reciprocate gestures, gifts, and service that they receive from another person over the course of their lifetime. However, as Lamb has documented, maintaining the moral compulsions of reciprocating gestures, gifts, and services were always qualified by the idea that the obligations of juniors towards their seniors (known as *seva*, or service) could never be completely satisfied. 'According to many elders, juniors can never give enough, in the right way, at the right times. [...] At the same time that *seva* overtly signifies the superiority of the elder being served, more covertly it reveals the elder's declining domestic power and bodily strength' (Lamb 2000: 61–62). In this conception of household relationships, there is no authority without reciprocity and service, and there is no meaning to service and reciprocity that does not also affirm authority in relationships.

Organisations like JS intentionally nurtured a feeling of *attiyota* (family feeling) through their intimate and long-standing location in the lives of people and rural communities. The demands of mutuality, reciprocity, centrality/peripherality, and hierarchy placed upon family members were placed in different ways upon members of this organisation. In other words, the relations of rule that struc-ture Hindu households were used to fight the compulsions of class, gender, and caste segregations, even though households are sources of material and representational inequality themselves. As relations of rule, these simultaneously order everyday life and provide a structure of ethical action. JS members who used terms like *attiyota* to describe relationships within the organisation often told me that it would not be easy for me to reciprocate what the organisation had done for me. My anxiety and theirs regarding my inability to reciprocate was a function of my middle-class position, my externality, and location in a North American University. After all, mutuality was contingent upon the creation of a relationship that lasted long enough to see reciprocity through by being there at the right place to give 'in the right way, at the right times' (Lamb 2000: 62). JS members applied to the research relationship the same principle they applied to their interventions in rural lives. That is, it was bound to be an instrumental intervention unless it was founded on long-term relationship of *attiyota* with all its implications of hierarchy and ethical reciprocity.

Hierarchy was legitimate when it came with reciprocity to make a relationship. Otherwise, it was quite simply authoritarian control, a monologue, and not a relationship. Consider Durga Pal's experience with one NGO which invoked the discourse of *sansar*, but failed to live by its ethics. In the late 1990s, Durga, a member of JS since the mid-1990s decided to withdraw her membership from an organisation called the Agricultural Labourers' Committee (ALC). ALC was one branch of a larger NGO, funded by the state and international organisations, which combined service-oriented development projects with grassroots mobilisation. She recounted the time when the leaders of the NGO refused to help her mother-in-law without a fee. All she had asked for was the NGO leaders' hospitality in Kolkata for her mother-in-law while she got her eye operated, the medical expenses for which Durga herself would bear. I quote her at length to show how she brought the challenge of reciprocity to the heart of her critique of participatory community development.

> We used to work with ALC. Having worked with ALC I saw their thing, their way of working in two-four meetings. They had kept me there as a member of the women's group, Women Labourers'Committee (WLC). At Milon Mor there was a meeting once every month. Members had

to pay a contribution, I even gave that. There was a fund there. I mean just one rupee or two rupees at a time, and if anyone from the group was in financial trouble, then that fund was used to help them. [...] But the three meetings I was at, they say to me, 'I feel for the poor, I do work for society' but it is all about what they say; they don't actually live by these words.

[...] I have evidence for this. Their children live there, they work, they stay there and go to good schools, they get into good cars and they eat well. We run around for this organisation so much, and when my mother in law's eye had to be operated [...] I had gone to them and I said that we are getting this operation done for my mother in law. I have done a lot of work with you all, or I am a member here and I make contributions and so on, so please make arrangements for her stay during the operation. We will pay for the operation and the medicines. We need your help when it comes to the meals and the accommodation. If I stay in the city and eat a meal, if I eat a meal outside it will cost a lot of money, could you cover that bit of the cost? Whatever other expenditure comes our way, I will take care of that. At that time WLC and ALC were together and the head, her name is Asha Tiwari, she said 'I can provide the food but you have to pay the price of the meal'.

Before that in my home the kind of trouble they have created ALC and WLC. From that, I felt very hurt after that meeting. I say a man stayed at my home for one month and built an organisation from that (generosity), he stayed, he used to eat all day, he used to eat in the afternoon, he ate breakfast, he came back at night and ate again — a gentleman called Shiva Pramanik. We give him so much food without asking for money, and now my mother-in-law is ill and I am asked for the price of her meals?

I was very hurt by this. I did not go for meetings for the next two months. They called me repeatedly. [...] They wanted me to tell everyone, in front of everyone the reason why I was letting go of this work. I said 'The person whose home you so freely use, the person who puts in so much time, effort, work without payment[...] so, that person's mother in law needs some looking after, and I have to pay for the meals? This is my difficulty, my hurt. What did I do? For whom? [...]

She said 'this person just pretends that she does not work for pay'. She said this. Because of this hurt I will not work. That is how I left that work. No one had to tell me to feel this way. It is my pain, for my mother in law. That is why I won't work. Children, their children, I see in front of my very eyes that they go to good schools, they wear good clothes, it is these things that make me feel bad, and that's why I will not work. [...]

Durga is talking about the hypocrisy of working for a 'household' with no semblance of reciprocity. The ALC household invokes the ethics of *sansar* from a position of hierarchy. The organisation appropriates the meaning of *sansar* and reworks this emic category into their definition of 'development'as self-help (*cf.* Yudice 2003). In fact, the *sansar* and future that benefits from ALC's practice is a narrow *sansar* belonging to its urban, middle-class component. Not only does Durga show how the poor work for NGO models of development, she talks back to an NGO's cynical capital accumulation through the expedient invocation of NGO as *Sansar*.

Notions of reciprocity, authority, and hierarchy were tied in with notions of caring, respect, and security in future relationships. And these notions were difficult and precarious in contexts of migration, commodification, unemployment, property-less women, the hypocrisy of arrangements with social work organisations, research and teaching commitments, and the hierarchy and asymmetry that marked relations with politicians and leaders. Durga questioned the dishonest appeal to social service, building community, and working for the poor when interactions failed to measure up to a minimum of reciprocity. Making an uninvited comparison, in closing her commentary on leaving ALC, Durga said, 'We really like JS's work, this Theatre work, the way they say things, they act with the same kind of feeling'. JS can claim a tentative place in her household and work-day as long as they struggle towards daily lived interactions which materialise the hypotheses and imagined equality they claim as rhetorical solutions on-stage.

On the one hand, long-term relationships allow dishonesty and discrepancies in claims about 'family feeling' to be confronted as Durga's narrative shows. On the other, JS's long-term presence makes Forum Theatre engagements not interventions that are one-time experiences, but regular processes through which alternative norms for living are performatively constructed. In a post-workshop and performance discussion between participants and JS leaders, this is how Ganguly and one of the discussants put it:

> **Sanjoy:** Another thing that happens sometimes, in villages those men who beat their wives at home come into the Forum and start talking very righteously about finding solutions to this problem, replacing the protagonist and behaving like a saviour of sorts. This piece of acting on his part sometimes affects him positively. We can cite at least five or six examples of this. Those who come before the Forum in this way receive a lot of applause [...]

> **Ratna:** So he understands that if he sides with the Oppressed wife in the Forum he will be applauded, that's why he does it?
>
> **Sanjoy:** Yes. At first its pretense. But when he sees that people are applauding him, he thinks to himself that this may be the way to be. So gradually a change comes about in him. (Ganguly 1998–99: 54)

An on-stage intervention can turn into reality over time as spect-actors confront the duality of a habitual norm of hierarchy off-stage and the applauded and publicly witnessed alternative norm on-stage. For Ganguly, the task at hand is not to change the oppressor conceived as individual, or isolated interactions, but rather the oppression accomplished in a relationship.

Mahesh Pal used this understanding of on-stage pretence and gradual performative materialisation of reality as a way of understanding the research relationship. This is an illuminating example for many reasons, but here I use it to show how he tied hierarchy and difference in the research relationship and how enacting a long-term relationship can performatively materialise reciprocity over time. Early on in the research relationship, Mahesh asked me about my plans for the future. I gave my usual vague and non-committal reply, 'Well, I don't know. I have wanted to teach for a while'. To that he said 'Can't you teach here somewhere so you can work with us part-time? It would be really good if someone like you worked with us'. I asked him what he meant by 'someone like you' although I presumed he meant someone with a degree education. He responded:

> There are things that you can understand that we cannot and it's always helpful for certain kinds of work. Not everyone can study. And in our work, it is important in our work to study. I have realised that. I used to think that it is not important to study and it is enough to do the fieldwork but I realise that the research aspect is also important.

Mahesh was entirely aware of the possibility of enrichment from getting a researcher's and/or an outsider's perspective. While he believed in this possibility and was encouraged by the nature of my interaction with people, he nonetheless suggested that enrichment by an outside perspective was not a necessary outcome of outsider involvement. The crucial component was spending time enough for the veil to come off, for a performance of interest to turn into involved commitment.

> The number of researchers who have come here are not few. Sometimes people are very friendly initially, but soon that mask (*mukhosh*) comes loose and the fact that they were acting is revealed (*beriye jaye je shudhu dekhate chaichhilo*). You can act out your effort to be a part of something even if you don't really feel it. On the other hand, sometimes what happens is that you want to be a part of it all, if for no other reason at least to be able to do your research work in peace (*nishchinte tothho jogaar korar jonno shobaar shonge mishle*), with the feeling that you are making an effort that in some ways goes beyond your research (*tomar dorkarer cheye beshi ektu amader kaaj-ta egiye dile*). On the other hand sometimes, as you keep acting you become the person that you have been acting and you find that you can hardly be any other way (*aar tarpore sheyi manush-tayi hoye gele, sheyi aager lok-ta aar hote parcho na*). Of course that's if you have spent enough time in the place.

I could sense the infinite significance of Mahesh's words at the time even though I did not quite understand them fully. In a research relationship, just as for those engaging in Forum Theatre interventions like the one Ganguly described above, for an individual to be persuaded that a normative change is worthwhile depends on collective witnessing, mutual encouragement, and affirmation.

To use Mahesh's words, the possibility that we can 'become the person that [we] have been acting' on-stage might strike a social scientist as an unlikely or anomalous occurrence, an ephemeral safety valve, rather than a 'utopian performative' that works as an engine of social change (Dolan 2005). However arguably, it is precisely the ephemerality of performance that makes kinetic representations powerful dramatisations of malleable structures. Performance shows that hierarchies are contingent and stability only assumes the air of inevitability. To sum up the lessons from examples outlined above, discrepancies between representation and reality, role-playing Oppressor and Oppressed, and acting and living against the norms of segregated and unequal living can be kernels of social transformations. In these experiences, I see the formation of spect-actors of history, not just on-stage spect-actors.

Although in some ways JS work relies on a universal humanism, they also draw on ethical sources of interaction such as *sansar* that belong to the life-worlds of its members. Seen from the point of view of universal humanism, this ethic of *sansar* where hierarchy can be one outcome of mutual and cooperative construction of respect and equality, will likely be judged to be regressive. In JS's practice however, the starting point of dialogue with 'the oppressed' rather than monologue opens up the possibility of recognising and inhabiting different histories of power as political practice. Here, incorporating difference has less to do with recuperating a stable subjectivity of 'the oppressed' than with representational equality for historical difference. Drawing on these multiple ethics of action and interaction, JS dramatises oppression as a relationship and constructs solidarity and historical possibility as a long-term struggle rather than as the practice of rehearsing revolution from the standpoint of the Oppressed.

Praxis of Failure

Ambiguity and failure are a significant part of JS's everyday stories and practice. Failure as praxis (not just practice) defines the process of making spect-actors of history. In this section, I argue that their approach to failure is complex and cannot be captured with any sense of closure. When participation fails to produce preconceived notions of empowerment, Robert Chambers (1997) describes it as bad practice. Chamber's view does not allow us to critically reflect on what gets constructed as errors or success in the first place, by whom and with what consequence. JS does not try to make success out of its failure by addressing isolated problems and relegitimising organisational strength (Ferguson 1994). But it does construct praxis out of dead-end interventions on-stage, and failures experienced off-stage.

For example, while JS prides itself for having worked consistently with village women, at the same time, its leading activists are regularly heard saying 'these patriarchal values were instilled in me, are in me even today. You can't wipe them out completely. That I have understood. I did not know this before. While working with women for so long, all this came to light' (Ganguly 1998–99: 65). There is an insistence through such claims that the very people who recognise the importance of anti-patriarchal work know that they cannot count on erasing the patriarchal imprint in themselves. Here, failure is part of a reflexive praxis. It is not a debilitating point that generates apathy, nor something to be recuperated as eventual success. Failure is simply one part of the struggle and process of constructing social change, something to be reflected upon rather than rejected.

For instance, what happens when failure to live one's real life by a new commitment learned on-stage is voiced in a reflective moment to one's group members? As an actor and activist, Amulya had questioned the wife-beating habit in many JS performances. However, at one point in time, he said to his Theatre team that he had lost the credibility to do Theatre with the others since he had hit his wife a couple of days ago. What do we miss by interpreting this as failure? If the efficacy and power of performance is measured in terms of a husband who no longer beats his wife, domination overcome, then Amulya failed. Seen differently, the process of generating discrepancy between reality on-stage and representations of normality off-stage were having an effect on him if he felt he had lost the 'credibility' to do this theatre.

JS men who refused dowry at the time of marriage are frequently cited as examples of what the learning process within JS can accomplish. At the same time, men who refused dowry at the time of marriage sometimes failed to resist subsequent pressure from their families post-marriage to bring in things from the wife's natal home. Structures of expectation and political economy constraining norms do not disappear in the face of newly witnessed or learned norms. For this reason, neither failure nor success, neither liberation nor oppression can be judged in terms of one-time manifestations. To understand spect-actors of history as process rather than liberated persons, failures must be recognised for their complexity, understood as a constitutive force that reinforces relations of rule, and can also generate learning for collective political action.

One JS play called *The Brick Factory* is particularly suggestive of the need to problematise the notion of success and failure. The engagement with this play animates most vividly that stepping on-stage to become a spect-actor does not happen in a vacuum. The play is a story set in the Birbhum district of West Bengal. It is about women's experience of work, exploitative wages, and sexual violence at a brick factory. Scenes in brick factory show men and women working for an unambiguously oppressive factory owner who withholds wages at will, exacts favours from men, and blackmails and sexually assaults the women workers. The play also has a scene where the men and women mobilise for a better wage but remain divided as the men workers fail to rally behind women's call for an equal wage.

More than any other JS play I witnessed, this one performed in Forum Theatre format, showed me just how unambiguously spect-actors can reinforce 'structure'. Young men stepped on-stage to argue that the solution to bonded women labourers is to disallow women from leaving the home. These views are antithetical to what JS leaders believe. Yet, suggestions of women's liberation can meet such 'dead ends' on-stage, so that they get reassimilated and the 'disorder'of their bonded labour or sexual subjection is brought back into the protective care of a domestic patriarchal structure. On other occasions, the 'dead end'was not quite as obvious on-stage. Take this seemingly heroic moment of liberation in the words of a female spect-actor. She intervened at a point in the play when the female worker subject to routine sexual assaults, Phulmoni, decides against returning to work in the factory.

Factory Owner: Why didn't you come today?
***Spect-actor* as Phulmoni:** I don't need your money.
Factory Owner: What do you mean?
***Spect-actor* as Phulmoni:** I mean I don't want your money.
Factory Owner: Oh! So you mean its okay with you, you wont get work, you wont get money and that's okay with you?
***Spect-actor* as Phulmoni:** Yes I don't want your work. I pee on your work! *Audience laughter.*

Uplifted by watching this spect-actor intervene, I followed the spect-actor, Lakshmi, off-stage to ask get a better sense of the meaning of her heroism. She explained her intervention on-stage, 'So the lower women fall, the more men will oppress them from above. So what we have to do is that for women to progress no men should be able to enter the home other than the husband' (15 February 2001). Is her rejection of the violating contractor's offer of work and her subsequent cry for protecting women necessarily conservative or liberatory? Forum Theatre performances are moments of this kind of complexity, marked equally by contingency and historical constraints, opening the possibility for further conversation among all seeking progress and liberation as well as those seeking protection within patriarchy. Such theatre may be theoretically intended as rehearsal of revolution (Boal 1979), but in practice it cannot be a unitary learning process nor fixed assumption about what the revolution will look like.

We could view Lakshmi's on-stage voice as liberation and off-stage voice as dead-end failure condoning apathy. If we merely read multiple spect-actor interventions as so many solutions to the same problem, Forum Theatre technique risks being equated with the kinds of military games which calculate multiple possibilities and 'large numbers of contingencies to control a situation' (Taussig and Schechner 1994: 24). Rather, making praxis out of failure implies that instead of viewing Lakshmi's on-stage and off-stage perspectives as success and failure respectively, JS assumes the task of constantly problematising both successful liberation and seemingly dead-end failures *in relation to each other.*

I present these interventions in JS Forum Theatre to reveal how my expectations of seeing 'rehearsals of revolution' were frustrated. After watching endless spect-actor interventions and series of 'dead ends', if not downright reactionary and conservative 'solutions', I asked Sanjoy Ganguly what he thought the solution to the bonded woman laborers'problem could be. He said without pause that 'There is no solution to Phulmoni's problem. Unless there is radical restructuring, there can be no solution to her problem'. I was confused by this because JS members distinguish their work as one that highlights mobilising against representational inequality, by redistributing the means of representation rather than mobilising around means of production. I had thought that redistributing representation was a constituent element of radical restructuring. Ganguly admits that 'economism has contributed much to the labour movement in the past. I do not deny the need for that even today' (2004: 230). But faced with Phulmoni's situation, he admits that working towards representational inequality fails to accomplish change in the face of unequal means of production. Again, this kind of acknowledgment of failure in JS's conceptualisation of political action around redistributing representation does not lead to apathy, nor render the task of fighting material and representational inequality meaningless. Rather, it is a reflexive recognition of the complexity and enormity of the task as much larger than themselves.

In the article quoted above, Ganguly compares the play *The Brick Factory* and its main character Phulmoni with another play called *Sarama* written earlier (see chapter three). It is about a fiercely independent woman who is raped by ruling Party-supported criminals, abandoned by her lover, subject to intense press coverage, and becomes a pawn in the game of Party competition. As the plot unfolds, when Sarama 'finds herself pregnant as a result of the rape, [she] ignores the social taboos and the strictures about the purity of the female body, she decides to have the child' (Ganguly 2004: 231). Among all the forces holding political–economic power in her context, Sarama only has the support of NGOs in this moment of multiple betrayals. The numerous and contradictory class and gender politics embedded in the play receive greater elaboration in chapter three. Of significance here is that Ganguly realises the limits of providing an assumed liberatory message through his plays.

Sarama was a very popular play when it was first performed. But when Theatre teams performed it in Birbhum, a woman called Phulmoni who worked in a brick factory, asked Ganguly to solve her plight as he seemed to have solved Sarama's. She said,

> in your play the woman is strong, very strong. People say you are doing good work. But tell me Babu, what are we to do when the contractor pays us less than our due and asks us to visit him alone? If we don't go to him, he will take away our job. You tell us, shall we give up our work from tomorrow? (Ganguly 2004: 232)

On-stage, Sarama had the backing of an NGO, off-stage Phulmoni did not. Ganguly describes this tension and dilemma of expecting people to fortify collectivity and self for protest, despite poverty. Phulmoni made Ganguly realise at this time that his Theatre should actively seek organisations engaged in struggles over land, labour, and resources. He saw his role as contributing to the work of these mass organisations across India by giving them the additional tools of 'Theatre of the Oppressed'in order to maintain debate and discussion as a regular mode of creative and democratic discussion.

He also realised that plays like *Sarama* written solely by him, not subject to discussion in the Forum Theatre format, were simply inadequate. That led him to conduct workshops and script Phulmoni's story in the play *The Brick Factory* which insists on the Forum Theatre format despite the 'dead ends'on-stage. The point of this statement is to highlight the praxis of failure in it. When 'dead ends'make Ganguly realise the structural constraints of Phulmoni's problems, he is encouraged to push the democratic practice further, despite and because of 'structure'.[4] Forum Theatre is often deployed because it is credited for its ability to construct solutions collectively. But as I see JS's practice, this kind of theatre highlights for community, collectivity, or person that solidarity is a contingent accomplishment, and that some problems cannot have an imagined solution within current terms of the problem or within the current historical conjunctures. In a context that assumes the success of pro-poor Leftist ideology and electoral democracy, there is a significant value to realising this in animated, public, and kinetic terms.

God Lies within Every Human Being

I conclude this chapter by attending to another significant source of ethical political action — faith. This section not only highlights my failure and inability but also my continuing struggle to access the meaning of faith in JS's practice.[5] JS fights the commonsense of a centralised culture built on the monologues of various superiors — state officials, village elders, fathers, husbands, academic researchers, rich landlords, and development professionals. Prasad explained that JS acts as if people are equal:

> Because JS believes that in every human being there is a talent. God lies within every human being. Every human being is a unique gem. No dispensable human beings. That is why JS does Theatre *of* the Oppressed. (Prasad, 28 January 2001)

Ganguly uses this language as well, 'inside every human being there must be a capacity for good, we must agree to that if we respect human beings' (1998–99: 54). In this sense, JS's transformative work assumes a universal humanism. These ideas about god in human beings resonate with Maya's idea that the 'light of the universe is for everyone'. Prasad's statement that 'God lies within every human being' is not about privatising god within individual subjectivity and practice, but about giving divine value to truth and equality as a mode of social interaction and involvement. These expres-sions of lived religion have long been expressed in the teachings of the medieval Sufi saint Lalan Fakir and the nineteenth century temple priest of suburban Kolkata, Ramakrishna. Ramkrishna, for example, said, 'wherever there is a living being, there is Shiva' (one of three main gods in the Hindu pantheon).

Blinded by my lens which I assumed to be secular, and by the secularism of development studies, for much of my fieldwork period I failed to pursue the question of what lived religion really meant to people. Numerous homes had preserved calendars with pictures of Ramkrishna, Sarada Devi (Ramkrishna's wife), Goddess Kali, and Goddess Durga from years past which they displayed on the walls of their homes as a substitute for the more expensive framed photos of gods and goddesses. These calendars hung alongside other calendars with pictures of historical figures and political leaders such as Vivekananda, Subhas Chandra Bose, Mahatma Gandhi, Jawaharlal Nehru, and Indira Gandhi — a pantheon of gods and leaders. I routinely saw people actively involved in making arrangements for religious festivals. These festivals seemed to me to coalesce issues of village politics and conflicts, neighbourhood cooperation and collective feasting, labour and status, new clothes and new friends. The fact that some of the long term participants in JS activities would observe every detail of every ritual often took me aback. During my years of fieldwork, I somehow assumed it to be a sphere of their lives that I could not access and would not have reason to understand. As I write this, the effects of this neglect on my part feels palpable. As such, I am forced to rely on the meaning of lived religion to JS leaders rather than its members, and to secondary sources on the meaning of Ramkrishna.

Sumit Sarkar (1998) has argued that popular religion was not so much a feudal vestige during colonial rule, as a significant source that helped an alienated urban, middle-class search for 'self'and 'future'. He has argued that Ramkrishna acquired valence for the Western-educated urban middle-class *bhadralok* in the last quarter of the nineteenth century (*ibid.*). At this time, *bhadralok* piety found expression in social activism of various sorts — 'patriotic history-writing, efforts to tap into folk cultural resources, satirical Theatre, introspective and emotional forms of religious devotion [...] [were] some of the ways through which inner tensions of the *bhadralok* found expression' (*ibid.*: 199). The *bhadralok* were also enamoured by the childlike '[r]ural retrospect, feminisation, a turning away from social activism towards the attractive irresponsibility of the child and *pagal* [mad person]' embodied in Ramakrishna (*ibid.*: 201).

Ramkrishna represents the inner anxieties of becoming middle-class in an age of political economic opportunities made available to traditional literati by the East India Company. By the 1840s, the literati that had migrated to Kolkata for jobs were finding it increasingly difficult to find jobs (Sarkar 1998: 224–25). The foreclosure of 'opportunity' by the mid-nineteenth century meant that not everyone with middle-class aspirations could become middle-class. At such a time, it was appealing to celebrate as iconic those who seemed to opt out of becoming modern through an irresponsible, childlike madness. Ramkrishna was likely to hold appeal to these middle-class aspirants to modernity. In Sumit Sarkar's words, '"Mad" to the conventional world, they are holy madmen who have opted out of the rat race for money and worldly success, emancipated themselves from the world of clock time and office space, and so can purvey divine truth in simple earthy language' (1998: 207). Girish Chandra Ghosh, a devotee of Ramkrishna and exemplary nineteenth century playwright, peppered his plays with characters glorified for having access to divine truth and shunning the materiality of bourgeois life.

Sarkar's interpretation of Ramkrishna situates him in the political–economic structure of colonial rule but neglects the fact that Ramkrishna's teachings about shunning materiality resonates with an older Sufi tradition. The particular implications of Ramkrishna's teaching for the Bengali middle class during colonial rule do not exhaust the meaning and power of shunning materiality in history. The division between 'great' and 'little' traditions, as scholars have shown, is an ideological one where the idioms of one imprint and evolve in relation to the other, transforming without any one rationalised goal. In meaning and power then, the idioms in circulation exceed and preceed the ideological containers within which they are fit at given historical moments such as the encounter with colonial capitalism.

The image of Ramkrishna, his relationship to Girish Chandra Ghosh, and the language of the poor as decent human beings (*daridra athaccha bhadra*) are familiar figures and tropes within JS. No doubt the Bengali middle-class legacy of Ramkrishna worship inspires the spiritual convictions of JS's urban middle-class leaders. Its organisational centre's name is Girish Bhaban named after the nineteenth century playwright. During JS 'ideological training' sessions, among many other sources of knowledge, Sanjoy Ganguly repeatedly recounts stories that reveal the interconnected lives and legacies of Ramkrishna, Girish Chandra Ghosh, and Binodini Dasi.

Stories narrate how Ramkrishna came to watch Girish Ghosh's plays, how Ghosh trained Binodini as an actor despite her background in Kolkata's red-light districts, and finally, how Ramkrishna touched Binodini's feet after a performance.

A key aim of these stories, as I heard their telling in JS space, was to mark reverence for the ethical actions and humility in prominent historical personalities. Sumit Sarkar's analysis captures the reasons for Ramkrishna's appeal for Bengali middle class of the nineteenth century, suggesting the legacy of Ramkrishna's lasting appeal today. However, Sarkar's argument should not be called upon to explain the totality of Ramkrishna's appeal today. I would argue that it is also the systematic exclusion of humility and faith from current political–economic culture that fortifies their appeal. Humility and faith are ingredients for a definition of a 'good life' and sources of ethical action, and have to be understood as such.

In my very first interview with Sanjoy Ganguly, he told me that he saw continuities between the foundation of Augusto Boal's thinking and that of Vivekananda (a figure of the nineteenth century cultural intelligentsia credited with the so-called Bengal Renaissance). In his words, the similarity lies in that 'Vivekananda's hypothesis itself is that human beings are perfect. Those who don't have this belief they very easily fall into a Stalinist kind of thinking and they think that if for one problem you discuss it with hundred people then that amounts to too many cooks spoiling the broth' (Ganguly, 5 June 1999). One might argue that Ganguly is latching onto liberalism not religion in Vivekananda's thought. Despite his statement, I have been inclined to treat liberalism and religion as competing sources of political action when in fact, what he really seems to be saying is that there is no inherent contradiction between them.

When Girish Bhaban — JS's organisational centre — was inaugurated, Ganguly spoke at the ceremony to mark the occasion. The ceremony included a small, intimate *puja* (devotional worship); a larger event with microphones, speeches, expressions of gratitude, singing; and a collective feast. Some members from JS's various Theatre teams had come to join in the celebration, although December being a busy month in agriculture meant that many had to savour the fruition of a struggle to build a space of one's own from a distance. The small *puja* in the office space sticks out in my field notes for that day. Here is an excerpt:

1 December 2001

> The puja [devotional worship] was held in the front room of the building. The room will become one of the offices of the organisational centre. One corner of that room was arranged with the picture of a saint. I could not recognise the man in the photograph. I realised later that not too many 'outsiders' [to the Ganguly household] did. Till the last minute of the puja starting, people were doing other things — cleaning, organising, arranging. In fact, Mahesh did not come and sit at the puja at all. He worked right through the puja. Sanjoy-da's father did the puja. There weren't many mantras [ritual chants] as far as I could hear. He only lit three dhoops [incense sticks] and circled them around the framed picture in front of him. He did that for a long time. He then prostrated himself in front of the images and did pronaam [gesture of respect for elders, ancestors, and gods]. When he rose and turned around, it was obvious that he had tears in his eyes. I realised then that so did Simadi. Rohini was sobbing into her anchal [the loose end of her sari]. I can only guess that the weeping is provoked by grief mixed with incredible joy, relief, memories of the struggle that produced this space of their own. Their tears seemed to be a tribute to their faith and strength.

Sima, Sanjoy, Rohini, and Sanjoy's father — each from urban middle-class backgrounds — were the only ones in that space. I tried to interpret their grief and passion in these notes, but my notes for the day are decidedly non-committal about the meaning of 'faith'in JS's political action.

After the *puja*, I tried to ask non-urban middle-class members of JS what faith meant to them. I asked Mahesh why he didn't come to the *puja*, and he said 'I am always calling god, I can't sit and attend to god'. I did not pursue him about his mode of 'always calling god' which could also imply secular faith in social activism. Members of the Ganguly household (Sanjoy Ganguly and his father in particular) were much more explicit about what faith meant to them. Invariably, the West Bengal government's political ideals and corrupted Communism came up as a rationale and point of comparison for their faith. Ganguly's father commented 'He [Ramkrishna] showed us that there will be as many paths as there are perspectives' [*jato path tato mat*]. Sanjoy Ganguly told me later,

> Today you saw an inner, hidden core of JS which outsiders can't see. No one knows of this spirituality in us. Could you tell that our core

> [he used the English word] is spiritual when you first met us? This force is what keeps us going. This faith is what kept my father going when he was poor and had to support seven brothers and make miracles happen. The faith that kept him away from corruption.

Ganguly reiterated later to everyone present, 'Today Dia saw our core.' And thus the 'core' of JS was constructed for me that day. What did it mean? That faith is a critical source for ethical political action? Or, that ethics is a central aspect of faith whether or not such sources of ethics are put to use in political action?

The reference to the force of faith in fighting corruption by Sanjoy Ganguly (a former CPM member) and his father (an adamant CPM member since the inception of the Party and through his recent death) is in part nurtured by an explicit critique of various forms of CPM Party corruption. Sanjoy Ganguly's evaluation of the importance of faith for political action is a critique of the dominant political ideology that is deeply uncomfortable with religious ethic as source of political action, a commonsense Leftist view that political action is sullied by a belief in god. Despite this view, the CPM has had its own complex negotiation with the ideology and practice of faith in West Bengal. Aditya Nigam's (2006) research shows that the Party has tried to accommodate minority communities and negotiate tense situations. For example, CPM local Party leaders meet the demands of *pujas* and *rozas* and thus engage in Hindu and Muslim ritual observances using public money and on official time. While its politicians accommodate religion and struggle to maintain the ideological purity of high Communism, they fail to capture the power of citizens' 'normal, unselfconscious way' of relating to faith in practice (*ibid.*: 283). In the context of rising religious fundamentalism and electoral competition, the CPM has turned to 'traditional resources' such as Ramkrishna and Vivekananda, reclaiming these figures as reformers from within rather than emblematic of the communal heritage that the Right-wing fundamentalist political party, the BJP, constructs them to be.

Yet, dissident CPM politicians such as Subhas Chakravarty believe that the overall exclusion of faith and the Party's inability to relate to citizens'everyday religious practices ultimately produce instrumental, superficial, misguided modes of battling religious fundamentalism. In the dissident politician's words, 'the more you "fight" communalism in the way it is being fought (by the Party), the more it tends to get strengthened' (quoted in Nigam 2006: 287). This ongoing failure is likely a *result* of treating religion as a separate category of social life. After all, can ethics be traced in some unproblematic and coherent fashion to entirely non-religious or entirely religious sources? Talal Asad has argued that 'the theoretical search for an essence of religion invites us to separate it conceptually from the domain of power' (Asad 1993: 29) which is 'a modern Western norm, the product of a unique post-Reformation history' (*ibid.*: 28).

As Nigam argues of CPM practice, despite the instrumental invocation of religion, the Party is unable to control its political community from turning communitarian because the faith of the leaders is historically inclined to icons and idioms of Hindu faith. Even dissidents within the CPM like Subhas Chakravarty who insist on the importance of religion cannot get past the normative Hindu idioms (Nigam 2006: 289). Here, the hegemonic Western norm of separating religious power from political power remains incomplete, as Hindu idioms remain the inadvertent representations used to make the case for 'secularism'on the one hand or for insisting on the everyday presence of faith in people's lives on the other. In both cases, 'different kinds of practice and discourse are intrinsic to the field in which religious representations (like any representation) acquire their identity and truthfulness' (Asad 1993: 53–54). Avowedly, secular representations of religion and religious representations infiltrate each other as if refusing to complete the analytical separation of religion as a separable category of social life.

Compared with the CPM form of duplicitous distancing on the one hand and defensive and instrumental incorporation on the other, in JS's political action, religion quite simply does not have to be relegated to the private sphere. Its political action makes ethics in faith modes of organising political action. Despite this general approach of accepting religious practices, it would be a mistake to cast JS's relationship to religion in any one way. The organisation cannot be characterised as equally inclusive of all forms of religious idioms and representations. Not that worship of other gods and goddesses is disallowed or discouraged. After all, its organisational structure cannot control who is worshipped in rural homes, spaces, and festivals. But within the organisation centre and at meetings where the director of JS is speaking, there is a dominant religious language of command that relies rather exclusively on the teachings and idioms of Ramkrishna and Vivekananda.

Clearly this is what Ganguly is familiar with, but this could conceivably lead to reproducing within JS the representational inequality among various religious epistemes and practices prevalent in the Indian context at large.[6] In short, religion is not a neutral source of knowledge within JS because it reflects the broader hierarchies in India. Nigam's words about the failure of dissident CPM elites like Chakravarty who cannot get away from a normative Hindu 'secularism'is applicable to JS leadership as well. For JS leadership as for the CPM, this failure, if we can even call it that, 'is probably inevitable. There is no Archimedean space available from where all experiences can be understood and reforms conducted' (Nigam 2006: 289). JS's political action is unique in the sense that they nurture the capacity of faith to provide a mode of thinking and action that builds a just, public life. If their practice could brave public struggles among various religious epistemes and unequal histories, then multiple pieties could inform constructions of a political community. At present, its invocation of piety and god in every human being gives JS a spiritual core aimed at fortifying an organisation and its members against corruption, and towards an ethical practice of political action.

In the spirit of the idea of a spect-actor of history, I must conclude on the note of my failure and continued struggle to understand the place of faith in JS practice. What stands out for me is that over and over again, I missed opportunities to pursue the meaning of faith, often feeling unsatisfied with accepting piety for piety's sake, whether among urban middle class believers or the majority of JS members. Ultimately, I view faith among JS middle-class leaders as a source of ethical political action and a publicised strategy for resisting the corruptions of contemporary politics. Had I asked better questions, I may well have found that its leaders are in fact following the lead of their rural members for whom piety and faith have multiple meanings, which are more or less rationalised into social functions for some believers, and which preceed and exceed their engagement in JS practice. If faith constitutes the 'inner, hidden core' at the heart of the organisational centre of JS today, I may have understood what exactly this means, if I had been asking better questions.

Conclusion

In this chapter, I have argued that JS members become spect-actors by scripting power against the odds that deny them representational equality in class, caste, gender and Party hierarchies. In part, scripting power is enabled through a theatrical process committed to breaking the ideological distinctions between the oppressed and the oppressor, as well as representation and reality through the emblematic figure of the spect-actor. Although this Theatre process insists on the category of 'the oppressed', JS practice on-stage and off-stage is insistent on identifying exceptions, and the capacity for oppression *within* those categorically represented as the oppressed. Its practice insists rather on a feminist vision of struggle that is akin to Nancie Caraway's 'crossover dreams' by insisting on making Theatre of the Oppressed an on-stage and off-stage practice that highlights the binary of Oppressed and Oppressor that we each inhabit and materialise in different ways at different moments in time (1991: 171–204). Here solidarity is a constructed outcome of engaged practice and political action, not assumed sisterhood.

In equally large part, scripting power is accomplished through JS's long-term commitment of living and interacting against the normative distance and deference that marks relationships in post-colonial rural Bengal. Drawing on multiple ethics of political action and practice — from Theatre of the Oppressed, to Ramkrishna, and *sansar* ethics of reciprocity and hierarchy — they act against Party political and patriarchal assumptions about what counts as progressive political action, refusing the normative divisions between liberal and secular, religious and progressive, and so forth. Against a universal modernity that assumes liberal secular subjectivity, JS insists on human proximity to god, the power of faith and ethical action, and the worship of gods as powerful modes of organising self, space, and rethinking possibilities for political action. Partly strengthened by faith and partly committed to lived democracy, they narrate and stage failure as sign of their historical reality and personal vulnerability to becoming oppressors as they engage in the Theatre of the Oppressed.

JS members know that their practice does not necessarily or absolutely transcend inequalities and hierarchies (within families, organisations, within and among societies, between god and humans). Indeed, not all hierarchies are conceived as detrimental despite their ongoing attempt to live the ideology of representational equality. And not all failures need be moved towards success, although failure is not cause for a debilitating apathy either. Facing hindrances and a breakdown of goals on-stage and ambiguity offstage highlights their struggles as struggles. For those living under Leftist rule which seems far too sure of its pro-poor ideology and success, publicly confronting, interpreting, and grappling with the meaning of failure constitutes a significant pedagogical process and makes these moments of 'defeat' profound. These experiences which highlight the ambiguity of liberation are also invaluable experiences in a neoliberal context which holds up freedom as the highest ideal of social life while paying little attention to the constitutive role played by exclusion and violence in the making of 'freedom'. In short, critically thinking about the meaning of defeat in these contexts reminds JS members to ask again, what kind of collectivity and freedom do we want and what makes these worthy struggles?

✷

Notes

1. *Gaajan* is a folk form of Theatre known for its subversion and humour. It is a common source of commercial entertainment and income in South 24 Parganas. All *Gaajan* actors are male including the ones who cross-dress to play female roles.
2. *Sindur* is the red vermilion powder worn by Hindu women as a mark of their marriage. *Alta* is a red liquid used to outline the sole of the married women's feet. Both cost very little and the person who sells these for a living is unlikely to meet minimum daily wage.
3. There are affinities here with living in an *ashram*. *Ashrams* are communities constructed to intentionally experiment with a particular ideology of living and working. In the enclosed space of an *ashram*, the discipline of sharing work is an experiment with political action on the one hand. On the other hand, it is also a test of one's own convictions about equality and freedom since the individual shares in a community that publicly witnesses the limits of a collective ideology in individual practice.
4. Arguably the CPM too recognised their 'feasibility frontier' when they cut back their revolutionary agenda of class confrontation and land redistribution, in favour of development with redistribution within parliamentary Communism (Ashok Mitra, Minister of Finance, quoted in Kohli 1987: 98, footnote no. 7). Unlike JS, through democratic centralism, the CPM retains control over scripting the future of peasants

expropriated from agricultural livelihoods, industrial development, and a deferred goal of socialism.

5. I owe much of my analysis in this section to discussions with Nosheen Ali.
6. As we will see in chapter seven on snake-goddesses and rural health-care systems, one way in which exclusion of religious practice becomes apparent is while managing the boundaries between spirituality and superstition.

Chapter Five

'Spoiled Sons' and 'Sincere Daughters': Schooling, Security, and Empowerment

Following international conferences in the 1990s, research and governance institutions joined in the call for education for all as basic to human development (Jeffery 2005; UNESCO 2000). In West Bengal specifically, recent policy initiatives and reports such as *The Pratichi Education Report* (Rana, Rafique, and Sengupta 2002) have contributed to the institutional push to increase primary school enrollment in general and female enrollment in particular, especially in rural areas. In January 2002, some scholars and policy-makers came to Kolkata, the capital of the Indian state of West Bengal, to reaffirm their belief and trust in the value of education in giving a sense of future security and in bringing empowerment to girls in particular.[1] The authors of the report on the conference claim that the 'workshop reached a consensus quickly that primary education advances human security', citing some of the 'enormous benefits of primary education — knowledge, information, skills, modernisation, socialisation, and the opening of young minds to "new worlds"' (Commission on Human Security 2002: 1).

Paraphrasing Amartya Sen's pivotal contribution, the report says, 'Amartya Sen described multiple linkages between education and human security: illiteracy is itself a human insecurity; education provides greater employment security; education enables people to exercise their rights; literacy expands the possibility for political participation; education empowers the underdog, especially women' (Commission on Human Security 2002: 2). Rather than recognising schooling as one more social practice and space constituted through operations of power, history, and hierarchy, Sen sees it as a relatively autonomous force to transform inequalities of caste, gender, and class. Giving particular attention to women's experience, he has elsewhere suggested that 'illiteracy is a significant barrier for underprivileged women, since this can lead to their failure to make use even of the rather limited rights they may legally have (say, to own land, or other property, or to appeal against unfair judgment and unjust treatment)' (Sen 2003).

Sen grants literacy profound transformative power concerning society, subjectivity, and cognition — embodying what Brian Street (1984) has called the autonomous model of literacy. New literacy studies pioneered the ideas that 'literacy may be implicated in the operations of social power, though not necessarily leading to social progress, and not as an autonomous historical force' (Collins 1995: 81) and that 'literacy may be implicated deeply in the forming of identities and subjectivities although not necessarily leading to profound cognitive changes' (*ibid*.: 81). This chapter applies a similarly tentative approach to the study of schooling by recognising the limits of its transformative power and highlighting how it is implicated in social and subjective power relations.

The Pratichi Report is a prime example of research on education which highlights problems of educational access and infrastructure but is less attentive to the implications of ambiguous value placed on schooling in lived reality. For example, in the introduction to *The Pratichi Education Report*[2] on rural schools in three districts of West Bengal, Sen decried the steady privatisation of public education, arguing that class divisions have been perpetuated through the 'evil of private tuition', which violates the Indian constitutional commitment to free education (2002: 8).[3] Research on educational systems in India construct 'the other' as produced by (and producing) experiences of schooling which discriminate on account of class, caste, gender, tribal, religious, or linguistic identity (Jeffery 2007; Jeffrey et al. 2004; Jeffery 2005). The Pratichi Report too captured rich data attentive to these forms of marginalisation and subjects of discrimination in the practice of the public education system in rural West Bengal. Nonetheless, Pratichi researchers seemed unable to listen when particular respondents from these marginalised groups described ambiguous experiences of schooling or when schooling was described as useless. There is evidence in interview narratives in the Pratichi Report that shows that people simultaneously take for granted the need for educating children as inescapable (thus affirming the value of schooling) while some also take for granted that education does not lead to salaried employment (thus contesting one of the most taken-for-granted purposes of schooling as leading to security).

Against claims of consensus, arguably, one of the primary challenges facing the 'Schooling for All' initiative in India, and perhaps worldwide, is that of recognising voices that claim that schooling has ambiguous value in their lives. I join numerous scholars to argue that schooling, literacy, and education are heterogeneous social practices, lived experiences, and emergent constructs with shifting meanings for various persons and contexts (Ahearn 2001; Barton and Hamilton 1998; Besnier 1995).[4] My analysis in this chapter draws on interviews, field notes, and recorded performances. I juxtapose these forms of evidence with survey data on primary education (Rana, Rafique and Sengupta 2002), human development indicators (UNDP 2004), and women's status reports (Bagchi and Guha 2005), placing side by side the evidence in these texts with the structure of feeling (Williams 1977) about spoiled sons and sincere daughters that I encountered.

As in most parts of India, preference for son and notions of virgin daughters as sacred are prevalent in West Bengal (Fruzetti 1990).[5] Despite these existing ideologies, I heard people make critical statements about their sons and speak of their sincere and hardworking daughters — representations that have always intrigued me. What was the meaning of these emergent feelings? I found that the representations of sons and daughters as deserving or undeserving of parents' attention and investments had to be situated within a constellation of significant relations and experiences (e.g., privatisation of schooling, rates of unemployment, informalisation of labour, and domestic violence) of which the institutionalised push for improvements in school enrollment for girls was just one.

Schooling provides one set of relations that mediate people's sense of worth and their definition of 'who is the developed woman' (Klenk 2004) or man. As I see it, the representation of spoiled sons and sincere daughters must be viewed as an educational issue when policy-makers push for schooling as a probable foundation for making secure and empowered women. Further, this language about spoiled sons and sincere daughters must be appreciated relationally if we are to recognise how being a schooled or unschooled son or daughter constitutes and expresses obdurate features as well as shifts in familial and gender relations in contemporary rural West Bengal. While there are numerous sources of insecurity in relation to schooling, for this chapter I view insecurity not only as the experience of unemployment, informalisation of labour, violent and short-lived marriages, and stubborn gender, caste, and class hierarchies. I also view insecurity as the uncertainty, contradictions, and anxieties about the future generated by people's inability, despite access to schooling, to make the contextual meaning and value of schooling matter in their struggle against the structural sources of insecurity named above.

The people I focus on in this essay also affirm the overall value of schooling since they invested in their children's education in the 1980s and 1990s. Still, parents, young boys, and girls also make contradictory evaluations of schooling, indicating that one's place within the family, regional educational and employment opportunities are key factors in constructions of the value of educating their children in schools. This suggests that analysis of education must be grounded in the specificities of people's felt responsibilities for the future within the particularities of their families. Schooling is not perceived as simply a neutral thing to be acquired. It enters people's lives bathed in notions of sacrifice, promise, and progress. It is a mode of becoming and belonging to particular places and times, within particular families and in relation to siblings and parents with dreams for shared or competing futures. Our analysis of schooling must take social norms into account to lend flesh and blood to its stochastic projections, security, and empowerment.

In this chapter, my methodological aim is to suggest the importance of looking in 'unlikely' places such as the stage to understand schooling within the larger forces and relations to which it belongs and to understand people's ambiguous views on it. Here, I focus on people's engagement with Forum Theatre to analyse emergent evaluations of schooling.[6] I am proposing that we rethink methodology and consider what we can learn about people's experience of school education when we are not looking directly in texts and contexts that are relevant to or require literacy or formal education. The play I will analyse here is not directly about school education. None of the improvised scripts I present below were prompted by questions about education itself, nor did they emerge in spaces institutionally recognised as relevant to school education. Yet they are illuminating — not that scholars should begin with serendipity and hope to end with insight. Ethnographies, however, must be conducted both by participating in the everyday experiences of schooling and by critically stepping outside this engagement in order to capture the multiple and contradictory rationales and histories that can help us understand the meaning and value people place on a social practice, in this case schooling.

Schooling, Gender, and Futures

Recent literatures that historicise schooling practices and ethnographic studies of how schools gain legitimacy and meaning in particular places have allowed researchers to focus on the highly contested, incomplete, and problematic project of making literate and schooled persons and societies (Barton and Hamilton 1998; Besnier 1995; Levinson, Foley, and Holland 1996; Rockwell 1994). While policy-makers claim schooling as engine of development, it is not a panacea that reduces high fertility rates (Jeffery 1998). Among scholars working on schooling in India, some show how schooling leads to devaluation of agricultural and manual work (Kumar 2000; Sarangapani 2003), whereas others show how it often fails to bring salaried desk jobs for men and is not always associated with conventional notions of empowerment or progress for women (Chopra 2005; Gold 2002) or men (Jeffrey et al. 2004).

Schooling is gendered not just because of inequalities in access to it (the focus of institutional initiatives) but also because young men and women face differential responsibilities for familial futures and therefore differential familial expectations about how they should use their schooling. This makes it imperative to think of gender, schooling, and futures as relational outcomes of (changing) familial norms. Here the concern cannot simply be about increasing female enrollment in isolation from other considerations. Restricting analysis to male bias in development policy and implementation (Elson 1995) entails a failure to consider how male and female identities emerge in practice (Laurie 2005).

Cecile Jackson (1999) draws attention to anthropological literature that has shed light on the relational aspects of unequal and changing power dynamics between men and women. Arguing that men often have 'contradictory relations with hegemonic masculinities' (1999: 91), Jackson asks that scholars recognise that the expectation that men choose strenuous work (rather than time-consuming women's work) in accordance with hegemonic notions of masculinity and men's own felt responsibility for choosing this work be recognised. This draws attention to men's work as gendered in ways that do not simply reproduce their advantage over women. Men's choices produce bodily self-exploitation in work, excess alcohol consumption (numbing the fatigue from work), high mortality rates from spent bodies, and lower body mass indices compared to women in their age group (Jackson 1999: 103–4).

Similarly, we must attend to how parental investment in sons' schooling adds to existing expectations that sons will provide for future familial and parental security as well as the ensuing judgment of spoiled sons who fail in their responsibilities. As Craig Jeffrey, Roger Jeffery, and Patricia Jeffery (2004) have recently shown, the inability of Dalit men in the northern Indian state of Uttar Pradesh to translate their schooling into secure employment as a result of caste discrimination in hiring, and despite the cultural capital and distinctions of being an educated person, has produced a culture of masculine resentment. The authors argue that development policy ought to recognise this sense of uselessness that educated Dalit men feel and that policy must address economic redistribution along with educational initiatives.

While I make a plea to view gender as relational, I do not wish to underemphasise the acute inequalities in girls' access to schooling in India. However, our challenge is not just to correct the lack of attention to gender disparities in experiences of education in institutionalised narratives about security, schooling, and empowerment, which Sen and others attempt. Rather, the task is to attend to the 'flesh and blood of people's lives' (Freeman 2001: 1009) in ways that 'challenge the very constitution of that macro picture' (*ibid.*: 1010) — of how, for instance, schooling is glibly said to empower and secure people in general and girls in particular. Indeed, the language of 'sincere' daughters (Rana, Rafique, and Sengupta 2002: 74) spells signs of an emic rationale for seeing girls' schooling as a 'new light in the house' (Gold 2002: 86).

This emic rationale for girls' schooling in rural West Bengal emerges in the context of patriarchal norms, where women are second in the West Bengal government's land agenda (Gupta 2002), and where small-peasant viability (Lieten 1990) is shifting towards decreasing productivity of land and land fragmentation (Rogaly et al. 1999). These political–economic inequities and insecurities play out in specific ways in women's lives. Therefore, apart from grounding analyses of schooling enrollment initiatives within familial trajectories and relations, we must also situate them in employment rates for men and women, average marriage ages, divorce rates, trends in violence against women, and displacement from agricultural work. These rates and trends that describe women's experience in rural Bengal's transitioning society must be viewed as 'educational issues' since the ability to provide for parents, children, and wives is a concrete expected outcome of schooling.

Educational Accomplishments and Challenges

Scholars attribute West Bengal's relatively high literacy rates in percentage terms (70 per cent for men and 60 per cent for women) to political leftism, economic redistribution, and female autonomy (Bagchi and Guha 2005).[7] Kerala, another Left-governed state, has even more admirable literacy percentages at 94 per cent for men and 91 per cent for women (Bagchi and Guha 2005). Seen another way, though, West Bengal also stands in the 18th position among 35 states and Union Territories in terms of literacy rates (Rana, Rafique, and Sengupta 2002). The United Nations' *West Bengal Human Development Report* claims that the state's problem is the neglect of girls in rural areas. Its population in 2001 was 82 million, 72 per cent of whom live in rural areas (UNDP 2004: 4). The proportion of households without any literate female in the state is 51 per cent for rural households and 31 per cent for urban households (UNDP 2004: 148). In Kerala, only 9 per cent of rural and 10 per cent of urban households are without any literate females (UNDP 2004: 148).

West Bengal confronted the challenge of improving education by building governmental and civil society alliances and initiatives, such as Shishu Shiksha Kendras and Shikshalaya Prakalpa, in urban and rural areas in the late 1990s (Balagopalan 2005).[8] For some, this led to marked improvements in enrollment and literacy rates, correcting some historical imbalances (Bagchi and Guha 2005: 50–52). Others have viewed this as a problematic move highlighting a two-tier division in perceptions between so-called real schools and (less than ideal) community-based non-profit schools that bring education for all (Balagopalan 2005: 92). In other words, educational initiatives embody and are met with complex perceptions about schools themselves, in addition to 'gender bias, gender-based role stereotyping and wage discrimination at work' (Bagchi and Guha 2005: 70).

Compared with these changes in education, economic growth in West Bengal has been obdurate and hesitant. While the state resisted the ideology of and wholesale incorporation into the new economic policies of liberalisation in 1991, it welcomed the removal of regulations and controls since it meant that the central government could not use partisanship to control the movement of capital (Sinha 2005: 113). West Bengal has by now moved to an explicit liberalisation agenda, aggressively inviting foreign and national capital investment (primarily in the service and retail sectors) to counter decades of capital flight, industrial stagnancy, and decreasing rates of agricultural growth. The state government has promised its citizens that the sacrifice of farmers' fertile land for retail industry and agribusiness will help counter rural unemployment by generating industrial growth. It remains to be seen how this trade in gains and losses for citizens will actually take shape.

The statistical and narrative evidence on shifting employment trends and its connection (or lack thereof to literacy) is telling because it reminds us that literacy is no guarantee of employment. Despite growing literacy rates in the 1990s in West Bengal, unemployment remains high for both men and women, with growing rates of marginal workers among men and women (UNDP 2004: 93–97; see Table 5.1).[9]

Table 5.1: Employment in West Bengal (as per cent of total population)

	Rural		*Urban*	
	1991	*2001*	*1991*	*2001*
Male Main Workers	51.18	46.00	49.34	50.61
Male Marginal Workers	0.91	8.30	0.31	3.47
Male Non-Workers	47.91	45.70	50.36	45.93
Female Main Workers	8.74	8.87	5.79	8.82
Female Marginal Workers	4.33	11.83	0.41	2.31
Female Non-Workers	86.93	79.30	93.79	88.87

Source: UNDP (2004): 90

Most of the growth in industrial development in the past decade has been led by small producers in both agricultural and non-agricultural sectors. Employment in industrial manufacturing and agriculture has stagnated while employment diversification in rural West Bengal has increased (conventionally viewed as both the means and end of rural development). However, this employment diversification has happened primarily in the category of marginal work, or work that does not offer up to 183 days of employment per year (UNDP 2004: 114; see Table 5.2).

This economic situation affects women, both at work and at home. Surveys have found that the rate of displacement of women from agricultural work and their insertion into informal household work has increased dramatically: 84 per cent of those displaced from agriculture between 1993 and 2000 were women (Mukhopadhyay 2005: 79). Furthermore, the South 24 Parganas region has relatively high rates of seasonal migration, which people commonly associate with the threat of marital desertion. A survey conducted by the West Bengal Commission for Women of 145 respondents in 10 districts showed that 50 women had experienced domestic violence, not one received wages equal to her husband's, six had active litigations against husbands who were in a second marriage, and 11 had been deserted by their husbands (Gupta and Chattopadhyay 2005: 124–27). The National Crime Records Bureau of 2001 notes the general increases in rates of dowry, dowry death, death by cruelty of husband and other relatives, and torture of housewives in West Bengal, even though the state as a whole has relatively low crime rates (*ibid.*: 116–21). The district within the state with the highest crime rate is South 24 Parganas. This statistical evidence suggests that people in the

Table 5.2: Occupational Diversification in rural West Bengal as per cent of total (main + marginal) Workers

	Cultivators		*Agricultural Labourers*		*Non-agricultural Labourers*	
	1991	*2001*	*1991*	*2001*	*1991*	*2001*
South 24 Parganas	33.1	18.8	33	30.4	33.9	50.8
West Bengal	38.4	25.4	32.3	33	29.3	41.6

Source: UNDP (2004): 99

areas where I conducted research live with multiple structural insecurities. They also inhabit two clearly competing realities: one where schooling is valued as necessary for a secure future, and another where people seem to live with the knowledge that access to schooling will not necessarily lead to employment and income security. I turn now to people's perspectives that animate these statistical trends.

'I have to Educate two Sons'

The literacy rate for South 24 Parganas district approximates the statewide 69 per cent. The female literacy rate is 40.6 per cent, compared with the statewide rate of 60 per cent (Bagchi and Guha 2005). As I got to know Jana Sanskriti (JS) members, I came to hear them voice their dilemmas and hopes. When I asked Bharati Manna, a landless, low-caste, agricultural wage labourer what her biggest hope was, she had this to say:

> When I have money from my daily labor, I will be able to educate my children. When I do not have the money, of course, I cannot educate them. But then even if they are a little less illiterate than we are, that will do. Then, they will not be as illiterate as we are. This is my worry. How should I raise my children? If I have to work night and day to raise my kids, to feed them, and you can *still* hear the sound of hunger in their stomachs then how can I educate them? After all there are a lot of expenses for teaching them to read and write. I have two sons at home. I do not have any daughters. Two sons. I have to teach two sons to read and write. My poverty is increasing because of this.[10]

Bharati uses the word for a foolish person (*mūrkho*) to refer to herself as illiterate (as many in rural West Bengal do). She also seems to suggest that teaching her children how to read and write (*lēkhā–pora*), which they can only accomplish through a combined practice of going to school and taking private tution classes in the evening, is central to raising them. Clearly she places a high value on schooling and feels that it makes one 'a little less illiterate' and takes one further. Beyond these projections, her words are ambiguous and intriguing because she emphasises the counterintuitive claim that schooling is a cause of poverty.

She ties her poverty with another thought of utmost significance: that she is burdened with sons. This is said in a social and ideological context where sons are treated as an indisputable boon. Although rates of female literacy have been increasing, parents will invest the utmost time, effort, and household income in the education of their sons, not daughters. Daughters are viewed as inevitably leaving their natal homes for household and agricultural work in marital homes. Giving dowry rather than investing in their schooling, people believe, gives their daughters a better chance at life. Since families go into debt to give dowry beyond their means, girls are seen as a higher cost to families.

But implicit in what Bharati says is a subtle re-evaluation of this commonsensical view (often shared by scholars) that it costs more to have daughters in the ideological context of son preference and compulsory dowry. She perceives the expectation and expense around weddings and dowry (the main expenditure for daughters) as somewhat negotiable because people can choose marriage prospects that suit their financial means. Schooling, however, seems non-negotiable because the compulsions of social expectations and expense combine with the commonsense assumption about the non-viability of an agrarian future reproduced in a devaluation of rural livelihoods, identities, and persons in educational narratives and curriculum itself (Morarji 2005, 2007).

Bharati does not speak explicitly in terms of connections between her children's schooling and a sense of security or empowerment. We might, however, understand her anxiety by situating her words in her biography. It is difficult to calculate how much transformation she has seen in her familial circumstance. The female members of her natal home were domestic workers while the men were agricultural labourers. Currently, she is a daily agricultural labourer. Bharati herself narrates transformation in her life not in economic terms but in terms of early married life when her husband got violent with her, which she explains as a consequence of her in-laws' influence upon him. She says she built her present domestic peace by impressing upon him the need to start a separate home with her. While she admits to the hardships of poverty in her nuclear family, she has discovered 'her lucky stars', evident, she believes, in her husband's emerging good nature.[11]

Her husband migrates seasonally to work in potato stores, where he transfers sacks full of potatoes up precarious ladders, endlessly and at relentless speeds. Working at such storage units was a primary quick source of income for those with able bodies in the village where I did my research. People spoke in no uncertain terms about potato store work in that only the really desperate risk work here. Stories about such risk — how it 'kills the body' and 'takes away strength' — are pervasive among families in this village. Thus people are often called greedy when there is a social perception that they do not need to put themselves through what seems like work that leads to rapid deterioration of health and strength. Bharati and her husband do not appear to have the luxury of taking such taunts into account. They are in debt to various shopkeepers and moneylenders. In this biographical context, Bharati must crave assurance that investment in her sons' schooling will come to fruition, contributing to her and her husband's future security. After all, a life of exertion by her and her husband will guarantee weaker bodies in the future. But does she have some assurance that this calculation of sweat and labour for cash, food, school textbooks, and private tuition will bring some future security?

The primary economic class in Bharati's village is made up of landless, agricultural workers and wage labourers who migrate seasonally. As Durga Pal describes this village of approximately 100 households, 'Other than ten to fifteen households, no more than that . . . other than them, we all have to put together numerous sources of income, and that means numerous types of work, to make sure that our households run, families eat all through the year.'[12] Seasonal work comprises harvesting, potato store labour, shrimp farming, and construction work in Kolkata. These labourers try their best to remain in their villages for as long as they can find work there, either on other people's farms or on parcels of their own land or by digging ground (*mātī-kātā*, literally 'cutting the earth') for road and pond construction. The primary migrants are usually married men. In the absence of their men, landless women somehow manage to labour for household food production and earn daily cash by labouring on others' land.

On-stage: Meanings of School

Sometimes folk and JS's theatre raised questions about present social contracts and familial expectations by presenting an imagined transformation of a social expectation on-stage. Huge crowds throng to watch productions in rural areas. Soon after the harvest of crops, people set up stages for *jatra* performances. Huge festivals are organised around these performances. The productions that currently frequent rural West Bengal are brought by urban, commercial *jatra* troupes. The stage occupies just one part of the space on the grounds of the festival. The rest is lined with shops selling everything from cookware to jewellery, furniture, and crafts. There are typically gambling tables and houses for adult male pleasure. This mélange of entertainment prompts some to say that these festivals (*melas*) are 'all kinds of unhealthy culture.'[13] Since young men frequent festivals, they have come to be characterised as embodying such culture. Yet mothers who complained about young men at the festivals were themselves addicts of some of these folk forms, as mentioned below.

A linked criticism suggests that young men are too enamoured of hypermasculine images of commercial Hindi cinema. They emulate fantastical heroes of the cinema, pursuing beautiful modern women while forgetting to pay due respect to aging parents. Modern women for their part are perceived to be skilled at breaking up the marital home. I saw a play in another folk form called *gaajan* in which the middle-aged, low-caste servant's soliloquy makes the son realise that he treats his mother cruelly. The mother's endless expressions of grief for the loss of a respectful and caring son are followed by the servant's emotional guilt trip that is supposed to rejuvenate the caring son. These themes, rehearsed in different forms and plots, publicly raise questions about spoiled sons and their relation to parental insecurity for the future.

Durga Pal has an avid interest in *jatra* performances. She is the wife of the oldest brother in a household of five brothers. This places her at the helm of the joint household. When *jatras* came to the region, she would wake up earlier than usual, complete all the work for her day, bundle up the money she had saved and some puffed rice in the loose end of her sari, and walk for hours to watch *jatras* that interested her. She did this, she told me, for a performance called *A Stitched-Up Bharat*.[14] She recounted to me the plot of the story as if she had watched it just last night: 'Can you imagine such a thing? Families where the sons do not even pay 200 rupees for a parent who needs an operation. This kind of thing is, after all, happening today.'[15] Durga was incredulous not because she felt that the melodramatic *jatra* depicted something unreal; rather, it corroborated her perceptions of the youth around her. She had educated both her sons and her daughter. But her eldest son had refused to finish school despite a great deal of coaxing.

> I mean he gave up school. That causes me a great deal of pain. His uncles had pestered him about that. They tried to explain to him night and day. I also tried to explain. I said, 'Son, when your grandfather could not educate your uncles, your middle uncle had to sit at home for one whole year. They barely had anything to eat; how could they study? Then he [the uncle] worked in a home in Diamond Harbour, tutored some children in classes junior to him, and studied himself. If he had been able to give the proper fees for a real education, then he would surely have a good job today. But this is how he studied. He would do the work in their homes, then teach the children, and then study himself. That's how he educated himself — through a lot of suffering. A lot of suffering.'[16]

Durga tried in vain to impress upon her son that he should continue to study so he would not have to suffer like his uncle (her brother-in-law) had in the past. Note that she does not use her husband as a role model for her son — perhaps because he is a farmer and, compared with all the brothers, spends the least amount of time in non-agricultural work. This uncle went on to get a Master's degree but still did not have secure employment. By most measures, the fact that he has a Master's degree and tutors students is ample sign of a good education. Yet, he is unable to get a steady income because he has such a 'soft heart' and is unable to demand money from the mostly poorer parents whose children he has tutored.[17] In Durga's estimation, he also has no physical capacity left for work on the field. Incapable of enduring the physical strain of agricultural work and without a hard heart, he does not have a stable income in spite of all the investment in education. In other words, this young man with a Master's education is unable to realise his felt responsibility of providing security for his family.

Durga's son chose to quit school and work at odd jobs, and today he is an assistant electrician for a shop-owner in a suburb of Kolkata. He spends most of his money on the cinema and on feeding himself. Is her son a 'spoiled son' who has access to schooling but fails to avail himself of it? Arguably he is a son who could not count on salaried desk jobs after school and chooses instead to work and meet present needs. Durga is probably aware of the familial trends that shaped her son's choices. Perhaps she feared her son finding the wrong path, learning from boys whom she described as spending 'the whole day roaming around aimlessly, watching bad videos, spending their parents' money.'[18] For her, the memory of times when her family faced hunger is not so remote — she vividly recalls the hard work, suffering, and sacrifice. Durga's feelings of insecurity as a parent become precipitous since she is surrounded by talk about today's uncaring sons who attend too little to aging parents, and about the coexistence of high literacy and unemployment rates.

When we step onto the JS stage, we see other constructions of sons and daughters that emerge in the process of audience engagement. Through this theatrical intervention, we can understand better what lies behind Bharati's and Durga's concerns about their children's schooling.

In JS's play *Sonār Mēyē* (The golden girl), a series of fairly one-dimensional stories weave a picture of the life of an average woman in rural India.[19] The play does not offer a well-rounded representation of women's power but shows their evolving powerlessness in their life course. Judged against Deniz Kandiyoti's critique of assumed and overarching patriarchy, this play does not capture the contradictory experiences of patriarchy. Kandiyoti's (1998) argument is that gender relations must be understood through changes in the course of people's lives. In the play, the woman protagonist by and large remains powerless. She is never seen as the mother-in-law she will inevitably become. This is precisely to provoke the audience to express their energy and anger about daily injustices against young brides, a statistically widespread phenomenon in this region.

On-stage, in the first run of the play, the female protagonist cannot play as much as her brother in her childhood, she must leave her studies to help with housework when called, she has to quit school when her parents are ready to get her married, she gets inspected from head-to-toe to determine her dowry, and she works all day and is beaten by her husband if she does not have the food ready on time. A telling song is sung in the scene when dowry is demanded that goes as follows:

> Since the prospective groom is well-educated, he refuses to take dowry (*Patro khubi shikkhito tai pon nebe na she*)
> He has simply asked the prospective bride for a few minor things (*shudhu kota jinish koneke cheyeche*).
> He has asked for one colour TV, one refrigerator, and one motorcycle (*cheyeche ekti colour tv ekti refrigerator*)

The song mocks education as a solution to the problem of dowry while highlighting the consumer goods desired by the well-educated.

Figure 5.1: 'I'll take a motorcycle for dowry'

In the usual format of JS's Forum Theater plays, after the first enactment, the audience members are invited to improvise and rescript scenes in the play by stepping on-stage and acting out reformed roles and expectations. The second enactment thus consists of audience members who take on parts of characters who they think can and ought to play a different role. During one such performance of *Sonār Mēyē*, an audience member intervened in the role of the daughter when the daughter was being pushed toward marriage:

> **Spect-actor as Daughter:** I am agreeing to the marriage since I am at that age. But I am not ready to accept marriage when there is a dowry involved.
>
> **Father:** So what is it that you want to do? You tell me.
>
> **Daughter:** I will get married without dowry. Without money, I will marry without money.

Father: You think anyone is going to marry you without money? Is anyone here in this big crowd who is going to marry you without money?

Daughter: All right then, I will study.

Father: You want to study, but there is no money to make you study.

Daughter: My brother can study, and for him there is money to study, but I cannot study. Why is that?

Father: But look, he is my future, you see.

Daughter: Why can't I be someone's future?[20]

This intervention on-stage is rich in meaning. One way of responding to the question posed is to invoke Hindu practices of inheritance whereby daughters typically do not own property and therefore cannot offer their parents either a sense of a secure future or a home. The assumption is that since women do not control property, nobody — in the natal or marital home — perceives his or her own future as dependent on her. Beyond structural disadvantage then, women intervening in this play usually identified the source of a wife's domestic problem in the daily disrespect the husband shows her and in the denial of opportunities for education in her childhood.

Typically older men, teenage boys, and teenage girls tended to be relatively reticent to make interventions on-stage unless they are already part of JS's off-stage political activism. However, young girls tended to speak with me after performances when they said things like, 'Girls are not only meant to play and do housework. Besides, if they study they can be better mothers.' I often heard young girls say, 'Marriage is all kinds of headache. All you do is work and get beaten.' One of the rare sights I saw was of a young girl saying to her stage-father, 'If you have money to send your son to school, you have money for your daughters. Divide it up!' The audience as a whole was typically divided around the issue of getting daughters married, with some claiming that girls should have access to equal schooling and others claiming that it was a waste of household resources. Both men and women argued for each side with equal vehemence.

In the course of my research, I was struck by the frequency of neighbourhood fights and community hearings regarding men with multiple wives, wives' anxieties about being abandoned by husbands who had migrated for work, domestic violence, alcoholism, and general domestic discord. In a context where marriage is commonsensically perceived as insecure and violent, perhaps schooling is the most acceptable and effective method of staying away from the difficult marriages that girls see around them, and expect await them. More recently, a young woman who was training to be a teacher in a JS preschool said, 'I will work part-time and go to study part-time. Can you tell me a way out? Does the government give money or something? We fall into Scheduled Castes. Because my father cannot afford the fees, he has said he only has money to get me married. But I want to study. He will get me married if I do not find a way to study.'[21] This woman's words show how reluctant poorer parents can be to spend money saved for a daughter's marriage on schooling and how keen some daughters are to find financial backing for further studies. Further, as documented by *The Pratichi Education Report*, teachers have a perception that 'girls are more sincere than the boys and they are more regular and motivated' (Rana, Rafique, and Sengupta 2002: 74). Even though there is a concomitant resistance on the part of teachers to think of girls as equally intelligent, they clearly think of them as more committed to their work (*ibid.*). Girls might well be capitalising on this perception of their sincerity to negotiate altered positions within their own families.

Consider, for instance, another intervention in the same play. Here the daughter is arguing with her father about why she has been ordered to help her mother in the kitchen when she has to study for her exams, which are fast approaching:

> **Spect-actor as Daughter:** Why? Why should I go to the kitchen? This is my study time. I have exams soon.
>
> **Father:** I cannot educate you any more.
>
> **Daughter:** Why not?
>
> **Father:** What will you do after studying?
>
> **Daughter:** Like everybody else, I will also work.
>
> **Father:** Look at Haripada's daughter. She studied so much, but what did she do after that? She got married and is now cooking keeping house.

Daughter: How are you so sure that your son is going to have a big job and that he will feed you?[22]

The taunt of the woman who intervenes (playing the part of the daughter) might be drawing on the prevailing attitude about young men as uncaring, errant, and irresponsible in these modern times.

These on-stage and off-stage words and worlds reflect at least three types of insecurity. The first is parental insecurity as expressed by Bharati and Durga, and in some folk theater that I encountered. The second involves male insecurity about the inability to live up to hegemonic constructions of what it means to be a man in rural Bengal, that is, to be responsible for, to be the sole source of present and future security for, and to provide for one's conjugal family and parents. The second intervener takes a jab at taken-for-granted notions of masculinity and familial arrangements by asking whether sons can be counted on for future security. The on-stage message is stark because the off-stage trends are not encouraging. Third, we can see the insecurity of young women heading toward precarious marriages and simultaneously being steadily displaced from agricultural work.

Figure 5.2: 'How are you so sure your son is going to have a big job and that he will feed you?'

Rima Das, a 23 -year-old high school graduate and teacher in a JS preschool, made a suggestive comment that indicates a relational shift in young boys' expectations regarding marital prospects, which I have yet to verify. She said, 'Nowadays boys prefer to get married to girls who have schooling; they even prefer girls who will work. Yes! It adds income, you see.'[23] The new trends of women's employment through local governmental programmes and non-governmental self-help groups give women with schooling access to credit for small businesses and some formal employment (UNDP 2004). Recently in an interview, Sanjoy Ganguly pointed out that with a Court ruling that mandates a 50:1 student-teacher ratio, West Bengal has a shortfall of 48,000 rural teachers.[24]

JS has responded to the defunct rural public education system in the state as described in the introduction and chapter one. It coordinates approximately 150 'learning centres' which are basically pre-primary schools servicing approximately 3,750 children from 150 villages and giving employment to 150 women in the age group of 20–35 years of age. JS's schools are primarily run by young unmarried and married women who have passed the Madhyamik examinations held after Class 10. As conduit of pre-primary schooling initiatives and teacher training in 150 villages, JS concretely addresses the problem of rural schooling while providing a temporary and fragile source of rural employment for women who have some schooling. Not going to school wastes a good chance at getting such jobs and credit, while going to it improves marital prospects, if Rima is correct, and provides some financial independence in marriage.

When schooling opportunities intersect with other opportunities such as employment, credit, and questioning norms about providing family security, there are some heartening signs for change. However, if we concede that at least some of these women's voices are motivated by fear of marriage and desertion, education has not fought the enduring lack of control young women have over the ideology that ties their place in society to men. The fear of desertion remains. Further, if we are to concede that women are women in part through their interactions with men, can respect for women be developed at the cost of respect for men? Is this pendulum swing inevitable? If we conceive of gender relations as a zero-sum game, we settle for discrete representations of spoiled sons and sincere daughters. Here, school education is assumed to have the capacity to reward committed daughters and teach spoiled sons a lesson. If, however, we understand gender as relational, we might be more attentive to how those sometimes disempowered by schooling (young men) can create the conditions for those who sometimes go without adequate formal education (young women) to articulate moments of bold transformation. Policy on education can take gender to be a relational vector of social formations by attending not just to statistics about low female literacy but also to female displacement from agricultural work, growing dowry requirements, violence in the home, and high male unemployment rates as educational issues.

Gender as Relational

When JS invites people on-stage, young men often intervene and sometimes enact a transformed role for women. There are many ways of interpreting such actions and the transformations at the level of social norms that can emerge out of such engagement (Mohan 2004). Our interpretation of the first intervention recounted above changes dramatically with the information that the member of the audience who intervened in the role of the daughter was in fact a young man. Recall the intervention and how the young man playing the part of the bride said things like, 'I am not ready to accept marriage when there is a dowry involved'; 'I will marry without money'; 'My brother can study, and for him there is money to study, but I cannot study'; and 'Why can't I be someone's future?' Here is further evidence that JS builds solidarity and crossover alliances rather than identity based on homogenous subjectivity and sisterhood as discussed in chapter four.

More significantly, here is a stark reminder of the possibility that men might be feeling disempowered as a combined result of their schooling, the dearth of available jobs, and the growing dissatisfaction of parents and teachers with boys' insincerity and lack of effort. The boy on-stage may be recognising the rights of an imagined disadvantaged sister, but he may also be coming into a realisation of his own inabilities and disadvantages regarding what it takes to be a man. His simultaneous identification with perceived female subjectivity (they are not their parents' future) and displacement from male subjectivity (they can no longer promise to be their parents' future) suggests that the quotidian forms for accomplishing male superiority and domination do not necessarily find fruition through schooling in rural West Bengal today. Here, educated boys fail to conform to hegemonic notions of masculinity because neither can they always secure employment nor do they aspire to work in the fields.

While agricultural work has decreased according to most surveys, it is strenuous work that is still available to the rural sons of West Bengal. Drawing out the conundrum, Karuna Morarji (2005, 2007) has asked, where does the rural educated person fit? And, how does this experience of rural men's failure translate into changing familial expectations and gender norms? Boys may be opting out of school, as Durga's son did, because they see currently unemployed educated male family members as harbingers of their own future, or boys might be encouraging their sisters' schooling out of their own sense of failure or dread, or just to be able to share in providing for parents.

Some might argue that girls' deferring marriage for later years is an intended and valued outcome of schooling. This view assumes that people consciously perceive deferral of marriage as a value of schooling. Rather, as the interviews and improvised scripts show, people are moved by perceptions of violent and insecure marriages, compulsions of seasonal migration, and displacement from agricultural work. Nor can women count on raising sons who will necessarily provide for them, as is evident in the lives of older women (Lamb 2000). In 1994, rural and urban West Bengal had 11.6 million and 4.6 million households headed by women respectively, including widows, abandoned wives, and wives taking care of households because of male migration (Banerjee and Mukherjee 2005: 24). Perhaps young women are persuaded to question unequal and unstable arrangements. Pushed out of agricultural work, largely unemployed, and increasingly made aware of fragile protection and security from husbands, they may find that the institutional push for schooling presents a way out to the extent that it enables them to access credit and jobs made available since the 1990s.

Conclusion

I have sketched people's particular struggles as they internalise and externalise the institutional push toward increasing school enrollment. These are not arguments that there is no value to literacy and schooling, but rather ethnographic evidence that school education is a 'contradictory resource', useful in varied terms, and more instrumentally useful to some rather than others (Jeffrey et al. 2004). Durga and Bharati's voices adequately capture the suffering and sacrifice involved in schooling children. I have tried to unearth the meaning and value of schooling from how people currently imagine their futures, especially in a context where access to it coexists with high unemployment and renders the institutionally stated value of school education ambiguous and questionable. Regarding institutional measures of empowerment, we can say that in this story, girls might well be gaining normative advantages because parents are changing attitudes toward girls' education in a context that forecasts no self-evident advantage in educating boys alone. But we must keep in mind that people exist within social and familial relations, and this reconstruction of sincere daughters still coexists with marital desertion, threat of violence, dowry deaths, unemployment, and the growing alienation of spoiled sons.

Research institutions such as the Pratichi Trust and the West Bengal Commission for Women must contribute to historically grounded understandings of empowerment and security rather than assume abstract claims as foundational truths which dispossess the complex and ambiguous meanings and value of schooling in people's experiences. In JS spaces of political theatre and activism, people often speak of the right to work in their villages as something that would be invaluable. Women and young children have marched against the governmental sanction of liquor production as an antidote to high unemployment because they saw it and its tie to liquor consumption as a direct drain on money available for schooling. These are some of their articulations of empowerment and security. If the stochastic claim is that schooling increases the likelihood of gaining employment, the conditions under which this is or is not an outcome deserve study.

In 2008–09, JS theatre teams scripted plays on education with a systematic goal of performing 700 shows of these plays over a period of 14 months. Each theatre team is documenting the kinds of interventions offered on the Forum Theatre stage so as to collect questions, information, and suggestions for developing rural education. This is evidence of JS democratising the research process itself. In doing so, they address the problems of rural education and employment by using corporate funding of social initiatives but *without* assuming dispossession of rural livelihoods and homes as a tragic condition for generating rural employment and enhanced opportunities in rural Bengal. Further, it will be interesting to note what JS's educational research reveals about people's responses to the spread of media and consumerism. There are significant opportunities here for using Forum Theatre as a means to address the problem of education pushing aspirations of young men and women away from rural futures and rescript education to construct futures within and beyond agriculture.

In West Bengal, where concerted efforts in economic redistribution and political decentralisation have been made, the alienation, insecurity, and marginalisation represented in words of parents and young men and women are haunting. Acquiring schooling is significant for girls, but its associations with empowerment and security must be measured in context. Where there has been little direct redistributive benefit to women and increasing violence against them, for the intervener asking why she cannot be someone's future, schooling is but one fraction of a necessary institutional response. Lack of redistributive equality, the threat of violence, and marital desertion also mark the ways women construct the meaning and value of their schooling. However, how should young men with their school certificates in hand belong to their families and communities as notional bearers of future security? They have had patriarchal protections of all sorts and live in a state with a pro-poor government that has been working for the benefit of historically disadvantaged people. Undoubtedly, alienation marks these men's present experience since for the young man asking why he cannot be someone's future, there is no available institutional response.

✷

Notes

1. The Pratichi Trust, the Commission on Human Security, UNICEF/India, and Harvard University brought together over three dozen academics, planners, educators, and government officials for the Workshop on Education, Equity, and Security. The Pratichi Trust was formed in 2001 through a donation from Amartya Sen's Nobel Prize money.
2. The Pratichi Report was the result of grounded and detailed research on 18 primary schools and 17 semi-governmental second tier rural schools in West Bengal — a state celebrated for its relatively high literacy

rates compared to the Indian average. The Report offered rich data on the neglected subject of educational experience for rural Indians, decried the steady privatisation of public education, and generated a list of recommendations for improving facilities and access in the second tier semi-governmental schools while critiquing the state-run primary schools and its tenured teachers.

3. In West Bengal, people increasingly rely on private tuition to compensate for poor quality instruction in public schools. While schoolgoing children attend free public schools, they inevitably need expensive, private coaching in the evenings to succeed in examinations.
4. Since the people whose lives and words I draw on did not always make a hard-and-fast distinction between literacy and schooling, I will specify implied meanings in the course of my analysis. In general I am referring to access to schooling (rather than literacy) because, although people's access to literacy or education is not limited to schools, socially and institutionally valuable forms of literacy are acquired through schooling. Thus, my interest lies in understanding words about being schooled, having schooling, or being allowed to go to school.
5. *Son preference* is a social phenomenon where, in part, families expect daughters to get married and belong to their husbands' families while expecting sons to provide for their parents' future security.
6. Forum theatre, introduced in chapter one, invites the audience to rescript enacted plays through improvised intervention in which audience members can respond to social problems presented in the first enactment of a play. Audience members step on-stage, choose a character whose role they wish to transform, and present a re-enactment of the scene they have viewed to create a different plot for the play.
7. See also Drèze and Sen 1997; Jeffrey 1992; Rajan, Ramanathan, and Mishra 1996; Kamath 1999.
8. The Shikshalaya Prakalpa programme is India's first collaboration between government and civil society that runs with the slogan 'a school for every child, every child in school' (Balagopalan 2005: 85). Shishu Shiksha Kendras are managed by rural local governments with help from UNICEF to set up primary schools that combat declining standards of government schools and their 'pathology of tenured teachers' (Balagopalan 2005: 95).
9. The United Nations Development Programme report draws on data from the census of India, which defines main workers as those whose main activity was economically productive work for 183 days or more in the previous year.
10. Bharati Manna, interviewed by author, 3 May 2001.
11. Ibid.
12. Interview, 3 May 2001.

13. Ibid.
14. *Bharat* is the Hindu mythological name for India.
15. Interview, 3 May 2001
16. Ibid.
17. Ibid.
18. Ibid.
19. The title *The Golden Girl* is a play on a familiar term of endearment, *sonā mēyē* (which means precious girl). The altered form, *sonār mēyē*, means the girl made of gold, indicating the gold that she is expected to bring as her dowry to her marital home.
20. Author's field notes, 15 February 2001.
21. Bhaswati Bera, interviewed by author, 12 June 2006: Scheduled Castes is a method of categorising lower castes inherited from colonial processes of rule and still used for government administration.
22. Author's field notes, 23 February 2001.
23. Interview, 6 June 2006.
24. Interview, 21 November 2008.

Chapter Six

Have they Disabled Us? Liquor Production and Grammars of Material Distress

In 2005, Jana Sanskriti (JS) mobilised a roadblock which was held along the main highway from Kolkata to Ramganga, a village at the mouth of the Bay of Bengal. Protestors halted the traffic of goods and people along the main artery of the local economy. Roadblocks are typically considered illegal by the government. The protests were signalling anger against liquor production in the region. Six men setting up posters and microphones for the protest were taken to the nearest police station even before the protest had officially begun. The microphone battery and glue were confiscated, posters and banners torn off the trees. But no one left the site. In fact, protestors poured in from neighbouring villages in the Pathar Pratima Block of South 24 Parganas district. They found a second battery and the protest raged on in the radiating heat of 38 degrees Celsius and what felt like 120 per cent humidity. The six young men returned in the afternoon, walked straight to the microphone and sang a JS song about collectively weathering every storm.

One of the six men — Prasad Sardar — told his captive audience about his interaction with the angry police escort who incessantly reprimanded them for illegal disruption of public life. Prasad had responded: 'You are spineless policemen. You find our work illegal, and you don't notice (*chokhe pore na*) the illegal production of liquor because it is in your self-interest. You think we are not intelligent enough (brain *neyi*) to understand what makes certain things legal and others illegal? You think we are children?!' He then challenged his audience, 'Have they disabled us?' (*Amader pongu kore rekheche, na ki?*) In Bengali, *pongu* means, 'to become physically disabled' — used for people with non-functioning limbs. Colloquially, the word *pongu* is used to describe drunks recognisable by their unsteady walk and loss of senses. Prasad was recalling the effects of alcohol intoxication as a parallel critique of disabling people's mental faculties.

Rural Bengalis, like Prasad, had been loyal voters for the Communist Party of India-Marxist (CPM)-led Left Front Government (LFG). Following the capital flight, high unemployment, and worrying decreases in the industrial working class vote by the late 1980s (Pedersen 2001: 656), the LFG has counteracted political attrition and alienation with policies for generating industrialisation, employment, and revenue. One such recent revenue-generation measure is the liberalisation of liquor licenses and therefore, legalisation of illegal liquor production. Considering the popularity of this government, its responsiveness to rural and urban labour issues, and the legalisation of liquor production, what does Prasad mean when he asks 'have they disabled us?', and when he objects to this illegality? Does he fail to understand that liquor production is one mode, now made legal, of generating rural employment and livelihood security for villagers? Why block the local artery of an already depressed economy and one of the few sources of employment available in this region? What explains the dramatic actions of a roadblock by celebrated beneficiaries and voting constituents of the LFG? From JS's perspective, this anti-liquor struggle articulates, rather than contradicts, their ongoing refusal to accept a world of shrinking possibilities.

In this chapter, my goal is to historicise 'choice' in the contemporary conjuncture as an explanation for Prasad's question to fellow villagers — 'have they disabled us?' Philip Abrams asks us to consider that 'what we choose to do and what we have to do are shaped by the historically given possibilities among which we find ourselves' (1982: 3). But Abrams cautions us, 'history is not a force in its own right any more than society is' (*ibid.*). He goes on, 'why the world is the way it is' has everything to do with 'why particular men and women make the particular choices they do and why they succeed or fail in their projects' (*ibid.*). Within highly constrained possibilities, people choose to act in particular ways — to produce alcohol or not. I contextualise the actions and various actors at the roadblock — anti-liquor agitators, police, local government officials, liquor producers, and liquor consumers' wives — to argue that the politics around alcohol production and consumption in West Bengal reveals competing definitions of legality, morality, livelihood, and political collectivity. Some of these definitions are framed as institutionally valuable and viable, and others excluded and rendered anomalous.

When the CPM grants liquor production as a livelihood choice even as a political collectivity for the poor, it colludes with a liberal rationality of 'choice' which excludes and disables the definition of poverty and development experienced and publicised by liquor consumers' wives. JS activists align with some of the liquor consumers' wives in refusing to abide by the institutionally thinkable choices and ideological norms for livelihood and political collectivity. I show how they both battle against social practices that attempt to affect material and subjective closures on the meaning of valuable employment, the meaning of material distress, and distribution of livelihood security. And precisely because these anomalous struggles challenge the political and economic commonsense of their time, they also reveal historically available alternatives or 'choices' for constructing livelihood and mobilising political collectivity.

I begin my interpretation of this struggle by considering Partha Chatterjee's discussion of 'political society', illegal action, and 'politics of the governed' through which he distinguishes democracy in post-colonial societies. I then combine accounts of political–economic developments in Bengal with liquor protestors' voices — Prasad and Bibek — to sketch the social life of liquor. In the second substantive section, I consider liquor-sellers' voices — Baisakhi, Dilip, and Nimai — to show the rationale for their livelihood choices and their critique of anti-liquor agitation. Final sections show the intimate collaboration of neoliberal rule with deep-rooted patriarchy through narratives of liquor consumers' wives — Naina and Medha. These stories from the 'intimate frontier' show how patriarchal familial roles are reworked as women perforate the comprehensive support for liquor as generator of family income and state revenue. Their narratives are the bedrock of my argument as they question the 'public' nature of the 'realism' of normative politics (and analytical discourse).

Through the narratives of JS spect-actors and liquor consumers' wives, this chapter makes the assertion that some rural Bengalis have no audience for their constructions of material distress, choice, and collectivity. The empirical focus of this chapter problematises livelihood choices, political alliances in villages, and emphasises the ways in which off-stage spect-actors script power against conventional norms of defining collectivity and choice in rural Bengal.

Tensions of Neoliberal Development

In 2006, key JS activists — Radha Das, Mihir Nahiya, and Bibek Haldar — walked me through neighbourhoods and helped strategise the research, providing insights, time, interview contacts, and homes to eat and sleep in. I conducted interviews in five Hindu and two Muslim neighbourhoods in two villages that I call Tarinipur and Sriramkrishnapur. Out of 28 interviews, 14 were with JS activists, 11 with participants in the roadblock, and three with liquor-sellers. Competing notions of legality and morality recurred as a concern in these interviews.

Given the massive capital flight, industrial decay, and inordinate rural unemployment accumulating through the 1980s, West Bengal's government officials are hard-pressed to deny the moral claim of people trying to survive, even if by illegal means. To keep their vote (for the ruling coalition of Left Front parties) or to win votes (for the divided opposition), the high ground of constitutional and official politics faces little choice but to allow, even encourage, illegal liquor production. Here, politics is negotiated between government and populations on the assumption that those who suffer distress resulting from welfare maldistribution *have no choice but choose* illegal, precarious, exploitative livelihood. As I will show, this assumption reinforces normative parameters of people's 'worth' based on actively and politically produced or excluded choices. JS confronts the question of livelihood by addressing issues of material and representational inequality. They do this by legitimising forms of rural work such as theatre, activism, and teaching on the one hand, and by questioning and debating what counts as valuable and worthwhile employment on the other.

In recent writings, Partha Chatterjee (2004) has made a crucial contribution to democratising the category of democracy by characterising 'illegal' and 'immoral' action in contemporary postcolonial societies as a marker of democratic political action. What he calls 'politics of the governed', has become a worthy rival to Eurocentric modernity (*ibid.*: 2004). Chatterjee's account of democracy is animated by a Gramscian distinction between civil society and political society operationalised through a Foucauldian lens of governmentality. In (post-colonial) societies where socio-economic policies of the developmental state combat poverty and 'backwardness', citizens are first and foremost enumerated as various population groups on governmental surveys (as landless, squatters, jobless, refugees, BPL card-holders, and so forth). Civil society, founded on ideas of 'popular sovereignty', equality, free entrance and exit, contract, deliberative procedures, rights and duties, is limited to those 'culturally equipped citizens' who have the privilege to realise idealised equal citizenship (*ibid.*: 41). The rest of the population are only 'tenuously, and even then ambiguously and contextually, rights-bearing citizens' (*ibid.*: 38). Outside civil society proper, yet enumerated and living within national territory, these populations are subject to control and potential claimants on state welfare and rights. These citizens are routinely pushed towards illegal action as a result of government inability to reconcile private property rights with the mandate of welfare for all citizens. The state in the neoliberal conjuncture faces an exacerbated tension as it has to invite capital, constructing a receptive environment for privatisation of various publics while providing citizen welfare from reduced public coffers.

Chatterjee's examples of 'politics of the governed' show how illegal action (such as squatting on public land, stealing electricity, travelling on public transportation without tickets) enables citizens to win government attention and collaborate with officials to form 'political society'. Two related processes constitute political society: first, a mutual recognition between populations and governmental officials of the instrumental power of the vote (Chatterjee 2004: 41); second, giving 'empirical form of a [given] population group the moral attributes of a community' (*ibid.*: 57). Thus, the governed reduced to enumerated categories resuscitate democracy in Chatterjee's terms, by making claims on the developmental state's grammars of welfare distribution. Articulating illegal action as necessary for survival incorporates 'illegality' and 'immorality' into a moral claim to governmental care. This is how marginalised citizens with or without the collaboration of 'parties, movements, and non-party political formations' carve out 'political society' in the face of historically entrenched odds (Chatterjee 2000: 46).

Chatterjee's insights suggest that, on the one hand, in light of capital flight, few livelihood alternatives, unemployment, and low household incomes, illegal liquor production is indeed 'democracy' at work. His 'political society' avoids pitfalls of a Manichaean conception of state–society relations as binary constructs much like Cooper and Stoler's (1997) understanding of the relational formation of the categories 'coloniser' and 'colonised'. Showing how the governed demand to be governed — by making stretched rules an organising principle of daily life with tacit cognition, participation, or even leadership of government representatives — is a crucial contribution to appreciating just how extensively state–society boundaries are blurred (Gupta 1995). The realism in this conception helps us recognise the moral and legal dilemmas of both liquor producers and protestors.

On the other hand, 'having no choice but illegality' is a trend in political action that works in conjunction with the economic reality of neoliberal globalisation and its race to the bottom. Both conceptions structure choice as little choice — seeing precarious, illegal existence and unjust, exploitative work as 'opportunity'. In my view, these theories privilege notions of value that sustain powerful legacies of colonial history, modernisation, and neoliberal globalisation. Together, they reinforce the idea that there are no other options for people designated as having less worth in the present. Indeed they risk buttressing the idea that certain people have less or more worth because they fail to recognise that not everyone chooses in ways directly calibrated to their 'low' or 'high' place in economic and political society. As I will show through voices and actions of JS activists, liquor consumer's wives, and the influential rich, reality is more nuanced.

Some wives of liquor consumers who are 'low' on the political economic spectrum, juggling multiple forms of work and desperate managers of meagre household funds should willingly accept liquor production as opportunity, but they don't. They actively refuse this and its structure of enabled 'choice'. Here, despite their poverty, women refuse liquor production as form of poverty alleviation which, they argue, exacerbates their material experience of poverty.

On the other end of the political–economic spectrum, the 'high' place of the influential rich does not compel them to choose liquor production as livelihood, but they do. Thus, they actively make livelihood choices that are not the only available opportunities for them, while normalising a destructive and divisive livelihood in the public sphere, and making the moral claim that the poor engage in liquor production all the more undeniable. Their political–economic status allows them to corrupt choice and delimit opportunity in order to manage electoral votes, adjust the rural poor to a neoliberal transition, and present the transition as an opportunity to alleviate rural unemployment. The politicians and police who turn a blind eye to illegal liquor production, and the effects of liquor production on social lives, could use their official power to distribute welfare, but instead they defer, deny, and corrupt welfare, and in so doing help construct the material distress that rules 'choice'. In so doing, they help construct consent for, and generate closure on the matter of, destructive livelihoods as both solution to and expression of poverty.

To pre-empt my conclusions, I am uncomfortable with Chatterjee's utterly unsentimental view of illegal action which chooses realism over utopia, or more pertinently, questions of justice. To be fair, he admits to saying little 'about the dark side of political society' (Chatterjee 2004: 75). Though he is aware of it, he cannot commit to a full explanation of 'how criminality and violence are tied to the ways in which various deprived population groups must struggle to make their claims to governmental care' (*ibid.*). Yet, this tension between illegal action demanding governmental care and illegal action that reinforces precarious, violent, and exploited existence is a fundamental one facing contemporary struggles against neoliberal development. Arguably, these dilemmas played out among conflicting citizens and politicians are an effective smokescreen for realising neoliberal (state) power.[1]

To reiterate, I am not supporting civil society's despair at sullying lofty criteria of deliberative democracy. The battle between political society and 'enlightened desires of civil society' is messy and contentious indeed, but can we say more than that (Chatterjee 2004: 77)? On the face of it, it is easy to view liquor producers as political society claiming that illegal liquor production is a response to material distress, while JS activists appear to be civil society defenders of 'healthy society'. However, as I will show, JS and wives of liquor consumers can also be viewed as constructing political society — fighting to publicise their sorrows and strife, proposing alternative norms, articulating possible grounds for building political society, and demanding to be governed through relational rather than divisive principles. Recognising the choices made by these actors within given historically available options shows how the framing of 'choice' occurs through an active political delimitation which makes certain definitions of welfare and distress subject to neglect, and renders certain bases of collectivity unthinkable.

The Social Life of Liquor

Liquor production has been reported to have dramatically increased in recent years. Recalling critical colonial histories about turning drink 'from custom to crime', initially I wondered whether protestors' perception was nurtured and exaggerated by a local moral police (Hardiman 1985: 185–251). At the same time, I was intrigued by Prasad Sardar's[2] conviction that 'Alcohol has a special tie with politics (*rajneeti*) today.' A glimpse of the political–economic dimensions of production helps understand the moral panic and liquor protestors' constructions of morality and illegality.

As mentioned in chapter three, by the late 1980s, the CPM was losing their crucial industrial vote as a result of capital flight, the close-down of sick industries, and increasing unemployment. In 1991, the 'licensing Raj' of the central government came to an end with formal neoliberal policies initiated in India. Bengal's moment for a phase of capital investment had arrived. Chief Minister Bhattacharya earned the name 'Brand Buddha' for inviting ambitious capital investments in sectors like petrochemicals, agribusiness, retail, and IT (P. Basu 2007). However, land and infrastructural support promised to investors generated conflict over the terms of industrialisation (Bhaduri 2007).[3]

Subsidising these investment opportunities have added to state budget deficits producing re-examinations of revenue-generation options. In 2002, the mainstream media criticised the government for losing revenue due to a faulty liquor policy. Reports argued that while the central government allowed potable alcohol to be made from 'sugar beet, beet root, potatoes and coarse grain', West Bengal state policy disallowed production from any other substance but molasses (*Times of India* 2002). Since the state does not grow sugarcane, liquor producers had no option but to buy sugarcane from other states. Additionally, bottlers had to get at least 50 per cent of their alcohol from domestic distilleries. All this raised liquor prices, increased tax evasions, decreased state revenues, while encouraging illicit liquor production. Responding to budget deficits and criticisms of its liquor policy, in March 2003, the West Bengal Finance Minister Asim Dasgupta liberalised liquor licensing policies in order to earn additional revenue of Rs 100 crore or $1 billion (*Hindu Business Line* 2003).

In 2006, Bibek Haldar[4] told me that 'Even three years ago there were about 60,000 people to a license. Now there is a license for every 18,000 people.' While the liberalisation of liquor licensing policies was likely to address state revenue losses and pricing issues, it increased perceptions and reality of government support for the capillary insertion of liquor in daily village life. It was now supplied through neighbourhood grocery stores in residential areas. People frequently complained about the stench, drunks lying around swaying on their way home, and fighting on streets.

Despite increased licenses, most liquor production in areas I researched is done without it. This is because this increase has showcased and legitimised liquor production as a lucrative business for those looking for opportunities. It seemed to be common knowledge that molasses-based liquor concentrate was diluted with great quantities of water, multiplying liquor quantity and profits. As an angry woman put it, 'In this business, you make a lot of money out of water. *Out of water!* Who wouldn't want to do it?' Medha Bairagi, a housewife facing alcohol-induced domestic strife accounted for this increase by pointing to businesses that hire motor vehicles to bring raw materials in and 'export' liquor out.[5]

These indicators of increase coincide with narratives about changing social norms. Combating my challenge that they saw more liquor because they looked for it, Prasad contrasted norms from his childhood (15 years ago), when 'there was not such a presence of alcohol. [...] At the very least, young children did not drink alcohol. 18-20 year olds never drank alcohol, didn't smoke *beedis* in front of people.' Brazen, public-drinking perturbed Prasad — starkly contrasted as it is to memories of his own surreptitious consumption of *beedis*, riven with guilt, shame, and fear of being seen by an adult.

This is the context within which Prasad challenged people to fortify critical and collective thinking against accepted wisdom that a lack of income opportunities disabled people, compelling liquor production. Roadblock mobilisers, including him, concurred that such actions were illegal. But theirs was a desperate effort to call attention to increased production of liquor and government unwillingness to regulate it. Prasad suspected Party politicians were negotiating with liquor producers:

> I don't know if it is because they want the vote advantage, or to hold on to their seat, but they seem to be supporting alcohol consumption. First of all, the government gives alcohol licenses. That's for country liquor. And then illegal alcohol runs effortlessly (*kono byaapar na*). We go constantly to the *pradhan* (local government or *panchayat* head), give our depositions, submit our demands, we submit a list of people who are selling, we even give names. All they tell us is 'Alright something will be done about it.' Having said that, they want to show people that they are doing something about it. So, they call the liquor businessmen and talk to them for a bit. And then two-three days later, it starts all over again.

The evasion and internal negotiations were never more palpable to Prasad and others than at the roadblock.

> **Prasad**: When police vans arrive and they are ready to *lathi*-charge us and put us in vans, the liquor businessmen are ready and waiting. They say from the sidelines, 'Sir, pick up this one. Take that one! This is one of them, this is another! And the police are following exactly their cue (*oder kotha moto korchhe*), picking up the ones they were identifying and putting them in the jeep.
>
> **Researcher**: Why are you telling me this? What is the significance (*gūrūtva*) of this?
>
> **Prasad**: The significance of this is that liquor businessmen already spoke to the police prior to the roadblock and they were identifying main mobilisers in the movement. Pick them up first and take them away. Hit them. And they verbally abused (*gala–gaali*) us as well. So the police are clearly supporting the liquor businessmen. [...]
>
> **Researcher**: Well, they too are citizens. So what if the police are supporting them?
>
> **Prasad**: But they are conducting an illegal liquor business. The liquor business is illegal. As a result, thousands of people are adversely affected in so many different ways. Financial harm, bodily harm, social harm, social environment (*samajer poribesh*) is harmed by it (*noshto hochhe*). So this kind of issue where police should really tear down illegal liquor production in two days, instead they are angry at us for conducting raids. [...] Saying nothing to liquor businessmen. If liquor businessmen are identifying us and police are catching us, when we identify liquor businessmen, why don't the police catch liquor businessmen? What should we conclude from this?

Figure 6.1: Two policemen holding rifles (on the right) publicly ally themselves with the liquor producers at the roadblock in 2005

Prasad concluded from this that police and local panchayat leaders have backdoor Party backing. I elaborate later why politicians occasionally, actively publicise these backdoor mediations at times like the roadblock. Ultimately, Party politics punished the innocent and freed the guilty. At the same time, JS activists frequently recounted how CPM panchayat official Ritika Haldar supported anti-liquor agitation, even breaking liquor pots with others. When I asked Bibek Haldar (Ritika's brother) about panchayat role in liquor protests, he suggested Party political constraints:

> **Bibek:** They participate till a given limit (*nirdishto sheema*) and they have done so in the past. [...] But they cannot dive into the movement as we can. [...] And I think that is because the party holds the reins behind them (*lagaam dhore aache*). There is a different power behind them. [...] If alcohol disappears, there is a problem in the market of votes.
>
> **Researcher:** What is the problem?
>
> **Bibek:** The problem is this, that today in India, the politician knows that they can buy votes with alcohol. If they drink alcohol, their minds

(*mostishk*) are not working. The person knows that I will not vote for Rambabu because in five years he has done nothing. But someone from Rambabu's party will give that voter a bottle of liquor and another fifty rupees and tell him to treat another five people to some alcohol. [...] So what you cannot do with money alone, you can do with alcohol.

Researcher: Is this your impression (*dharona*)?

Bibek: No, it is my experience (*obhigyota*). I live here. I have seen it. [...] Alcohol is a weapon for party politics. Meanwhile where do they get the money? Donations (*chanda*) from the alcohol business. Here, take five thousand rupees. And then the party uses that to encourage (*utshaho*) voters to drink. Go drink at that liquor store. Is it not a good weapon (*bhalo hathiar*)?

Bibek said that 'all Parties are thieves' (*shob* Party *chor*) and he was certainly not the only one with this conviction. Not surprisingly, protestors of every political stripe participated in the roadblock.

Prasad and Bibek's view of political–economic corruption and illegality, giving alcohol an indispensable presence in village communities, complements judgments of alcohol as a moral problem in behavioural terms. Bibek argued that gentlemen (*bhadralok*) don't drink. To him, drinking was a fount of vice and violence: gambling, domestic violence, theft, and murder. In making these associations, he constructed part of his notion of self and society: 'Since we are human beings, we want to remain distinguishable from animals. So in my social environment, among people around me, in my society, why would we drink something that is making other people healthy in mind and body (*shushto mostishko aar shoreer*) ill? Our aim is to keep that healthy human being healthy.' Bibek's morality combines upper-caste and middle-class notions with anger at corrupt political support for illegal work to argue for building self in communion with, rather than in opposition to, the construction of society.[6] Liquor production was understood as a moral problem by liquor protestors and producers alike. It is to the producers and their words that I now turn.

Drink and Desperation

The notorious 'Khara *para*' (Khara neighbourhood) — known as a 'CPM neighbourhood' — adjoins the bus stop where the roadblock was held. One resident calculated that 20 out of 35 households produced alcohol. Beyond numbers, people felt 'Break the pots there and it will stop everywhere else.' Radha described the challenging situation:

> It is a dangerous area and you cannot go there on your own. [...] The police tell us that women activists have to go along if the police are to go on a raid there because *para* people make false accusations. The women in their [Khara] homes tear their blouses and shout rape if we go there. So you have to be very careful with them.

Khara *para* producers had negotiated lasting alliances with Party officials, panchayats, and other powerful men such as schoolteachers. One resident, a schoolteacher, and former panchayat *pradhan* called Bolai Master, featured prominently in people's stories and he happens to be a renowned drunk. Since JS had contentious relations with people in this neighbourhood, I never made it to any of these homes. Instead, I spoke to one liquor-seller whose alcohol supply came from Khara *para*, and two other liquor-sellers who worked in Sriramkrishnapur.

Prasad's words about alcohol making people *pongu* or disabled were constantly with me as I conducted interviews. It seemed like an absurd coincidence when I realised that two of three liquor-sellers (one man and one woman) were actually physically disabled. The woman was 35 years old, unmarried, with an obvious limp to her walk. She initially told me that she produces liquor (*maal tūli*), making clearly connected statements to explain why. 'No one gives me food (*amake keo bhaat deye na*). I have not got married because my leg is broken, so I make liquor.' Her mother spoke for her when I asked why she remained unmarried, 'She fell from a tree when she was young. And she asked not to get married because she felt that she could not do housework adequately. She was scared that her in laws would get angry and beat her.'

Despite the mother's understanding, patriarchal norms had left Baisakhi to fend for herself. As cultivators had harvest rights on the land she leased out, she effectively had no source of food. The government's special welfare programmes for the disabled (*protibandi*) did not reach her. She said, 'Disabled people get rice. They get unemployment money. They don't give me anything. What can I do?' She encountered this denial of welfare from two schoolteachers — Bimal Das, a Congress panchayat leader and a former CPM panchayat leader, Bolai Master. 'They tell me, keep doing what you're doing for now. We will give you a disability card.

We will give you one (*debo*). It is the Age of "will give you" (the *debo* Raj) after all.'

The significant role of schoolteachers (doubling as panchayat officials) in mediating illegality on behalf of liquor producers fits well with Dwaipayan Bhattacharya's (2001) explanations for how the Left Front has accomplished continuous electoral success since 1977. He argues that CPM built alliances with key sections of a segmented society in order to maintain popular support after its land reform programme, Operation Barga. Rural schoolteachers were an ideal category as salaried people without vested interests or income from agricultural land, yet knowledgeable about rural society, and educated in Leftist ideology. As such, they were perfect conduits to help form 'socially extensive trust and reliance between communities and classes' and helped turn these relationships into 'tangible support for the party' (Bhattacharya 2001: 677). Just as they helped make the government 'local', they also subject it to popular scrutiny. Over time, alliances between party, panchayat, and schoolteachers produced a nexus of corruption. When I began fieldwork, honest schoolteachers were still held in the highest esteem. Others however were seen as getting rich on permanently protected jobs, building massive brick houses, buying motor vehicles, and with too much time for politics. Teachers such as Bolai Master and Bimal Das have this kind of reputation. Bolai Master gave CPM ideology local reality, but in doing so, he helped construct what Baisakhi refers to as a '*debo* Raj'.

Baisakhi grossly underestimated her profits from alcohol sale (at Rs 50–60 or $1.50 per month). She inserted distance between sale and source claiming that she bought it from her uncle in the Khara *para* who sourced it 'from outside'. According to Baisakhi, liquor production in Khara *para* had stopped because liquor protestors brought losses. She recounted telling protestors 'If you can give me rice, then you can break them. Otherwise, don't touch these.' When I asked her what benefit this business had brought to her, she said

Baisakhi: No benefit. But I have to eat, don't I? How should I eat?

Researcher: Could you have found any other type of business?

Baisakhi: No. If there was then why would I do such low work (*neechu kaaj*). Such dirty work (*nongra kaaj*)?

She wished that someone would employ her as a cook in Integrated Child Development Scheme (ICDS) centres like other women so that she did not have to do work that people looked down upon (*lok kharap bole*). Despite her anger at protestors who break pots, she understood their rationale: 'It is for the sake of peace around here. Otherwise, in homes there is beating, verbal abuse, people can't survive.' While distress drove her to liquor production, her words also underscored liquor as causing other forms of distress.

Baisakhi's livelihood choice indicates her economic and patriarchal compulsions. Being unmarried, unable to work freely, or do heavy labour, she chose a business at home done through familial connections to a wider liquor trade. Unwilling to take her disability card issue any further up the political ladder, she settled instead for police and panchayat understanding, while inviting the wrath of neighbours. In my interviews, I heard of three other women running liquor production units including a widow and another single woman with two sons.

Nimai Mondol is a 56-year-old liquor producer. He began by inviting us to sit in his 'dirty home'. When we objected pointing to the neat and tidy room, he said it might be neat, but the home was dirtied by his work. Each liquor-seller made reference to the moral judgment they assumed hung in the air. With that out in the open, Nimai described the desperation behind his trade: his wife died of 'some fever', he used the three *bighas* of inherited (Operation Barga) land to pay for his youngest son's thalassemia treatment in Vellore; his son, who died despite these efforts, left him with no help for farm-work, pushing Nimai to resuscitate a trusty business. Producing about 60–70 (500 ml) bottles of liquor per month, he earned an average of 50 rupees a day. When the panchayat leadership came to question him on his work, they left understanding this man as satiating his hunger (*pétér jaala*).

Dilip Patra is a middle-aged liquor-seller with a visibly bent leg, living with his wife, parents, and daughter in a small hut. His broken knee leaves him unable to do heavy labour. His son's employment at a sweet shop in Kolkata supplements household income. Dilip's father's Operation Barga land (1 *bigha* and 15 *katha*) was divided among his four feuding brothers now living in separate homes. He inherited no land, but as the eldest son, he has to look after his father. His monthly income from liquor varies depending on monthly debt. His distress was expressed as intimate duties of providing for his *sansar* (household) and aging father against the odds of physical ability and opportunity. Failing responsibilities made him feel less than human.

> If I go along with your position, how will my household run? Look at my father's age. And if my father cannot eat, and I am not with my household, then am I a human being? What shall I do? There is nothing to be done. I don't even get [his] old age pension.

Radha Das,[7] Mihir Nahiya[8] and I collectively interviewed Dilip Patra, asking questions according to no prescribed structure. Like Baisakhi, Dilip was forthright about the socially problematic nature of his work. He felt he had no choice because there were no other opportunities. He recounted how a pond-making loan opportunity available through the Sundarbans Development Board (local development agency) came to naught for him. He had even used a marital contact to place his name on the 'lottery' list for loan-receivers. Far from a matter of bad luck, Mihir added his impression that the corrupt *pradhan* had placed names of gold jewellery store owners to the 'lottery' list meant to enable double-cropping on farmland.

This is how the developmental state failed Dilip, also making clear that his illegal work could hardly be questioned by government officials. After all, those who deny and corrupt welfare cannot but reinforce grammars of distress since they help produce the distress. About (political) Party role in the alcohol business, Dilip said 'There is no Party role. They let everyone do their business.' He interpreted attitudes of Party officials and liquor consumers as mercy and explicitly disapproved of a movement that destroyed property and livelihood.

> They come and break your liquor pots. Even this sister (pointing to Radha) came once and did that. They broke and left. I am telling you there is nothing to do here. Do you know where I get money from? Those who drink. They say 'Poor people how will you eat, you go get some liquor. Like that. That's how we eat. Even they show mercy (*maya*).'

Radha tried to defend JS work but it only produced a crescendo of frustration from Dilip:

> **Radha**: Our organisation, or whoever comes to break your production, they are concerned about the spoiling of our social environment,

> the harm it causes to the body, the fights it generates in the household. Perhaps you can do something that does not harm another ten households.
>
> **Dilip**: You are telling me? I know all this.[…] What is it that I could do? […] That's why I am telling you, give me something to do and I will stop this. […] That's my guarantee.

JS is explicit about not being a service-providing NGO. Rather, they mobilise to hold state officials accountable to development planning and welfare distributions. As such, Radha assured Dilip that JS would mobilise for alternative employment for liquor producers at the *anchal* (regional) office. Despite Dilip's critique of JS work, he offered a stray comment of comfort, 'You have come here, not for my harm, but for my good. I have been able to understand this.'

The desperation of disabled bodies, lack of healthcare facilities, fragmented households, corruption in distribution of alternative livelihood opportunities, and financial need in a patriarchal agrarian society drives these three people into the liquor business. Their distress 'legalises' the work even if it does not take away its 'lowliness'. While recognising household distress caused by liquor as moral justification for anti-liquor protest, they see JS's road-block and destruction of private property as illegal, even merciless work. One activist had literally paid for damaging private property as someone had destroyed his betel leaf plantation by putting salt on the plants.

Though material distress drives liquor production for the interviewees described above, the backgrounds of liquor producers did however vary. Liquor businessmen typically belonged to Scheduled Castes and roughly half the producers are known as landless or near landless. However, about 20–25 per cent of named liquor-sellers are middle- to high-caste, landowning, influential politicians. Further, since everyone in Khara *para* had now become rich, initial landlessness was not at the forefront of people's imaginations. Landed and influential liquor producers are evidence that this was not necessarily the livelihood of the desperate; that 'choice' does not automatically calibrate to 'low' positions on political–economic scales. Normalising illegality of the poor liquor producers can serve as a façade that equates influential liquor producers' choices with the moral and material compulsions of the poor. In a recent clarification of his argument, Chatterjee has argued that 'unlike squatters in Mumbai or Kolkata', (2008b: 92), the middle class who engage in illegality do not have the 'moral stamp of legitimacy' (*ibid.* 91). He goes on to say, 'it is mistaken to claim that the dominant and propertied classes any longer set the standards of morality for society; rather, in a democratic age, the moral passion of entitlement and outrage is on the side of those who have little' (*ibid.*). But whose moral passion and outrage is on the side of those who have little? And what political action is this moral passion constructing?

In South 24 Parganas, contrary to Chatterjee's argument, the rising middle and upper classes are forcing the illegal actions of the poor. Chatterjee (2004) argues that the challenge of building a political society requires a 'mediator' who translates attributes of a population group into moral attributes that help form a community. The mediators for liquor producers are schoolteachers, panchayat leaders, police who are perceived as citizens, (liquor) consumers, and government representatives. Witnessed drunkenness and visible negotiations with producers at roadblocks perform the social function of stretching the rules, normalising illegality by making it public knowledge. Politicians who questioned illegal producers also publicly performed the pedagogic function of dissuading protest by discursively highlighting how distress drives liquor production. Yet, by stalling disability cards and denying alternative livelihoods, they materially reproduced distress in the community. Indeed, they essentially and discursively enabled producers to form an albeit uncoordinated 'community' with common conviction about moral dilemmas and circumstantial compulsions. That is, rather than distribute welfare adequately, the politically influential and the rich help give the material distress of the poor 'the moral stamp of legitimacy' which is then recognised as merciful care, to use Dilip Patra's terms (Chatterjee 2008b: 91). This is the rule of an episteme with its attendant disabling material effects on poverty and choice.

At the protesting end of the spectrum, as an organisation, JS are also mediators because they give people's disparate experiences collective form and the 'imaginative possibilities of community' (Chatterjee 2004: 60). Its activists speak variously as householders, agricultural workers, landless, seasonal migrants, women abandoned by husbands, and victims of domestic violence. In addition to travel for seasonal migration, they accrued cultural exposure and capital over years of translocal political action across JS theatre teams. The subjects of JS activism may be producing what Gidwani and Sivaramakrishnan have called 'regional modernity' with 'elements of a Gramscian counterhegemonic praxis: a symbolic and material vocabulary for challenging ruling ideologies' prevalent in villages (Gidwani and Sivaramakrishnan 2003: 187). As alternative mediators, they struggle to validate alternate bases of political society. Rather than assume that 'the moral passion of entitlement and outrage' is structurally inclined to 'the side of those who have little', it is worth considering when and how such moral outrage is mobilised, and who among 'those who have little' such mobilisation excludes (Chatterjee 2008b: 92).

On occasion, JS itinerant cultural activism across various village theatre teams translates into a perception that unconnected to agricultural incomes, activists are able to 'mercilessly' destroy meager livelihoods of the desperate. Yet, as inhabitants of rural homes, one of their first campaigns in the early 1990s was a Right to Work campaign which combated constant out-migration by emphasising need for jobs in their own villages. Today, with widespread land acquisition, its activists battle every effort to dispossess existing skills, meanings, lands, and livelihoods. In JS Director, Sanjoy Ganguly's words, 'Is issuing of liquor licenses the only way of the government to generate revenue?'

For JS activists, anti-liquor agitation is a battle for healthy livelihoods. Rather than accept *any* employment that generates exchange value, they unite people against revenue-generation that destroys other things of value. Fighting instrumental, ephemeral politics of soft legality exchanged for votes, JS takes on the massive challenge of constructing widespread unity to mobilise for worthwhile employment and healthy occupation. Recognising stories of liquor producers' distress as reinforcing rather than solving the problem, it refuses to buttress a grammar of poverty and welfare maldistribution by encouraging liquor production as governmental representatives have done. Along with liquor consumers' wives, JS activists help fortify the 'intimate frontier' in the battle between accomplishing an opportunistic politics, and perforating the commonsense grammars about distress and drink. For liquor protestors, the 'darker side of political society' cannot wait to be addressed after the 'public' disadvantages of being marginal citizens have been repaired. JS's critique of 'political society' as constituted in rural Bengal suggests that political discourse and its implicit preference for an artificial 'public' of political action must be expanded. Rather, JS recognises dispossessed meanings and other intimate rationales as a thinkable politics which can challenge the 'informal' legalisation of illegal work, the normalisation of destructive consumption, and the perpetuation of divisive livelihoods.

Sorrows and Strife on the 'Intimate Frontier'

Family, in its heteronormative form, has been a historically significant idiom and vehicle of social, political and cultural life in rural Bengal (Bannerji 2002; Chatterjee 1993; Sarkar 1984). In a normative environment that regulates women's work and activity outside homes, parliamentary Communism mirrored democratic centralism of CPM Party structure within the Bengali family, mobilising women's action by filtering Party work through family, and by constructing Party itself as family (Basu 1992). Purna Das, Executive Member of West Bengal Democratic Women's Association said 'We see the CPI (M) as our family. Like our family it protects us' (quoted in Basu 1992: 54). In so doing, the Party escaped problems of bringing women out of homes for action perceived as working against home.

More recently, CPM championed 33 per cent seats for women's leadership in panchayats in this devolution of state power (Munshi 2005). Thus, panchayat leaders such as Ritika Haldar are common, even if perceived variously as 'independent', 'novices' or 'puppets'. NGOs have also deployed family as idiom and vehicle for decentralising state responsibilities by invoking principles of reciprocity, obligation, and belonging within a Hindu *sansar* which means household in concrete terms, and universe or larger household in abstract terms (Lamb 2000). The remaking of legitimate spheres of women's actions is initiated by arguing that selfless work for community (*sansar* in its abstract meaning) is the best route to alleviating poverty in the home. In short, leaders, politicians, and NGO activists alike have used *sansar* to persuade women to work for neighbourhood, community, or country.

Such use of *sansar* is significantly out of touch with contemporary anxieties expressed about growing disunity and strife in families. Sons, constructed as invaluable, precious, faultless persons in the

Hindu patriarchal family, were routinely blamed for wasting away expensive investment in their education and leaving parents insecure (see chapter five). Brothers have been fighting over land inherited from parents, resulting in separate nuclear households with new insecurities, unviable livelihoods, and parental neglect. Like a mathematical constant, daughters-in-law in these homes are blamed for instigating fights among warring brothers (their husbands).

These anxieties around broken families have a political–economic face captured in the Bengal Chief Minister's 'objective' terms: 'It is time to assess the present situation of the state realistically and objectively' (Bhattacharya 2007). To summarise the agrarian crisis from the CPM perspective (*ibid.*): CPM-initiated land reform helped construct a stable social base but increasingly divided landholdings among children of land reform beneficiaries, neoliberal policies worldwide, and also costly agricultural inputs have rejuvenated landlessness. Agricultural growth has reached a point of ever-diminishing returns for farmers. The solution to this agrarian crisis is what Sumanta Bannerjee has called CPM's 'new jingle: Agriculture is our base, industry our future' (Banerjee 2006).

CPM's analysis of 'objective' dimensions of life in agrarian Bengal is relevant motivation for encouraging revenue-generation through means such as liquor production. Yet, fragmentation of land and family in rural areas is the very reason such production *as* solution is perceived as divisive, unsustainable, and harmful. For, along with land divisions within families, liquor production was seen as an added factor for dividing families and communities to create what people called an 'unhealthy culture'. While women informants were increasingly aware of their constant work for welfare and care of the larger 'public' household, they found that problems of their breaking families were ignored by the same leaders who sought electoral support or mobilised participatory development. As primary caretakers of *sansar*, community, and seasonally even agricultural work, women have become difficult subjects in the 'accomplishment of rule' and transition to neoliberalism (Li 1999a) amidst seasonal male migration, liquor production, and consumption.

In interviews, without exception, people cited domestic strife and violence as the main repercussion of liquor. Women and adolescent children bore the brunt of decreasing household incomes (for schooling) and increasing domestic violence. Radha Das told me of a village where women had been breaking liquor pots on their own, without any mediators and mobilisers. For her, this was impressive evidence that JS anti-liquor protest was organic work. Despite patriarchal assumptions that women's protest betrays family, in fact women expressed an unshaken resolve to bring security and peace to a *sansar* reeling with sorrow and strife.

I interviewed Naina Middha because I remembered her anger at the roadblock in 2005. She was unafraid of the police, cameras, and the alcohol producers. She is approximately 40 years old, living in a *sansar* of six people. She lives in the Khara *para*. Naina supports two sons, and a husband who drinks a lot. She works on others' fields, tying up ropes lining tomato plants, cutting the rice harvest, and growing rice on her 10 *kathas* of land. Naina's neighbour and relative told me that Naina was very brave to speak with me because Bolai Master (schoolteacher and reputed drunk) is her neighbour from whom she borrows money when she is desperate.

Figure 6.2: Naina (standing on higher ground midst policemen) has a captive peripheral audience of women, while the policemen read newspapers, feigning distraction

Naina spoke to me in whispers but needed no prompting with questions. 'What can I tell you? We (wives) are the ones who are telling people of the oppression we face from this. The shouting, the beating.' She said sometimes her husband drinks for three or four days till he is completely unconscious although now her sons curb his drinking. 'We do after all have to run a *sansar*, don't we? If your husband drinks then all the money is with him. If I have to go to my husband every time I need books for their school. If I have to go to my husband every time I need to go to the market to buy rice, or food. Then as a woman where will I go? You tell me!' Neighbours rarely respond to household fights any more because, 'These days, there are fights in house after house (*bāri-bāri te*) so many households, should neighbours help sort out all these fights?'

Naina offered her analysis of why officials too remain unperturbed despite pervasive domestic strife. She recounted her words to policemen at the roadblock,

> If you don't do anything when people tell you of their difficulties and problems with liquor, then what interest do we have in telling you our problems? What interest (*ki shartho*), you tell me?! You tell me who should I complain to about conflicts in home after home? They don't say anything. Only once there is great pressure like a death or a murder at home, then they come and casually take a look, ask questions. That's all. They take bribes behind the scenes (*pechon theke ghoosh*), that is why they cannot find a solution to our problems.

Naina's seemingly tepid challenge about pointless recounting of sorrowful domestic stories is a concrete assertion that government representatives negotiating 'political society' with liquor producers and consumers are guilty of patriarchal neglect. She knows that police corruption perpetuates violence, bodily harm, and impoverishment at home. Despite highlighting these intricate connections for the police, Naina believes she has no audience for her complaint.

Her public protests generated further fighting at home. Her husband had asked her why she was participating in 'these women's organisations'. She had retorted, 'Why shouldn't I go? They [liquor businesses] are making money from a poor household like ours. That does not hurt you (*antore laage na*)? It does not touch your conscience (*bibek*)? You go there and they buy land, they grow rice, buy cars, based on our pain, our difficulties. This is what you want. Is this the solution (*samadhan*) to our household's sorrows (*sansarer dūkkho*)?' Responding to her husband's judgement of going public with 'private' problems, she questions his conscience for worsening financial hardships through drinking. Implicitly, she claims that he already made their problems public by spending *sansar* money on drinking and enriching liquor-producers.

Naina was in despair when I asked whether Khara *para* had in fact stopped making alcohol as Baisakhi had suggested. Her response went straight to Party politics, returning seamlessly to liquor production.

> This is a CPM *para*. If you say anything about liquor production they shout at you. [...] We are divided. That's the other thing. The people in this neighborhood are partly in our camp, and another half in the Khara camp. The parties will not let us talk to each other and sort it out. The party wants to talk to both sides. But the parties say different things. They sing one song in our camp and another song in their camp. Now which song will you listen to?

While the grammar of distress counts on people 'racing to the bottom' against each other, reaffirming beliefs in lack of choice and diminished sense of worth, Naina believes people can unite against a production process and politics that blatantly gains from divisions. Yet her faith in protest was wavering, 'nothing has changed in fifty years. [...] We continue to labour for fifty years. In this life, I will not have happiness. We will only have *jala-shasti* (literally, burn and punishment) of a husband, burn of *sansar*, burn of children.' And then back to resolve 'we have to work together in a family, right? That's why I protest. I take blows from my husband, why not take blows from police?'

Here, Naina makes an arresting challenge to conventional meanings of 'working together' for a *sansar* and bringing 'family dishonor' by revealing continuities between experiences in her private and public households. Notwithstanding her rather normative view of family roles, she believes that causing losses to liquor business is essential work to strike a blow against the profit they make from addictions, impoverishment, and conflicts in poor homes.

Medha Bairagi is a 35-year-old woman who lives with her two teenage daughters and her husband. Married at 15, she had a son who died two or three years after marriage. Her husband farms six *bighas* of their land and labours on other people's lands. She cooks, cleans, and works on rice and vegetable production for consumption. She participates in anti-liquor agitation when she can '[...] so that everyone, so that *I* can get peace (*shanti*) and live in peace. [...] So that there isn't war at home day in and day out'. As in Naina's home, where sons fight the father, Medha's daughters fight with theirs — over money, marriage, school, and liquor.

I asked if liquor was solely responsible for disruptions at home. Medha drew distinctions: 'Can there be disruption (*ashanti* or literally the lack of peace) without liquor? When there are fights without liquor you call that a misunderstanding (*bhool bojha-bojhi*). In our homes, it is liquor that causes problems.' Her husband primarily drinks at Khara *para*. Medha believed that even the police are afraid of them since Khara women take 'their clothes off in front of police and then accuse them of robbing their honour.' These women challenged Medha, 'Well, why does your husband drink? Do we invite him to drink?' Medha continues to fight her husband's reasoning — sadness at their son's death — by asking 'Is drinking going to bring him back? Is it a solution?'

Medha had been to Congress panchayat leader Bimal Das 'at least hundred times'. Now her daughters were sensitive to domestic fights becoming public knowledge. Medha continued participating in agitations despite disapproval because for her, public agitation was just one strategy towards a better family life. Her neighbours and relatives refuse to join in unless they suffered the same, claiming that 'Our lives will end, but liquor will not.' For her part, Medha is convinced that she has to try. 'It isn't always CPM rule or Trinamul rule. Things *do* change. Similarly, I don't accept that liquor is here to stay.' JS mobilises support for this alternative norm of political action towards ethical, collective living.

Naina and Medha's ongoing struggles to unite people mirror JS challenges in mobilising protests. On one liquor raid, villagers gathered in support of the producer who was a widow. They argued that she would have nothing to eat without the business. Radha Das recalled her response to them:

> **Radha:** She would not have anything to eat? How many families in your village? At least seventy, right? Now this one person's business is causing harm in hundreds of other homes and you are coming together to support her. But all of you in seventy homes have not found a way of coming together to say that we will all take turns to support this

> widow! That we will take turns — whether it is rice, or vegetables or whatever it is! Instead you are supporting an illegal business which is breaking up another twenty homes. [...] I said this to them.
>
> **Researcher:** What did they say?
>
> **Radha:** They all agreed that this is definitely bad work, but argued that government and the big fish (*boal maach*) should be attacked for giving licenses, not small fish (*pūti maach*). I said to them that in order to attack the government we need men and women from your homes. Where else am I supposed to find the strength to take on the government? We have to be together in this.

In light of a destructive but lucrative business, necessary in the vote market, as it tames hunger while disabling conscience and collectives, JS activists hold up a mirror to people's porous logic of support for liquor production.

In the end, people can choose to act differently. Consumers' wives highlight their belief that husbands can choose to fight sadness and frustration considering wives live through similar pressures. These women believe that neighbours can choose to stand in solidarity against a destructive income source. In so doing, these protestors are reclaiming the right to define the meaning of the 'social' in social relations. They want police and politicians to be accountable to domestic sorrow and strife. As such, with or without JS's mediation, they help raise profound questions of alternate meanings of material distress and constructions of political society that remain historically available but dispossessed of meaning.

Conclusions

I have tried to recount lives and meanings of liquor as they offer competing constructions of meanings of legality and morality in contemporary rural Bengal. JS and protesting wives reveal liquor's 'inner' meanings and perforate commonsense definitions of choice and worth reinforced by political economies and grammars of distress and distribution. While 'having no choice but pursue illegal action and exploitative jobs' is a political and economic reality of neoliberal development, JS argues, precisely for that reason, that it is deeply problematic to reinforce this evaluation of people's worth and work, conceptually and politically. Chatterjee's study of illegal action as sign of democracy and political society may not propose such a reduction, but his agnostic description of political society arguably lends implicit support to it. His elaboration of political society remains ahistorical rather than situated within the conjuncture of the present to reveal the tensions *within* the 'politics of the governed' and the illegalities of political economic power and rule.

JS views this labelling of 'having no choice', as the foundational destruction of self-worth that perpetuates unjust forms of exploitation and rule. Lack of income-generating opportunities combined with patriarchal constraints, physical disability, death/absence of young male farmhands no doubt push people in an agrarian economy toward distress and options such as liquor production. While fully cognisant of constraints that drive such production, JS activists take the mediating support of well-heeled politicians and the police for liquor producers as evidence that collective action is all the more imperative.

The influential and rich have given socially-embedded reality to governmental ideologies of distribution and welfare in the past, and they similarly embed distress as justification for a race to the bottom today. As such, they help construct neoliberal development through the veneer of a 'merciful' politics. All of this is done in relatively public view, legitimising specific ways of earning votes, livelihoods, welfare, property, and attention for distress. Based on the evidence presented above, I ask: what stops 'political society' from forming based on forms of material distress experienced by liquor consumers' wives? While liquor producers' distress is certainly thinkable as constitutive force of 'political society', Naina and Medha's distress do not count because they are messy for the patriarchal state that conceives of materiality through a male optic. Other scholars recount examples of 'dark democracy' in gender- and caste-based political actions (Breman 1999; Hansen 2001; Menon 1999). Instead, I argue that competing legalities and moralities, variously rationalised and challenged by liquor producers, protestors, and consumers' wives, make for divided political societies — tensions and divisions that are effective in realising neoliberal development.

Contrasted to influential mediators, JS is an alternate mediator of political society and community. For them, illegal action is a convenient construction that realises development by reinforcing assignments of 'low' worth and allowing communities to implode with unhealthy livelihoods, exploitative jobs, and 'transgressive consumption' practices in an increasingly commodified world (Liechty 2005: 7). JS activists are an inconvenient reality for governmental mediators of development because they insist that uniting to demand peaceful, constructive rural livelihood is possible if people have united to support a widow's liquor business. They puncture naturalising practices and double standards of influential mediators like rich liquor producers to show that livelihood choices are not always calibrated to people's 'low' or 'high' place in economic and political society. Revealing opportunistic political–economic constructions of distress and 'having no choice' undergirds JS's alternative moral basis for community and political society. Prasad's challenge — have they disabled us — is at heart, a hope against hope that people can be brought together to believe that together they have a choice, and a chance.

Chatterjee's intervention is powerful. Still, it is one thing to identify social processes navigating distress; to recognise the brutal choices people find themselves making; and to reveal opportunistic divisions and alliances that governments nourish as a way of reconciling dilemmas of private property and welfare provision. But, in leaving aside the problem of the 'darker side of political society', his academic realism is susceptible to reinforcing a myth that particular people, lands, and livelihoods *are* bearers of low worth because of which they have no choice but to produce a politics of stretched rules. In the end, Chatterjee's political society does not provide a framework for interpreting 'merciful politics' or neoliberal collusions with patriarchy. Moreover, this amounts to deserting the problem of social justice within democracy.

I hope I have shown that distribution of welfare and experiences of distress, strife, and marginality are not always in 'public' terms. Nor does the threshold between public and private household remain unchallenged. JS is invested in fighting 'public' definitions of 'low' worth by constructing critical, collective action from the very sites of alienated action. Can we conceptualise 'political society' in this more sentimental vein of political possibilities, warts and all, now rather than later? Here, Naina's political action is instructive. Her voice is far from a casteist or elitist disregard of desperate choices. She is convinced that protesting and disrupting public life and private property is valuable. Above all, her words show that she is at a loss for where to go. Nobody seems to be listening — 'not *panchayat* officials, big people (*babu-ra*), the police, nobody. Who do you go to?' For those who taught her an older politics of selfless contribution for the public *sansar*, she now flouts patriarchal norms and the grammar of distress to say that she prefers to be governed in ways that take cognisance of the relational sorrows and strife in her (public and private) *sansar*.

✷

Notes

1. For example, Jan Breman has shown how extraordinary violence against landless Dalit by high caste men and ensuing illegal collaborations by governmental representatives goes unpunished in part because of interparty competition and intraparty divisions where Congress party 'old-style leaders who remain faithful to tested ideals favouring upliftment of the downtrodden are opposed by operators and brokers prepared to sell their trade and themselves as floating politicians to whoever offers the best deal and the highest profit' (Breman 1999: 12).
2. Prasad Sardar is a 29-year-old man — one of the key actors/activists in JS since the early 1990s. He lives with six others in a landless house-hold in a village called Bhimpur in Kulpi district. He has done all kinds of daily wage work such as selling *alta–sindur* and snacks on local trains to working knee-deep in the deltaic waters of the region picking out shrimp larvae on shrimp farms.
3. I have reflected elsewhere on recent protests against Left Front land acquisition and the Left Front's defence against the charge that it is becoming a neoliberal state (Da Costa 2007).
4. Bibek Haldar is a 39-year-old male. Central to the anti-liquor agitation in Sriramkrishnapur, he led other men in scripting the play 'Hai Re Mod' (The Bane of Drink). He lives in a 'CPM household' of ten: his wife, two children, his two brothers, their wives, a nephew, two sisters and his mother. Collectively they own twelve *bighas* of land. He has led efforts to pressure his sister and *pradhan* Ritika Haldar to address the liquor problem.
5. In these areas of Bengal, local trade largely relied on forms of transportation run on human labour. Use of (petrol-driven) motor vehicles for local trade was considered a sign of a flourishing business.
6. JS activists recognise different drinking norms among tribal populations and problematic histories of censoring tribal custom (Hardiman 1985). In future research I hope to study tribal populations' response to anti-liquor agitations and JS belief that the history, logic, and meaning of tribal liquor consumption, differed markedly from those animating youth in communities recently initiated into alcohol.

7. Radha Das is a 31-year-old woman in the Central Coordinating Committee of JS since 1994. She travels frequently for JS work returning to her parents in Sriramkrishnapur. Her landless and indebted parents supported four daughters. Her involvement in the anti-liquor agitation had caused conflict at home when her father was a heavy drinker.
8. Mihir Nahiya is a 35-year-old, male JS activist since 2002. He has one and a half *bighas* of land. An active participant in the anti-liquor movement, he helped write the play 'Hai Re Mod' (The Bane of Drink).

Chapter Seven

The Snake-Goddess and her Antidote: Compelling Collectivity against Inequality and Uncertainty

In the introduction, I suggested that this book addresses the contentious relationship between culture, development, and dispossession as viewed through the lens of rural political theatre and activism. Given the spirited turn to culture in development thinking and practice, it is particularly important to ask about the limits of 'culture' in general, and religion in particular, in development's cultural turn. Studying Jana Sanskriti (JS) work provides a glimpse into how development is constructed and critiqued when we are not looking. That is, as a neglected site for understanding development the lens of theatre allows us to understand alternate constructions and practices of political collectivity, development, and democracy in a place where electoral success has contributed to epistemic closure on the meaning and materialisation of these terms. I have argued that JS engages in cultural work, wages epistemic battles, and fights the structural and normative closure on the very meaning of collectivity, development, and democracy in this state. In this chapter, I argue that although JS is interested in constructing alternate collectivities, livelihoods, and rural futures their work misses a significant existing collectivity as constructed by the snake-goddess Manasa. Again, my aim here is to identify the possibilities already embedded in everyday social relations which shed light on the relationship between capital and culture though they may not readily strike the social scientist as spaces of development.

In June 2005, when Radha and I were at a tea stall flanking the bus stop on the main Ramganga highway, we heard that a girl from Radha's village, Srirampur, had died of a snakebite. We rushed through our tea to take the 50 paisa boat-ride across the river to Srirampur. As the boat approached the other bank, we saw that a crowd had gathered around what we imagined was either the victim or her family members. But why here, midst commuters and thoroughfare, I wondered. Radha drew my attention to the platform that was being made out of banana leaves and barks. 'They will put her on that and set her body afloat on the river. They don't burn or bury people who die of snakebites, they set them afloat', Radha said. 'Why not?' I asked. 'Who knows? Because they say that their life (*praan*) can come back, that's why you have to set them afloat, set them free, can't burn them (*bhashiye dite hobe, khola chharte hobe, poratey parbe na*).' A fellow passenger asked me 'Don't you know the story of Chand Sadagar and Ma Manasa?' I had meandered into the realm of popular legends and stories of which I knew next to nothing. I shook my head and swallowed my questions till later.

I had never seen a young person dead before. She was not more than 15 years old. She lay lifeless, with evidence of a foaming mouth, glassy eyes, and her head resting on her wailing father's lap. We walked another 20 minutes towards Radha's village in Pathar Pratima Block of South 24 Parganas district picking up pieces of the devastating event. She had chosen to sleep on the cool mud floor to fight the punishing heat of June. The snake bit her at night. To complicate the picture, the snake seemed to have bitten her in the pelvic region. The girl, who had her period at the time, was initially unsure whether she felt acute period pain or a sharp bite, and then she became too embarrassed to seek help. She gave her family little time to react to her rapid loss of consciousness, and the poison overpowered her before they knew it.

The sight of the girl and her sobbing parents stunned me. I knew nothing about snakes, antidotes, or snake-goddesses. A familiar line from a JS play that I had seen numerous times now took on haunting dimensions. It was a line from their first play (discussed in chapter three) *Gayer Panchali* or, Song of the Village[1] — 'Snakes live in the village, and the antidote lives all the way in the city.' The comma is crucial. The performers always took the pause between the two parts of the sentence very seriously — one full second to communicate distance and despair. It was a familiar and memorable line, designed to effect drama. In my early years of research (1999–2001), I had asked participants and members of the audience whether they liked JS's plays. The most common refrain was 'Yes. Because we can see our lives in these stories. They tell our stories, our reality (*bastob*), they tell of daily events (*doinandin ghotona*).' 'Which of these is a story from *your* life?' I used to ask in order to coax respondents to go from general identification to particular life experience. Not infrequently, they quoted this line and proceeded to tell me how someone they knew died of a snakebite.

My encounter with the young girl's death from snakebite in 2005 made me realise that my relative indifference to Manasa, the snake-goddess over the years of fieldwork was a mistake. I had not practiced a theoretical commitment to understanding material and cultural realms of social life, and to examining how ideas turn to matter and how material transformations are value-laden conventions that rule (Williams 1973; Gramsci 1971; Comaroff 1985; Comaroff and Comaroff 1993; Sahlins 1976; Taussig 1980; Thompson 1971; Hall and Jefferson 2006; Scott 1976, 1987, 1990). In part, the secular time of social science and capitalist history had blinded me to the meaning of Manasa (Chakravarty 2000).

I only returned to question people about their beliefs in her in February 2008. I wanted to understand whether the worship of Manasa was ubiquitous, what she meant as one of the many goddesses that people worshipped during the year, and whether any of her devotees correlated this worship with the lack of proximate health centers. I found that her worship was ubiquitous, but largely in poor households and neighbourhoods. I found too that men and women spoke with equal passion about worshipping her. While I was not able to watch an actual ceremony, it seemed to me from descriptions that men and women had significant (if not equal) roles in propitiating the deity and fulfilling her expectations. She was an exacting goddess who reserved special demands and bestowed distinct favours upon the poor. Her devotees called her *kacha khekho debota* which means that she was a goddess that could eat you alive. They also called her *Ma Manasa* which means Manasa, our Mother. Fear and love combined to produce the belief that she worked both as an antidote and insurance against the threat of snakebites.

The idea of a snakegoddess as antidote and insurance strikes the normative secular social scientist studying development as faith in the *absence* of science, superstition working *in place* of medical advance and good healthcare. Notwithstanding the rhetoric of inclusive secularism and participatory development, certain types of religious belief and practice continue to remain identifiably 'other', far too distant from rationality and modernity to tolerate.[2] This understanding of biomedicine and snake-goddesses as occupying oppositional positions on the spectrum of tradition and modernity is a striking example of Saurabh Dube's (2002a) concept of 'enchantments of modernity'. Dube has recently argued that:

> The idea of modernity rests on rupture. It brings into view a monumental narrative — the breaching of magical covenants, the surpassing of medieval superstitions, and the undoing of hierarchical traditions. The advent of modernity, then, insinuates the disenchantment of the world: the progressive control of nature through scientific procedures of technology, and the inexorable demystification of enchantments through powerful techniques of reason. [...] Yet processes of modernity also create their own enchantments. Enchantments that extend from the immaculately imagined origins and ends of modernity, to the dense magic of money and markets, to novel mythologies of nation and empire, to hierarchical oppositions between myth and history, ritual and rationality, East and West, and tradition and modernity (Dube 2002a: 729).

The active mobilisations that construct and maintain belief in these distinctions produces a performed and embodied 'myth of origins' story of modernity that claims rupture from tradition. Ongoing, embodied, and performed, Dube's idea of 'enchantments of modernity' is an approach that does not dismiss modernity, modern subjects, or many other essentialisms of capitalism and colonialism as exclusively European, simply unreal, or merely ideal. Rather than dismiss the ideological distinctions which constitute the 'enchantments of modernity', for Dube the task is to '[stay] with the modalities of power that inhere in such difference' (Dube 2002a: 743). He urges that we attend to such a task by 'carefully querying and ethically articulating tradition and community, colonialism and modernity, memory and history, the secular and cosmopolitan, and the subaltern and the nation' (*ibid.*).

This chapter focuses on enchantments in the health sector. I highlight how certain forms of belief in health and healing are read as villagers' superstition and alienation in the face of material hardship. In the conclusion, I juxtapose this belief with the equally faith-based beliefs in insurance systems and biomedical treatment which are naturalised as 'modern' and not understood as matters of belief and alienation to the extent that they are. The larger debate to which this research addresses itself is the question of the limits to 'culture' in development's spirited turn to culture. Although the World Bank is increasingly comfortable with religion as conduit of development in a striking return to colonial missionary work (Clarke 2007), can it use its honed powers at selective incorporation (Rademacher and Patel 2002) to see snake-goddesses as antidotes for and insurance against snakebites? Is the Bank's move to re-situate development's affinities with culture and religion a break in the otherwise constantly refurbished myth of modernity's rupture from tradition? Or, when push comes to shove, will the 'stubbornly superstitious' villager remain guilty of 'blind' beliefs, and be subjected to discipline and exclusion?

Much of the chapter is dedicated to an ethnographic analysis of belief in Manasa in rural Bengal, studying the articulations between rural healthcare systems and modern medicine, healing practices and 'good' doctors, superstition and antidotes. Here I develop the insights into Manasa worship provided by historians and anthropologists of religion. In A. K. Ramanujan and Edward Dimock's account of the Manasa legend, she is described in the classic split terms common to representations of Hindu goddesses — she has a capacity for destruction and regeneration (Dimock 1962; Dimock and Ramanujan 1964).[3] Feminist theorists of South Asian religion have provided an exemplary critique of this split representation of the ideal Hindu woman mirrored in goddesses by focusing on everyday practices and segregated oral practices where complex relationships and creative play with norms of womanhood, sexuality, and domination were articulated (Raheja and Gold 1994).

With similar attention to indeterminacy, Manasi Dasgupta and Mandakranta Bose have analysed the Manasa tale foregrounding the themes of sovereignty of feminine energy (*sakti*) and women's powers of moral persuasion (2000: 148–49). These authors argue that the lasting popularity of this tale is because of its capacity to capture the fundamental ambiguity of women's power in a patriarchal society where men have to endorse women's mysterious powers and moral strength for the latter to be considered powerful. The tale also points to the ethical indeterminacy of norms (*ibid.*: 159). In different moments of the story, we learn that the powerful male and female figures are both subjugated by and autonomous from social ideologies and the divine control of gods (*ibid.*: 156). The moral of the story for Dasgupta and Bose is this ethical indeterminacy whereby despite the 'the enslavement of humanity to unjust gods', human action can and does on occasion transcend enslavement when people find grounds for common affection despite patriarchal customs and social control (*ibid*.: 159).

Apart from lessons for understanding women's power and suffering in a patriarchal society, the legend of Manasa also offers revealing attention to political–economic locations of her worshippers as well as those who neglected her worship. While recognising the significant gender dimensions of Manasa worship and its historical tie to the battle to establish the worship of female goddesses (*sakti*) and recognising the injustices women face in a patriarchal world, in this chapter I attempt to situate her worship in the political and economic context of its practice. Here too, ethical indeterminacy lies at the core of the story for the poor are required to worship her in ways that nourish cooperation, sharing, and interaction among people otherwise segregated by social ideologies and inequalities.

Studying people's belief in Manasa made me recognise that the secularism of development continues to blind critical examination of popular religion. In the context of West Bengal, mistaken recognition of the meaning of Manasa as illiterate villagers' stubborn belief in superstition misses notions of health, collectivity, and development. This misrecognition speaks of alienation and exclusion from both capitalist history and representational equality. Not only does this produce the enchantments that Dube refers to, it also obscures our under-standing of alternate and more rooted social collectivities and knowledge that can fortify struggles for equality in a time of capital. By attending to the political–economic aspects of her worship, I do not mean to reduce Manasa to a set of material concerns and produce a functionalist explanation for the meaning of 'the time of gods' within the 'time of capital' (Chakravarty 2000). Rather my aim is to highlight how the histories of power that are animated in the world of Manasa worship coexist and intersect today with other histories of power (such as a modern healthcare system) that compete as ideology, source of inequality and subjugation, ethics, and faith for her worshippers.

My research of Manasa as antidote and insurance against snakebites also shows that lived religion is an important but not sole cultural register for rural social life and political critique. Lived religion provides an epistemological system that aggrandises critique of government hospitals, private clinics, and inaccessible health care. Belief in Manasa's power and respect for ancestral rule and knowledge historically precedes and exceeds an encounter with modern healthcare. Moreover, Manasa worship currently coexists as cultural register with people's trenchant critiques of privatisation of healthcare and discrimination by hospital workers in West Bengal. Villagers I spoke to demanded equipped rural health centers with better attitudes among its doctors, even as they stated unambiguously the limits and irrationality of allopathic medicine.[4] I argue through the ethnography that certain forms of belief in health and healing bear ambivalent relations to multiple and intersecting, if unequal, histories of power.

By way of a conclusion, I present a contrast between the belief in Manasa and another context of belief that revolves equally around health, risk, survival, and love — the recently liberalised health and life insurance industry marketed to urban Indians. This contrast allows me to return to Dube's concept of 'enchantments of modernity' and consider the kinds of mobilisations and socialisations which produce the superstitions that persuade consumption of 'national' and 'modern' health and life insurance products. Through this comparison, my aim is to recognise the degree to which modern privatised health insurance and Manasa worship might be two different forms of insurance — similar in what they provide, while relying upon the construction of distinct social formations.

My argument is not simply that Manasa is the kind of worship or belief that flourishes in contexts of suffering, although this is in part her function. My point is that she cannot be reduced to a form of alienation. She produces knowledge about uncertainty, the inexplicable, and the unquestionable dimensions of life while constructing collectivity in ways that help weather suffering. The task for the social scientist interested equally in historical difference, social inequality, and social justice is to understand what lessons for addressing social inequality and constructing social justice lie within daily practices of rural moderns.

Death, Distance, and Expertise

In the past, I have always insisted on semi-structured interviews with individuals, conducted one at a time. Over and over again, in the four different villages where I conducted interviews about Manasa, this proved impossible. My research assistant was Lata Mondol, a leading JS activist in this region. We began interviews in her village and travelled to three other contiguous villages with which she was equally familiar through her work. She took me to the households she thought would best be able to provide information, and people in those households assigned me to talk to particular family members. Typically I was directed to speak to women, older kin, and on occasion, the patriarch of the household. Yet, listeners gathered quickly no matter where we sat and they could not help but intervene. Lata tried to request silence and sequence, but I had never encountered this kind of eagerness before. The interviews turned into semi-structured discussions, focusing sometimes on one person's commentaries, and turning into a cacophony of responses at other times. This was neither focus group, nor group discussion, nor individual interview — but a combination of formats. I requested only that they try not to drown out each other's words, considering the limited hearing capacity of my recording device. I spoke with 25 individuals in four different villages in the Kulpi block of South 24 Parganas district. In addition to these interviews and field notes, I draw on secondary sources such as census and survey data.

Even though I knew that rural 'remoteness' was constructed feature of place, stories of death from snake-bites belied this kind of deconstruction (Tsing 1993; Pigg 1997). Villagers were ambivalent about the distance between city and village, variously expressed in relief, anger, and fear.But during the monsoons, this ambivalence turned into unmitigated anger and helplessness. In the Sundarbans, the monsoons drastically change people's relation to mobility because time spent on travel increases exponentially. This is especially true in the villages where I did my research where most roads are not made of asphalt or even brick. Unlike the terrain further south towards deltaic Bay of Bengal, navigation here is not primarily reliant on rivers and boats. In the monsoons, residents of Pathar Pratima and Kulpi blocks tended to brave the outside only for their most pressing needs.

The dark, heavy silt of this region turns the landscape into a massive pit of clay. Everyone is forced to walk barefoot and pull clothes up at least till the knee, taking one slow, sticky, slippery step after the other. Getting produce to the market becomes a daily struggle and economising on time an absolute challenge. While human mobility is slowed down, snakes slither across village paths as they are flushed out of the ground during the monsoons. While those working in paddy fields and shrimp farms are particularly vulnerable, the danger cuts across class divisions. If you are bitten by a snake during the monsoons, it would take three times as long as it would normally take to get to a hospital that has the antidote. As one landless woman from a Hadi[5] neighbourhood put it invoking the JS play in her speech, 'I mean if snakes are primarily in the village, and the medicine is in the cities, then by the time you reach the city, you can harvest the vegetables you have sown!' She laughed in disgust. I asked her what change she imagined might help. She said:

> If there is a health centre here it will be helpful. By the time we take people for treatment, they die. Other than that, the roads in villages are so inconvenient that by the time you take people you will die. [...] all this path here was full of mud (*pointing all around her hut and the neighborhood path around her pond*), and you couldn't even cycle over it. So you have to carry the person if you want to take them anywhere. The person dies half way along the way. Look at that tubewell there! (*It is not more than hundred meters away*). In the monsoons, mud upto your waist. Women can't bring water. So just to get water from there, it is such a problem. So, if you have to take patients to the doctor carrying them on your back, you can imagine.

Prasad Sardar, a young man belonging to a landless family from Kulpi block and a leading JS activist asked: 'The people who are in brick buildings, in two storied or five storied or ten storied buildings — will they be bitten by snakes?' Prasad has been a day-labourer for much of his life doing everything from selling *alta* and *sindur* in villages, consumer goods on trains, and picking almost invisible shrimp larvae from muddy deltaic waters. In 2000, he described to me how his nephew died of a snakebite.

> It had bitten him at dawn. He was still alive. I mean, by then of course he was foaming at the mouth. We took him to the village clinic and they told us he has to be taken to Calcutta immediately. But there are no provisions for a vehicle from the hospital to take the patient to the city. They couldn't even tell us where, which hospital to take him. The thing is we are poor. We don't have the capacity to immediately shell out two, three thousand rupees and rent a vehicle that will take him to the city. We just don't have that capacity. I mean we have to first collect that kind of money, then find and hire the vehicle, then go to the city

> and find a hospital. I mean it's a huge, long, process . [...] So, while we were taking him [...] [*he finishes the thought in silence*]

For Prasad who lives in a hut which is a five-minute walk from the state highway running from Diamond Harbour to Kakdwip, there is an unbearable reality to distance and the way in which common needs turn into extraordinary emergencies.

For the cluster of four villages that I did research in within Kulpi block, the closest primary health center was in Belpukur (between 5 to 15 kilometres away depending on the village). Karanjali has two sub-centres (between 7–15 kms away depending on the village) and the closest hospital is in Kulpi town which is up to 30 kilometres away from the furthest of these villages. Corroborating interview accounts, Tables 7.1 and 7.2 draw on 2001 Census data to show that the sparse distribution of health centres among villages in Kulpi block make the distances to these centres from any given village quite vast.

Table 7.1: Distribution of Health Centres

No. of inhabited villages in Kulpi block	*Total number of villages with health centres in the village*		*No. of villages with allopathic dispensary*		*No. of villages with primary health centre within village*		*No. of villages with primary health sub-centre within village*	
	1991	*2001*	*1991*	*2001*	*1991*	*2001*	*1991*	*2001*
172	**1**	**1**	**1**	**7**	**1**	**5**	**2**	**29**

Source: Census of India 2001

Table 7.2: Distance to Health Centre in kilometers if not available within village

Health centre < 5 kms	*Health centre between 5–10 kms*	*Health centre between 10+kms*
51 villages in Kulpi block	**64** villages in Kulpi block	**52** villages in Kulpi block

Source: Census of India 2001

It is worth recalling that monsoons multiply these distances exponentially. This is the situation despite the fact that the World Bank has invested in the West Bengal health sector since the early 1990s (Soman 2002). Diamond Harbour and Kulpi towns (the closest towns to these villages) are notorious sites of mushrooming private clinics that charge absurd prices for entirely unregulated medical treatment. For patients who need surgical treatment that no shaman can claim to do, selling or mortgaging land, cows, and others assets, or going into debt are the only way to pay.[6]

In another interview I conducted with Prasad in 2008, he told me of the poor quality of facilities, 'the doctor stays for two hours, rather than the mandated six.' Typically, health centres have medicines like paracetamol and antacid but the life-saving drugs such as medicines for dog-bites, snakebites, in his words, 'the medicines that are very important, you need them immediately, you don't get those in villages.' I asked 'Can't these medicines be kept in the village?'

> **Prasad**: That is our question. There are no medicines. That's why people are inclined towards *ojha*, *guneen*, (*shamans and other indigenous healers*) towards god. Now what happens with these is that most people die. This is what happens.

Prasad's view of shamans is that villagers suffer from a lack of consciousness because they suffer from a lack of options. I have heard this critique of traditional healing at JS meetings before. For example, at a Human Rights Committee meeting in Srirampur in the summer of 2005, one JS leader seemed to reduce traditional healing practices to superstition when he said 'We have to fight superstition with the belief that jaundice needs a doctor and not a string of sticks.' Like Prasad, this member, who led the Committee in his region, sometimes viewed doctors and shamans as mutually exclusive beliefs, defining one goal of their human rights and development work as making the transition from 'a string of sticks' to a doctor. While they emphasised an unequal system of rural healthcare, such statements also misrecognised a long history of indigenous health practices and goddesses of health in people's lives, posed the access to modern healthcare in mutually exclusive relation to lived religions, and neglected the fact that villagers' often had coexisting, complex beliefs in modern medicine and 'traditional' healing while critiquing the limits of each in its contemporary practice.

I asked Prasad what JS had done to address the problem of healthcare.

> **Researcher**: Have you told politicians and leaders about this?
>
> **Prasad**: We show it through our plays. [...] We have also taken these issues to various health departments and offices. We have submitted

deputations saying that at least snake-bite medicines should be kept in the village health centres. They listen, but they don't devote any work to it whether it is the local government or the state.

Researcher: Maybe the thing is that these medicines are not found in the villages because they need refrigeration. And there is no electricity in the villages.

Prasad: Well that's what the hospitals say. But I think that if it takes refrigeration to keep these medicines in the village, then that is what should be done. After all, these medicines are most needed in villages. There is no electricity. Surely they can make any kind of alternate arrangements (*bikolpo byaboshta*) for electricity to make sure that these crucial medicines are available. They say often that we don't have a fridge and you need a fridge for antidotes. But if our government wants to have refrigeration for this kind of purpose, do you think they cannot do it? These are simply lame excuses (*shudhumatro ojuhaat*).

Researcher: You think they are doing it on purpose?

Prasad: I think the issue is actually that I have my suspicions whether our government or the people in power actually consider villagers human. We live like cows and goats. *Somehow* think of the absolute minimum needs and give it to them, or deny them these things. Give it or not, it all speaks of the same [attitude] (*Dile o dao, na dile o na, byapar ta eki*). And yet, it is with villagers that they constitute their collective (*othocho gramer lokeder niye i oder shongothon*).

For Prasad, tolerating healing by shamans, inaccessible and unaffordable urban healthcare, 'quack' doctors, poor rural health centres, and lack of political will to change the situation, all ultimately come down to a dehumanisation of villagers in the eyes of governmental power. None of the steps in altering the situation seem insurmountable to him.

After all, West Bengal is known as one of few states in India that generates surplus electricity which makes it an attractive port for capital investment. Moreover, Kulpi town,[7] which is a small port town in Kulpi block, was in the news as it was slotted to become an economic zone with room for an 'environmentally friendly' ship-breaking yard, developed port facilities, and an integrated hub of port activity (I-Maritime Research and Consulting Division 2003).[8] The juxtaposition of pouring capital into certain infrastructural developments such as ports for agricultural retail and export, rather than roads and healthcare for villagers is palpable if you live in Kulpi block of rural West Bengal.

In Praise of Manasa

Every year, at the very end of the Bengali month of *Bhadra* (roughly translated to 15 August–15 September of the Gregorian calendar) and the beginning of the month of *Ashween* (roughly 15 September –15 October), households in the south 24 Parganas region engage in an elaborate three-day worship of Manasa. This is at the end of the rainy season, while the *aman* crop is growing and a month before its harvest.[9] This puja is alternately referred to as Manasa puja (worship of Manasa) and *ranna* puja (worship through, or of, cooking). This puja is done in the 'chosen' households where some family member has seen Manasa in their dreams and been instructed to do her puja. The dreams themselves bore remarkable similarity across villages. Once she appears in a dream, the puja was done every year and passed down to children. Passing of the 'fire' from parents to children enables the patrilineage to continue worshipping Manasa. Once you have the fire, or once the puja is done in a household, no one can ever choose to skip it. I asked what might happen if someone did miss it out of some compulsion, and I was repeatedly told that no one would dare to find out. Durga and Kali pujas, other goddesses in the Bengali pantheon, simply did not command compulsion of this magnitude.

On the last day of the *Bhadra* month, men and women in the household prepare for a night of cooking for the following day's cold feast. The preparations include buying new cooking pots (earlier clay pots, now metallic), new kitchen baskets, carving out a new oven in the mud floor of the kitchen. As every interviewee describing the requirements emphasised, 'everything has to be new.' They added that those things could be subsequently used daily, but for the Manasa puja, once a year, they had to use new things for the kitchen and for the puja (worship). Men of the household would do the shopping for the puja, buying vegetables and foodstuffs not already grown, saved, or otherwise acquired. They talked about doing other preparatory work such as cutting the wood for the cooking and the puja fire and cutting the various vegetables and fruit for the meal. A landless young man in the low-caste, Midde neighbourhood emphasised how household tasks took on an almost meditative dimension during this puja, 'Those who are doing this, this is an incredibly powerful thing. When the women are cooking for her, they don't speak. 'When we cut vegetables for her cooking, we don't speak.' Some women told me that someone had to recite Manasa *mangal* while cooking.[10]

As soon as the sun rises, cooking would have to cease, the oven would be cooled down with water, household members would have to bathe before the puja was started. The cold feast gets its name from the food cooked all night and eaten cold for the rest of that day by kin and other invited guests. On the third day, the oven is lit again for the feast of hot food. The idea is to follow the cold feast with a hot one the next day featuring steamy rice with vegetables, and other meat dishes if the household is able and inclined. If meat is affordable, the expectation is that ducks are sacrificed for Manasa's hot feast. This cycle completes the three-day puja. Worshippers of Manasa are required to maintain the scale of the puja at the level at which they started it. Bringing down the scale was believed to surely incur her wrath. If you cooked six vegetable dishes to go with the fermented rice in the first year, every year Manasa would expect at least six, or more, but she would not tolerate less.[11]

The idea is to dedicate to her, each according to ability; share the blessed food among household members, kith, kin, and other invited guests; and also commit to maintaining this degree of giving and receiving through time. Yet, at other points in conversation, the same interviewees also asserted that what was important was doing the puja every year, even if it meant you could afford to serve nothing more than fermented rice to Manasa and the immediate family. In multiple interviews, there seemed to be no contradiction in knowing that it was compulsory to worship her every year, and that it was equally dangerous to do the puja out of pure compulsion. Sanatan warned: 'Say, if you don't feel like doing the cooking, you are just forcing yourself to do it, then the next day you will see a snake dead in the *panta* (fermented rice) or in the vegetables. That means Ma is saying you don't have to do this. This has also been seen.' Need, belief, conviction, and desire coalesce to create worthy devotion.

The mind is oriented towards Manasa puja a month in advance. People start balancing immediate needs with the shelf-life of resources. They put aside a pumpkin here, a coconut there 'in Ma's name.' The emphasis on begging complements the importance placed on the compulsory nature of Manasa puja. Quite simply, 'This is a puja that is compulsory. Even if you have to beg.' I provoked an explanation by saying 'So Ma Manasa is demanding? Stubborn?' The answer came immediately from Sharmila, a devotee, 'Oppressive (*atyachari*).' When I pressed her to tell me whether all classes worship Manasa and why, she said only the poor initially and later smiled and said she didn't know why and still later argued: 'Maybe god loves us more. That's why she likes to eat in our homes more. Other than that I can't give an answer.'

In Scheduled Caste neighbourhoods (Keora) with largely poor households who have no land, where men migrate to work in Kolkata or Bangalore, or do daily wage labour on shrimp farms, I asked people how they procure things for the puja and what if they can't afford it in a given year.

> **Rita**: Still you have to buy it. You have no choice. However, difficult it might be. I mean in any case, we have to find a way of bringing rice into the home right? This is the same thing. Somehow, in any way you can, you have to bring rice to cook for Manasa even if it means begging for it.

To Rita, thinking of feeding Manasa is the same as the compulsion to feed yourself. In other words, just as you would not give up on survival, you cannot give up on feeding Manasa. When I asked Vishnu, another person in Rita's neighbourhood why the goddess orders people to worship her, he said 'Maybe she ordered them, or perhaps she asks those who can't eat, to beg for food for her worship? Somehow you have to do the puja.' Rita and Vishnu tied respect for the struggle to survive and subsist with respect for and worship of Manasa. In another Scheduled Caste neighbourhood (Midde), when I asked how people procure things for the puja, they emphasised the relational compulsions of beggar and giver while giving higher meaning and collectively fortifying hope.

> **Researcher**: How do you procure them (jogaar)? Do you buy things?
>
> **Tanusree**: Yes we do buy things. We don't have much of our own, so we have to buy it. Or, say sometimes you have to ask people for it because you can't buy everything. Say for example, you don't have rice at home, you have to ask people for at least one fist of rice and do it [the puja]. Or, if you don't have vegetables, or if you lack something, then you have to ask people for it.
>
> **Paromita**: As long as you use ma's name, they will have to give.
>
> **Uttara**: When they hear ma's name, people will give.

Manasa thus dignifies begging by compelling the giver rather than highlighting the compulsion of the beggar. Bhakti thus gives dignity to need. As Tanusree put it:

> **Tanusree**: Bhakti is everything, right? You have to have a good mind and do this. If you don't have good bhakti then you will see harm.
>
> **Researcher**: What do you mean by good bhakti?
>
> **Tanusree**: Good bhakti meaning I might give a tiny bit, but I have to give it with a clear conscience (*porishkar bibek*), with peace (*shaanti*), with a pure heart (*bhalo mon*). I have seen that if we don't have much, somehow we are able to improvise (*jogaar*) and find things for the puja. Leave it to the goddess. I don't know how it happens. But we find it.

In other words, while Manasa has high expectations for her puja, she is equally the resourceful and surprising provider. Perhaps most significantly, she is the source of ethical action of giving with a 'clear conscience, with peace, with a pure heart'. This notion of 'magical' and ethical provisioning of food is a common means of combining religious worship, offering food to gods, and redistributing food within South Asian communities. When I asked the question about why Manasa demands this mainly of poorer households, an elderly lady in the Midde neighbourhood emphasised not Manasa's love for them as Sharmila had, but rather their love for the goddess: 'Poor people have it [the puja] more. But poor people don't mind begging to be able to do the puja.' Manasa puja simultaneously dignifies giving food to those who beg for it and inculcates an ethic of subsistence and sharing in the village community — by displacing the compulsion onto the fear and wrath of the mother, rather than the need of the family. Such findings about inculcating and negotiating social, ecological and subsistence ethics are far from new or specific to Bengal (Scott 1976, 1987; Gold and Gujar 2002; Gold 2009).

Those who are better off in the village tend to interpret the worship of Manasa differently, explaining their neglect of her worship in a statement of classic multiculturalism in rural Bengal. That is, there are different worshipping traditions for various communities within a village. Mukesh is a middle-aged man who has worked for an adult literacy NGO for 23 years. His family owns ancestral land and he never has to worry about buying rice or other food supplies. He said,

> It's not that it [belief in Manasa] isn't there [in rich households]. Maybe they don't have this tradition. Not everyone prays to Kali. Some people worship Christ, some Kali, some Ramkrishna and some do Manasa. This is just a question of personal peace of mind. Which turns into a tradition. It's not anything more than that.

Pushing him further, I asked him whether he was not afraid of snakes since he does not worship Manasa. His response was as follows:

> Well, the thing is that there is fear of snakes and there is also not a fear of snakes. Everyone has fear of snakes and there is also no fear of snakes. If snakes bite us then of course humans will die. Now those who are completely unconscious (*oggyo*) their thinking is different. Those who have education they think differently. Or, the thinking of a modern, scientific mind is different (*adhunik, boigyanik monta alada*). For instance, we read the newspapers, we watch the news on TV, radio. Or, in various meetings and workshops we know from that, that 50% of snake-bite victims die of fear. After all, not all snakes are poisonous. Now we can see from that the rest die of poison. So in the villages we have *ojhas*.[12] And they bring the poison down. And the other thing is that it is only in Diamond Harbor that you can find the serum. So what happens is that people just take the patient to the ojha instead of trying to go all the way to Diamond Harbour. But I can say that I don't really understand how you can cure with chants. And that which I don't have enough understanding of I cannot say I believe or not.

Mukesh asserted education, consciousness, and rationality as the explanation of his belief in medicine and his agnostic attitude to *ojha* (shamans). According to him, in addition to being dissuaded by the immense distance to the hospital, the lack of education and rationality took 'unconscious' villagers to shamans before they went to hospitals. He believes that the risk-averse poor will choose the local *ojha* to the serum available in the unreliable hospital far away. But he was also convinced that a hospital in the neighbourhood would not be enough to make the puja stop — consciousness-raising and education would have to complement the arrival of the hospital. In this school of thought, the moral economy of the risk-averse peasant is not a 'mere' function of their structural location. Even once access to biomedicine is proximate, the rationality of adopting and using biomedical notions of health still require pedagogical persuasion.

Despite the gestures towards multiculturalism and agnosticism, Mukesh made classic statements about the stubbornly superstitious villager still surviving in remote areas. 'Can you see too many ojhas these days? It is because people's belief in them has died down that their numbers have decreased. In the remote areas there are people who believe in ojhas. We have not been able to bring consciousness to people.' In his view, the *ojha* is a cynical practitioner who is conscious of capitalising on 'blind belief'.

> There was a well known ojha, who treated patients alone in a room. And then did the rest of *jhar-phook* in public (*hocus-pocus with linguistic reference to broom and blowing air*). Then later in an interview that ojha said that humans have a blind belief (*ondho bishaash*) that if snakes bite, then ojhas alone can bring the poison down.

Later, when pressed to go beyond multiculturalism and the claim that the uneducated worship Manasa, he offered a popular Bengali saying (*gareeber ghora rog*) which asserts that the poor have all the illnesses of the world. He explained that this did not mean that illnesses did not afflict the rich, but rather shows that the effects are greater for the poor, because the treatment, costs, contacts with Members of Legislative Assembly who guarantee a hospital bed, are relatively inaccessible for them. Meanwhile the rich have an entirely different set of options:

> I mean I saw Tarun when his father was ill. At that time, when they had to figure out where to find two thousand rupees, they were going crazy with that.[13] But at the same time, there are people who will not keep their parents in the very hospital bed that Tarun was so desperate for. My father cannot stay on this bed. In the course of my work I have seen a lot of hospital situations you see. My father will have to stay in an AC [air-conditioned] room. That means that they have the ability to spend money on this.

For Mukesh, this comparison highlights why the poor fear illness as much as they do. In his sociological imagination, he explains this fear as the reason why they seek solace in the worship of goddesses of health such as Sitala, Manasa, Chandi, and Shashti. Before I turn to the Manasa legend, I return to interviewees in poorer neighbourhoods to show that their reliance on traditional healing was not mutually exclusive from their relation to biomedical healing systems.

The Ojha, Manasa, and the Hospital

Not all deaths from snakebites were hastened by distance from antidotes and health centres. Like the incident I began this chapter with, a number of people told me of children dying because the parents didn't notice when the snake bit the child, or didn't understand why their child was crying because the children themselves could not speak yet, or did not know what had happened till it was too late. Still others died because they did not know the name of the snake and doctors either refuse or delay treating victims if they don't know what kind of snake bit their patients. In other words, doctors and hospitals assume that victims will see the snake, recognise it, be able to describe it, or better still name it. It also assumes presence of daylight and electricity at night (which is rare in these regions). Rita Sardar (Prasad's sister-in-law) was particularly troubled at the thought of children being bitten. 'Now, they are children, they play in all kinds of places. Sometimes in piles of straw, sometimes in bamboo forests, in all sorts of places. They are young. They don't know what snake bit them. They can't recognize them.' Her inability to constantly keep track of children's whereabouts aggravated her feelings about doctors' expectations.

This tall order from medical institutions compounded with the distance travelled to get there explained why most respondents thought it sensible not to waste time on hospitals. There was just one case recounted to me where a man did not believe in shamans. Sixty-eight-year-old Lalita Sardar (Prasad's mother) told me that 'The snake bit him at night. And he went at night to the hospital. He killed the snake, put it in a bag, and then took a van. He went in a motor van to Diamond [Harbour]. And towards daylight he died.' Each factor highlighted by Lalita signals this victim's choices while situating him in class and education terms. This man insisted on going to the hospital rather than to the village *guneen*. He had the presence of mind to take the snake along *and* he could afford a motor van run by private businessmen who routinely capitalise on midnight emergencies. Despite succumbing to poison, this man was able to choose things that Lalita herself would not choose, or be able to choose for financial reasons.

Lalita's daughter-in-law Rita reinforced the moral of the story by abstracting particular details from it: 'He even had the snake with him and it was still no use. You have to say what snake bit him and without it they will give you all kinds of medicines. So by the time they try out all the medicines, the patients can die. [...] That's why we go to the *guneen*.' I asked them to explain what the *guneen* does to patients. This is how the conversation proceeded:

> **Rita**: They use their hands to sense how far the poison has traveled. And then they bring the poison down. Then they have medicine and they feed that medicine to you.
>
> **Reseacher**: Is that Ma Manasa's medicine?
>
> **Rita**: Yes.
>
> **Researcher**: What medicine is it?[14]
>
> **Rita**: I wouldn't be able to tell you the name.
>
> **Lalita**: Those who know medicine hardly tell patients the medicine names. If I know it, I will not tell you that if you take the roots of this plant, it will cure you.

Although Lalita's son Prasad, like Mukesh, seemed to think that the *lack* of medicines and proximate health centres went far in explaining belief in god and shamans, his mother and sister-in-law had a *comparative* mode of explaining their choices.

The exchanges quoted above highlight comparative experiences of healing expertise in addition to factors such as distance, cost of travel, and hospital costs which combine to make health centres and hospitals an unreliable option. While doctors seem to irrationally rely on patients for names of snakes before administering medicine, the *guneen* gives medicine regardless of the snake. With the indigenous healer, people are assured of some treatment. This healer's expertise and faith in the power of his own business is reinforced because they refuse to reveal the names of the medicines. This is because the medicines are derived from local plants which people might begin to administer for themselves depriving the traditional doctor of business. If this is *guneen* control over their trade and profiteering, it also reveals confidence in the efficacy of their knowledge and skills. To patients and their family, this is surely a significant marker of expertise.[14]

This is not to say that *guneens* always recuperate victims of snakebites and other ailments. The fact that they fail is widely known and acknowledged. The explanation for it is typically that they are bad healers. A bad one is understood as plain incompetent or as holding a personal grudge for the patient or their family, and letting it interfere with effective practice. Like Stacey Leigh Pigg's study of shamans in Nepal, the comparative perceptions of effectiveness and expertise of medicine and the *guneen* in West Bengal too, is ultimately a matter of belief based on what set of experiences and circumstances make up the foundation for a given judgment. Madhuri Haldar, an elderly lady from a middle-class household in a Hadi neighbourhood in Baras village, summed up her hierarchy of options 'take them to a *biswasi guneen* (trustworthy *guneen*) or straight to the hospital.'

In each interview, regardless of what else I had been told, I asked whether the presence of a well-stocked health centre right near their homes might result in Manasa puja dying out. In retrospect, the question reveals more about my assumptions than anything else. But the response was unequivocal and unanimous. Every time, people responded saying that this puja would never end. Our ancestors have done it, and we will never stop it. Manasa clearly has a longer and integral history in these lives than provider of insurance or healthcare alone. But the functionalist comparison in the question proved fruitful because it highlighted that some did not trust the existing health centres, some did not trust modern medicine, and some trusted modern medicine more than they trusted *ojhas*. For example, one set of respondents argued that well-stocked government rural health centres with doctors who cared to treat (and touch) low-caste, poor people would make a big difference. In other words, health centres needed to be modernised to treat patients of various class and caste equally.

Researcher: If there is a health centre in the village?

Madhavi: That will be good.

Daughter in law: That will be good. Now in Jamtala people are going to private clinics. If they go to hospitals, the supervisor sitting there they give you diarrheoa medicine for fever. There isn't a doctor to diagnose the problem. She asks me 'what's happened to you?' I say fever and she gives some medicine for stomach problems. I mean unless you inspect the patient with your own hands how can you diagnose the problem? You didn't even touch the person? No they send you to the private clinics. Now we are poor people. Can we pay sixty rupees, sixty five rupees, seventy rupees, hundred rupees to be treated in private clinics?

> If the government has built a hospital and the doctor sits in private clinics instead, then how will we manage?

These are critiques of the continuing practices of untouchability that deny adequate healthcare to low-caste patients because the doctors refuse to touch them for medical examination. Madhavi is equally frank about how the privatisation of the healthcare system discriminates on the basis of class. At the same time, she also criticised the flourishing trade of 'traditional healers' minutes later when she said 'all kinds of people have learned the science of possession (*guneen bidya*)'. For her, like Prasad, if health centres were built, then people's reliance upon traditional healers would surely diminish. But for her, unlike Prasad, the belief in Manasa would not waver, whether or not there were hospitals and health centres around.

Manasa was equally a protector against harm, risk, and uncertainty that came *from* rural health centres and modern medicine. Consider this excerpt:

> **Lalita**: No way! This puja will continue for twelve eras ahead of us. When I die.[...]
>
> **Rita**: No, no! If there is a rural health centre.[...]
>
> **Researcher**: One at a time so I can catch each of you on tape.
>
> **Rita**: Ma, hold on (*to her mother in law, Lalita*). If there is a health centre here then perhaps when the snake bites we will go to the health centre. Then we will be able to go to the health centre and that's true. But there is no guarantee that if it bites and we have medicine that we will survive. It is only when you have Manasa Devi's medicine that you survive. It's good if there is a health centre. But then you still have to tell the name of the snake. And if it takes too long to get the right medicine, then the patient can die. And here the *guneen* will not ask for the snake's name. They will use the power of their hands and do something. And whatever it is, it is a puja of our ancestors, they will not be able to abandon it.

Apart from reiterating her commitment to Manasa and value for ancestor rule, Rita also reveals that snakebites are a special kind of affliction, one that deserves special treatment by *guneen* and *ojha*, the conduits of Ma Manasa's medicine for her worshippers. Health and healthcare simply cannot have a one-size that fits all treatment philosophy. The problems vary in nature and so too must the mode of medicine.

The Suffering of the Rich

While traditional healers are judged in contrast with biomedical provisions in rural healthcare, Manasa worship is a different story. One might argue as Mukesh did that Manasa worship by the poor is eminently receptive to a Marxist interpretation of religion — necessary protection for those who have slim means of security from a range of illnesses. My conversations do suggest that the poor worship Manasa because she expects it of them. Yet, the Manasa legend itself is about the complete destruction of property and family that befalls a rich and ostensibly protected merchant who has seven sons (a great boon in a patriarchal society). The legend, as known to people socialised in the oral tradition of this region, tells the story of Manasa's birth, her quest to be 'worshiped in the world of men', the promise of Siva's help in accomplishing this, and the constant hindrance she faced from Siva's devoted disciple, the merchant Chand Sadagar, in accomplishing her goal. The legend focuses on her power as bearer of snake poison and destroyer of the same as the combined means of overcoming Chand Sadagar's revulsion for her.

According to the legend, Chand Sadagar was a rich merchant and trader in medieval Bengal who is simply repulsed at the thought of worshipping Manasa. Given his wealth and widespread influence, Manasa is convinced that if he worships her, everyone else on earth would as well. To convince him, she strikes at random, killing people with her poison and saving them with her 'soma' — the sacred liquid that renders poison powerless. In this, Manasa represents the core principle of the medical philosophy of homeopathy, as Dimock and Ramanujan note: 'with poison do I slay thy poison' (1964: 301).[15] In the course of the story, Manasa destroys Chand's enormous estate, wrecks his ships at sea, and kills his seven sons. She also saves Chand from death and later in the narrative, saves one of the sons called Lakhindar because of Behula's wifely devotion for Lakhindar *and* her steadfast devotion to Manasa. It is only because of Behula's devotion that she sets Lakhindar afloat on a banana bark platform on the river, which convinces Manasa to bring him back to life. Eventually, she saves Chand's six other sons as well. These demonstrations of her abilities to take and give life finally win Chand's respect and fear although in the end, he only promises to worship her with his left hand since the right is devoted to Siva's worship.

Historians have interpreted Chand as a symbolic representation of Siva where he embodies the essential humanity of Siva, his power and influence, his struggle in the face of something more powerful, and his defeat in dignity. I argue that apart from insight into the history of Hinduism and the growing worship of feminine power, the way in which interviewees in contemporary Bengal described the story and the meaning of Manasa in their lives moves me to consider other lessons as well. Chand is also symbolically taken to represent the rich and influential who are believed to be and believe themselves to be protected from life's random disasters. In fact, this seems to me to be one of the core messages of the Manasa story itself. In one version of the legend, Neta, Manasa's companion, advises Manasa to make all people realise the unpredictability and uncertainty of suffering by subjecting them to suffering:

> Hear me, O merciful one. The snakes are your constant and powerful companions. [...] It is by your snakes that your worship will be established here on earth. Hear me, O Jagati: you can defeat no one except by showing him the consequences of your wrath. If he is not in trouble, no man in all three worlds will worship you. Therefore, O mother of serpents, slaughter your enemies! Show mercy only to those who worship you. As many men as you destroy, so many more will worship you (Dimock 1962: 318).

In this excerpt, Manasa is advised to kill people with her snake poison and her army of snakes, to put them in trouble so that they remember her. It is no accident that the key conflict in the legend is between her and a rich, influential trader devoted to a male god. One might argue that even here, a Marxist interpretation of religion is coded into this selection because Neta suggests that where there is suffering, there will be worship and god. However, even though Manasa is primarily worshipped among the poor, it is worth remembering that Neta's advice is given to the goddess of snakes (a relatively random source of harm that cuts across social strata). The Manasa legend is centrally about the destruction of property and family that befalls a rich and protected merchant. The legend and its continuing oral circulation is a striking example of the certainty of uncertainty, chance, and risk of harm, illness, and disaster. The recognition of human fallibility and vulnerability, as I see it, is the core purpose of worshipping Manasa. It is a reminder that we each are vulnerable — moments away from losing what we have or steps away from a bountiful blessing. Thus, as we pursue wealth and health, we must give, ask for, receive, and share in recognition of this uncertainty. Admittedly, while recognising Manasa as piety for piety's sake, I also find myself reading Manasa as one who ties recognition for uncertainty by compelling constructions of collectivity. Manasa's antidote in the face of this human vulnerability is to compel cooperation among the poor and give and take between people of disparate social classes.

Conclusion: Counting on Collectivity

I have argued that predominantly poor, low-caste households worship Manasa, while negotiating their demand for and critique of both biomedicine and traditional healers. Although the well-off and well-educated perceive this to be a result of need, survival, and lack of education, the worshippers themselves spoke of multiple, and sometimes contradictory inter-relationships between need, desire, conviction, and love for Manasa. No doubt she must be understood in contexts of grief and material distress emanating from an unequal, if not absent, healthcare system, inadequate communication infrastructure, and lack of electricity. Even with favourable Leftist policies where the political common sense is that the government is pro-poor, healthcare systems are defunct, and villagers in particular are far from free of class and caste discrimination.

In snakebite cases, doctors make literally impossible and irrational requirements of complete knowledge and control — they demand to know which snake bit, assume there is light and visibility at night in villages that have no electricity, expect that patients will get to hospitals on time and with enough cash in hand. For villagers living in South 24 Parganas, heading to the hospital entails putting faith in the possibility that there will be a doctor willing to treat and touch the patient — a faith often betrayed. This journey from moment of snakebite till the time that the doctor administers an antidote and the patient recovers or dies, is marked by a series of miracles and blind convictions that the system is likely to work for the poor, low-caste villager. That is a leap of faith that most villagers have learned to treat with scepticism. In part then, Manasa worship functions as adaptive strategy in the face of state neglect, privatisation of healthcare, and daily discrimination.

Villagers do not choose the traditional healer because they blindly believe in him or her. Rather, they refuse to choose hospitals blindly, knowing the demands of distance, money, and information. Nor do villagers always trust a traditional healer because they recognise their limited range of medical expertise, greedy profiteering, and personal vendettas for what they are. Even as Manasa's presence in lives precedes and exceeds the encounter with modern medicine, she herself is not free of devotee judgment since she is seen as oppressive, demanding, and devouring.

The 'enchantment of modernity' becomes apparent when we consider why *this* adaptive strategy is viewed as superstition whereas faith in biomedicine and life and health insurance is naturalised as rational and modern. In 2008, before heading to West Bengal to ask questions about Manasa, I spent a few days in Delhi. In the evenings, I was glued to the television, savouring Indian advertisements and catching up on the newest obsessions of the urban Indian. What stood out in early 2008 were endless advertisements for insurance companies. As I view them now, these advertisements in liberalising India are potent enchantments of modernity, mobilising faith in the ability to buy health and relatively certain futures while callously hiding from view deeply unequal access to medical care.

When I try to recall memorable insurance advertisements prior to 2008, I can recall one which was persistent from my visit in early 2007, and of course the Life Insurance Corporation of India (LIC) ones during school and college years.[16] The LIC was one of those rock-solid institutions of the Nehruvian developmental state — solemn, strong, and from a neoliberal perspective, downright stodgy. Its advertisements however conjured little. In 2008, these advertisements had a different mood. A revamped LIC promises to be there through 'rain or shine' in its advertisements. Others are more contained in telling audiences that while some things in life are unavoidable, insurance can help guard against most forms of misfortune or ill health. In all of these advertisements however, biomedicine's hidden affinities with faith are made apparent as they reveal the health insurance industry's enchanted and ideological assumptions about control over human life.

These advertisements told me that if I was the kind of person who understands the importance of combining healthy activities such as yoga and running on the treadmill with a demanding work life, then I should choose the Reliance India 'health and wealth' plan. Another company, Nationwide Insurance, has commercials that tell audiences that 'life comes at you fast' — that people grow old, that they get caught in extramarital affairs, and that your children could become rappers in foreign accents instead of being fluent in Hindi.[17] It asks the audience to be financially prepared to meet each of these possibilities that life might bring. Other companies such as Met Life India or ICICI Prudential offer to help you love your child by being prepared for every turn of life, every educational cost, every source of sadness that comes their way. ING Vysya Life Insurance advertisements explicitly warn against letting 'moments of happiness' — getting married, women holding letters of acceptance to MBA programmes, and new fathers holding their babies — turn into 'sinking feelings' of heavy (financial) burden. In each of these advertisements, humour plays a significant role in dissipating the crassness of exploiting images of love for children, youth, education, and security in old age. Like Mastercard advertisements in North America that tell you that money can't buy love even as they spell out exactly how much it might cost to express love, Indian insurance advertisements are blatant in exploiting fear as expression of love. Buying insurance mitigates fear while helping people express familial love and felt responsibilities.

In this narrative, the god of the consumer citizen is control. She is the heart of a heartless world because worshipping control in a free world presents the option of mastering (or suffering) the risks endemic to a free society. Perhaps expensive, but never extravagant, spending on insurance is prudent spending to plan against an uncertain future. The moral thing to do is to insure what is yours — your property, your future, your family. Recently the Guardian reported that the UN is considering micro-insurance schemes for farmers in Asia, Africa and Latin America to address the age-old problem of bad weather. Trials are on with 600,000 farmers in Kolhapur, India with funding from Bill and Melinda Gates Foundation where comic books are used to explain the schemes. These insurance plans emerge in times of heightened fears around climate change and uncertain weather patterns while the schemes themselves are tied to international climate change deals and treaties. They are founded upon the logic of providing low premiums in times of low risk. In this model of rationalising agricultural security, to not have insurance then is to be an irrational, inept, and immoral citizen — not a modern one. But should calamity hit you, what is it that insurance ensures? If Hurricane Katrina is anything to go by, insurance can't buy you the love of a president, judge, mayor, or the media even in times of greatest need. Certainly it doesn't always guarantee money from your insurance company. Did they simply capitalise on fear of risk, of the future, of uncertainty? Private insurance might simply be comfort in a comfortless world.

Consider that belief in private insurance companies is mandatory for the citizen who lives in and understands life within capitalist modernity. Rather than infuse capital to address unequal medical care, massive infusions of capital attempt to persuade citizens that their access to healthcare is only morally and materially available through increasingly privatised insurance. This is increasingly true in rural India where health insurance industry is taking off (Mukherjee 2008) while the central government attempts to relax caps on foreign direct investment in the insurance sector as a whole (Chandrashekhar 2009). All the while, health-care itself remains largely inaccessible to the poor, and neither modernised nor equalised. This normalisation of health insurance is considered rational, 'learning nothing' from the fraud and failures of national and multinational insurance companies (*ibid.*). Moreover, the normalisation of health insurance is considered rational even if we happen to recognise that faith in human ability to control death, uncertainty, and the future is a blind belief, a superstition — a foundational enchantment of enlightenment thinking. This should enable us to rethink the value-laden judgement of the label of superstition for traditional healing and Manasa worship. More importantly, it counters the assumption that superstition, rather than inequality, is obstructing development.

Does the fact that Manasa might be part adaptive strategy in face of material distress and state neglect mean that belief in her is simply 'false' consciousness in the absence of 'real' medical advance and equal access to medical care, replacing one mode of alienation with another? I think not. She is not merely an adaptive strategy because Manasa worship began well before an encounter with what we know as modern medicine. Today, villagers claim that Manasa worship will not die out despite the arrival of good health centres. This is echoed in Ralph Nicholas's study of surviving Sitala worship (the goddess of smallpox) in 1981, a decade after the widespread availability of the smallpox vaccination in rural Bengal. There is more to Sitala worship than inability to control this disease which still exists in rural areas of the state today. Nicholas's explanation is that popular religion accomplishes what science fails to do for humans: 'The sciences have not provided a root answer to the "why" of human suffering. It is to provide a meaningful, that is to say, fundamental and adequate — answer to the "why" of smallpox that Sitala comes to be fitted into the already crowded Bengal pantheon' (Nicholas 1981: 36).

Manasa helps the person suffering (frequently the poor) understand why they suffer and how to suffer. But cognitive control over material and social circumstances does not entirely capture what Manasa is about. She must also be recognised as agent of social formation and producer of knowledge. When I asked Madhuri, a devotee of Manasa, whether worshipping her saves people from snakes, she said 'That's in god's hands, how can I say anything. Our ancestors have been doing this puja, so that's what we do. That's god's hand. God perhaps thinks that I should be bitten here, so who am I to say "save me"? That's god's wish, ma.' In other words, even human worship cannot save you from snakes and she knows it. She ascribes agency to Manasa making a case for accepting parts of our world and life where the power and effect of causality, principles, and human will remain unknown and unknowable to humans. Manasa teaches people to know and recognise their fallibility in the face of uncertainty and risk — regardless of which system of healing treats their ailments. Further, precisely because they know the fallibility of modern medicine, the only antidote and insurance against uncertainty is *bhakti* and collectivity. The rituals of cooking together each according to their ability, dignifying begging by the poor, and giving by the rich for Manasa constructs collectivity in contexts of socioeconomic inequality while it reminds us all of unquestionable fallibility. To use insurance scheme-speak, in times of low risk, rather than charge low premiums, Manasa compels cooperation and sharing in preparation for times of high risk when the financial and emotional resources of the individual might prove woefully inadequate.

People nurture belief in Manasa as antidote and insurance against uncertainty through their *bhakti* and collectivity. She is an antidote and insurance because she helps form collectivity in the face of ultimately uncontrollable sources of illness and death — of which snakes are an important example in rural Bengal. Manasa worship offers a powerful lesson that for each of us, regardless of our immediate and apparent social and material environs, there are ultimately uncontrollable sources of illness and death. In the face of cosmic or ecological uncertainty (depending on our beliefs), she teaches us that having money to pay for a vehicle at midnight, or for hospital bills, or having the ability to buy expensive health insurance can be fragile fictions, brittle sources of comfort.

Does fatalism capture this view adequately? Mukesh, the educated well-to-do social worker said something similar relying on scientific rationality: 'If snakes bite us then of course humans will die.' And as Cecilia van Hollen is reminded all too painfully, despite being able to afford advanced healthcare in North America, 'the biomedical myth of the possibility of conquering death' is just that — a myth (2003: 217). Ultimately, whether we can survive a snake-bite is not entirely in our hands. All the more reason that those facing multiple disadvantages of class, caste, and gender seek comfort in collectivity, in the dignity and rationality of sharing, in proximate healthcare centres free of caste-discrimination — all the while calling upon divine protection. When leaders and activists of JS describe such belief as superstition, they miss a significant possibility of understanding collectivity embedded in lived religion. While they battle with government officials for access, quality, delivery of health services, in this case, they do not step off-stage, so to speak, to wage a concurrent struggle to count modes of healing and healthy societies that co-exist with the drastic need for biomedicine in rural Bengal. The collectivity that Manasa constructs does not count. The presumption of Manasa as superstition becomes another reason for defining development as accomplished only when we leave behind village culture. Rather than address material and representational inequality, dispossessing meanings in the life-world of the villager is a principle mechanism through which epistemic closure on the meaning of development is affected.

The larger question I raised in this chapter was: Does development's spirited turn to culture have room to understand how snake-goddesses might work as antidotes and insurance for frequent deaths from snakebites in rural Bengal? If what Manasa teaches us looks to development practitioners like superstition more than reason, traditional fatalistic thinking rather than 'modern' logic, blind belief rather than human reasoning, then perhaps the neoliberal 'turn' to culture is a contemporary variant of the embodied enchantments of modernity. Or perhaps, Manasa might become an insurance advertisers' icon or a World Bank emblem — their goddess of healing and comfort — counting on and profiting from collectivities not of their making. Now that's the spirit of capitalism.

✷

Notes

1. This play weaves numerous stories about panchayat corruption in distributing development in villages, migration for dangerous work in the cities, and lack of healthcare in villages. The larger message of the play was villagers' claim to the right to live and work in the countryside throughout the year.
2. For example, Akhil Gupta (1992, 2002) notes that social theories of childhood, progress, and development make little room for conceptualising reincarnation. He argues that theories of life course are foundational assumptions of capitalist modernity and its myriad contracts which rely on the conviction that an individual is allowed one life. Theories of time embedded in ideas of a life-course assume linear movement from birth through growth and maturity towards death as the final ending of an individual life. Linear time defines the careers of nations from birth, to take-off to advanced states as development. The idea that time moves forward then is inextricably linked with one of the central enchantments of modernity — progress. Excluding some beliefs, such as reincarnation, as fundamentally 'other', beyond reason and causality, is a valuable construction that helps reproduce the monumental narrative that poses a rupture between enchanted past and reasoned present. The idea that snake-goddesses can be antidotes for snakebites becomes an inadmissible claim to reason because of similar enchantments.
3. Edward Dimock (1962) argues that Manasa *Mangal* is neither folk, nor classical, nor court poetry but rather an evolving combination. This echoes a decisive argument made about the interdependent emergence and development of the oral and written traditions, or the great and little traditions in India (Marriott 1990). Dimock presents two perspectives on the legend: one that argues that it offers profound clues to understand ancient Hinduism developing from indigenous myth to Brahmanism, and another perspective that suggests that Manasa's legend represents the 'struggle of decaying Savaism [worship of Siva] in Bengal against the growth of Saktism [worship of feminine power]' (Dimock 1962: 310–11; Dasgupta cited in Dimock and Ramanujan 1964: 319).

4. Stacey Leigh Pigg (1996) has brilliantly argued that Nepali villagers are equally discriminating in their belief in shamans and modern medicine. Ann Grodzins Gold (2009) makes a similar argument about the simultaneous belief in miracles and rationalised agricultural practices in Rajasthan.
5. The Hadi caste is a Dalit one whose members are variously scavengers, street-sweepers, drain-cleaners, or who remove carcasses, and pull rickshaws or trolleys. They are frequently referred to as *mathor* to identify them as those who remove other people's excreta from inhabited environs.
6. See Rana and Johnson 2003 for similar findings on villagers in debt to pay for healthcare in District Bardhaman. The unregulated nature of private medical practice exacerbates issues of accountability and legal recourse. This situation is common to other West Bengal districts such as Birbhum and Jharkhand (Soman 2002; Rana and Johnson 2003).
7. On the other side of the harbour from Kulpi port town is the Haldia petrochemical industrial park. Further east of Haldia lies East Midnapore, the site of the recent protests against land acquisition. Proximity to port makes these lands particularly good for business, making the villages in the region particularly vulnerable to displacement.
8. The estimated costs of turning into a dynamic port are roughly US$ 235 million, http://www.thehindubusinessline.com/2004/08/12/stories/2004081202760600.htm (accessed on 24 May 2008); http://www.imaritime.com/backoffice/published_files/India_Port_Report_Numbered.pdf (accessed on 24 May 2008); http://www.3inetwork.org/reports/IIR2007/01-The%20Infrast.pdf. (accessed on 24 May 2008). Although the project awaits environmental impact assessment approval, if pushed through, the Dubai-based port operator DP World holds 44.5 per cent stake, Keventor Agro (an agribusiness company) of Mukund Steel hold another 44.5 per cent stake, and the West Bengal Industrial Development Corporation holds the remaining 11 per cent stake in this public–private partnership (*ibid.*).
9. *Aman* crop is planted in June and harvested between November and January. This crop is planted in the summer agricultural season for which farmers rely on the monsoon rains to feed crop growth.
10. *Mangal kavya*, as Edward Dimock defines it, is poetry eulogising one of the gods and goddesses in the Hindu pantheon: 'They tell of the power and magnificence of a particular divinity, how man prospers by the worship of that divinity and suffers by denying it' (Dimock 1962: 307). Such poetry is neither romantic nor focused on the intricacies of language. Depicting everyday experiences of people in 'field and village', unlike the lofty and inaccessible gods in the Brahmanical tradition, mangal poetry shows that '[e]ven the gods partake of [...] essential humanity' (Dimock 1962: 310).

11. Some told me that because Manasa required them to cook fish for her in the original dream, their family had to add fish to the vegetable dishes.
12. *Ojha* and *guneen* are types of healers working in the village who are variously defined as traditional healers, exorcists, quacks, and witch-doctors.
13. Tarun brought me over to Mukesh's house for the interview. Although they are immediate neighbours, they belong to opposite ends of the village class and caste spectrum. Tarun, a 23-year-old, lost his father to illness a year ago. I interviewed his sisters for this study. Both are employed. Urmila works at Mukesh's house as domestic labour, and Sharmila is a teacher for JS's pre-primary school. They are both unmarried despite their age (28 and 33 years) because the family cannot afford the dowry demands.
14. Surprisingly, they make no mention of the *sij* tree which symbolises Manasa worship in household and neighbourhood courtyards. This tree also appears in the Manasa legend. It is believed to have emetic and antidotal properties. In the Teor neighbourhood, interviewees walked me over to their *sij* tree and talked about its properties and described its role in Manasa *puja*.
15. Homeopathy is Janus-faced in its relation to human innovation and science on the one hand, and religion on the other. It is fascinating to note in passing that homeopathic principles, which inform some of the guneen remedies, are quoted in Vedic texts (Atharva Veda) — 'with poison do I slay thy poison' (Dimock and Ramanujan 1964: 301). At the same time that it is present in authoritative Hindu texts such as the Vedas, the homeopathic principle also appears in Muhammed Iqbal's (1877–1938) poem where the poet both celebrates and distinguishes god's work from material achievements by human beings:
    You created wilderness, mountains and ravines
    I the flower beds, gardens and groves
    I make mirrors from stone
    I find antidotes in poison
16. LIC is the nationalised insurance company that controlled 100 per cent of the Indian insurance market till as late as the year 2000, much later than most other sectors had undergone formal liberalisation.
17. Hindi is the language spoken in some states of northern India.

Conclusion

We live in times that harbour profound ambiguity about accepting praxis as foundation of collectivity. We also live in a time when we can only tenuously and tentatively trust culture as political process because culture is thoroughly implicated in right-wing hatred, wars, imperialism, and commodification. In this book, I have tried to interpret the work of rural political theatre and the living labour of meaning-making in daily life off-stage not as somehow overcoming this tension, but as embodying it, struggling against its limits, and sometimes reworking possibilities delimited by this constitutive tension of our times. Rather than assume that 'small' spaces of hope are weak and ineffective signs of social transformation, *Development Dramas* has insisted on considering the meaning and modalities of a number of development anomalies such as rural political theatre to consider its relation to epistemic struggle, the formation of collectivity, and social change. I have fought assumptions about what counts as political action by studying political theatre as normal political action, as no more extraordinary and no less effective site for constructing social relations and social change.

The work of Jana Sanskriti (JS) has been a constant struggle to make meanings real and immediate to them count as a representation of the state of their world. In paying attention to the on-stage dramas and the intended cultural work of giving particular meanings moral and institutional weight, I have shown how the Left Front Government (LFG) hegemony is constituted and/or otherwise rendered incomplete. While theatre has been used in myriad ways to buttress political and economic struggles for sovereignty in India, rural political theatre remains largely invisible to theatre canons and metropolitan audiences despite its existence and popularity among villagers.

This book theorised this neglect and documents one significant construction of rural political theatre in JS's work. Their method of Forum Theatre plays with the ideological distinction between representation and reality as a way to move people past real and imagined separations such as subjects of power and subjects of oppression, artist and audience, leader and follower. In playing with these distinctions, JS's method on-stage gets people to live a reality in which representations are no more or less malleable than reality off-stage. In this way, studying rural political theatre offers telling insights into the social life of development by representing everyday experiences, hopes, choices, and politics of reconstituting futures.

The realm of 'off-stage' plays an equally significant role in this story. In *Development Dramas*, off-stage refers to both ethnographic context and metaphor of unintended action. In each chapter of this book, I have tried to describe forms of dispossession of meaning, epistemic exclusions, and representational inequality. I have used these terms interchangeably to signify processes through which particular historically available meanings, values, actions, and processes come to be written out of dominant imaginaries and institutions of development and political action. By reconstructing a world of dispossessed, anomalous, anachronistic meanings, I have tried to study the formation of this thing called 'structure'. Rather than accept that devalued meanings do not count because they are excluded from'structure', I have situated these meanings in contexts and relations of their making to suggest that alienated meanings and representations can be generative of social formations and transformation, whether we are looking or not. JS's commitment to building theatre teams as nodes of critical pedagogy, play and political action in villages required collective living against the segregations of class, caste, gender, and rural–urban life in modern India. Their construction of a long-term public sphere for spect-acting and scripting plays required that villagers share in controlling the means of political representation. Every part of the JS outcome however, cannot be considered an intended goal of mobilisation, nor even a coherent one. Yet it can be characterised as social formation.

Similarly, preparing food for Manasa constructs social collectivity by requiring cooperation across caste and class. While Manasa may not intend to mobilise social transformation against the multiple forces of inequality which her devotees face, she inculcates an ethic of survival and sharing. This kind of political action slips under the radar in many studies of social change because of a Gramscian optic to see intentional social engineering and visible mobilisation as the primary sign of power in transformation. When we view intended social change as sole indicator of political action, the accomplishments of JS and Manasa do not count because these are largely constituted through daily self-making, multiple sources of ethical action, and normative convictions. JS reminds us that it is never redundant to ask: how we know development when we see it.

Following Timothy Mitchell (2002), I consider it imperative to go beyond the liberal assumptions that intentional social engineering is the sole sign of transformation. I found multiple 'off-stage' meanings and practices that participate in constructing collectivity and social transformation. Anomalies, anachronisms, and dispossessed meanings documented in this book are examples of suggestive engines and outcomes of transformation, even though they are not immediately visible as nodes of mobilisation and embodiments of power. These examples reveal the power and efficacy of JS's cultural work, while showing how it remains incomplete or otherwise participates in reinforcing ruling epistemes. In presenting the off-stage labour of meaning-making, I have suggested methods for interrupting glib assumptions about inevitable market epistemes, individual freedoms, ideological collectivity, and democracy by reimagining where we might look for the 'political' of political action and the space and site of social change.

Although I have focused on JS's theatre, this book sees the neglect of political theatre as just one telling drama of how 'development' and political action comes to be naturalised in the current conjuncture. By studying the daily labour of meaning-making as political action, I also theorised the dramas of dispossessing other meanings (of materiality, collectivity, and choice) in the ongoing making of 'development'. Reworking the ideological import of equality, by representing different and unequally valued meanings, is difficult work in a time and context where material distress disables and reinforces an impoverished political imagination. But the labour of reimagining political action in rural Bengal dramatises the value of seeing domestic violence and liquor consumers' wives' livelihoods as a problem of material and representational inequality. In other examples, lived conceptions of 'development' highlight what persons and relationships are alienated when schooling and modern healthcare systems turn into articles of absolute faith and 'basic needs' wisdom while disregarding the contexts within which these development ideals are experienced. These alienated conceptions should be taken into account in conceptualising development and social change.

When Marx described the process through which the social character of labour came to be expropriated from humans, he captured the fact that inequality is ideological as much as it is based on calculation of profit and wages. After all for Marx, commodification is a foundational abstraction of living labour without which there is no capitalism. His emphasis on the unprecedented way in which capitalism organises and represents relations of production explains why and how capitalism comes to exert force as modernity. His is clearly not a purely economic history of capitalism. However, a Marxist understanding of the political force and efficacy of capitalism relies exclusively on the history of capital as starting point and explanation. I have drawn on the work of various scholars to understand 'capitalism' and 'culture' as outcomes of shared histories that intersect with and refer to capital's original misrepresentation.

Persevering with the ambiguities that mark experiences of development in people's lives I showed how, when, and why multiple histories of power — such as histories of capital, ideologies of equality, worship of gods, *sansar* ethics — intersect with, exceed, and differ from each other. They provide multiple hierarchies and resources for ordering social action. Studying these intersecting histories of power, ethical and normative regulation, and agency, I showed that the efficacy and legitimacy of 'development' often lies in how people choose to negotiate the constraints they face given the historical availability of multiple, if unequally valued, possibilities — whether as wage-labourers, peasants, upper-caste politicians, rural patriarchs, liquor consumer wives, or villagers without healthcare.

Marx's explanations for transformation focuses on seeing the quantitative impoverishment of wage-labour brought to a boiling point when qualitative transformations become possible. For him, the engine of transformation cannot lie in the process of representation. But perhaps, this process lies at the heart of naturalising the idea that capitalist modernity is inevitable and the work of representation lies at the heart of subverting this normative closure. It may not accomplish transformation without say redistribution of resources such as land, but equally land struggles without representational equality can reproduce status quo and reinforce the market episteme as inevitable. The work of representation is not always visible and 'other' histories of power are not granted modernity, efficacy, or legitimacy. But this does not rule out the living labour of meaning-making which gives these histories constitutive force in contemporary lives, action, and social relations.

While the focus of this book has undoubtedly been JS's political and cultural work, my aim has been to show what it means to build a struggle around means of representation, rather than means of production. Their work no doubt raises the question of whether a social movement that chooses not to reorganise production relations (the doctrinal view of class struggle) but rather focuses on reorganising means, practices, and relations of representation can be thought of as progressive. While this is a matter of perspective and politics, I hope I have shown how and why some who engage in JS's work in rural Bengal came to be persuaded by what might seem to others like a huge leap of faith — the idea that representation can lead to transformation, that representational equality can generate new definitions for the 'social' of social relations.

Small spaces of hope and reimagined political action such as those captured in this book can be used to generate claims of subaltern autonomy and cultural difference, but they can also be significant expressions and struggles against dominant epistemes. I hope I have shown that multiple cultural registers of action coexist in rural Bengal and within JS political action. These intersecting histories of power never defer to each other in any all-encompassing sense, nor does this render any one space of struggle a stable emblem of cultural difference and autonomy. Rather, viewing political theatre as I have tried to do in this book, as 'everyday forms of collaboration' (White 1989: 56) as much as everyday forms of disloyal enactments, and refusals to play normative scripts loyally (Butler 1990) allows us to critically scrutinise 'those who want to limit freedom' as well as 'those who want to extend it' (Mahmood 2005: 10). People go about interpreting, organising, and living their daily lives despite exploitation, marginalisation, and disillusionment. Living and acting against normative closure is a trace on power relations and the power of our imaginations. The work of political theatre in democratic polities embodies ethical indeterminacy, even as it is testimony to the daily cultural labour of playing with and protesting the rule of epistemes.

Bibliography

Abrams, Philip. 1982. *Historical Sociology*. Ithaca: Cornell University Press.

———. 1988. 'Notes on the Difficulty of Studying the State', *Journal of Historical Sociology*, 1(1): 58–89.

Afzal-Khan, Fawzia. 2001. 'Exposed by Pakistani Alternative Theatre: An Unholy Alliance', *Social Text*, 19(4): 67–91.

Ahmad, Aijaz. 1992. 'Introduction: Literature among the Signs of Our Time', in *In Theory: Classes Nations Literatures*, pp. 1–42. New York: Verso.

———. 2000. 'In the Eye of the Storm: The Left Chooses', in *Lineages of the Present: Ideology and Politics in Contemporary South Asia*, pp. 209. London, New York: Verso.

———. 2004. 'Imperialism of our Time', in Leo Panitch and Colin Leys (eds), *Socialist Register*, pp. 43–62.

Ahearn, Laura M. 2001. *Invitations to Love: Literacy, Love Letters, and Social Change in Nepal*. Ann Arbor: University of Michigan Press.

Alexander, Jeffrey and Philip Smith. 1993. 'The Discourse of American Civil Society: A New Proposal for Cultural Studies', *Theory and Society*, 22: 151–207.

Ali, Nosheen. 2005. 'Pidgeonholing Piety', review in *The Herald*, October.

Appadurai, Arjun. 1990. 'Disjuncture and difference in the Global Culture Economy', *Theory, Culture, and Society*, 7: 295–310.

———. 2004. 'The Capacity to Aspire', in Vijayendra Rao and Michael Walton (eds), '*Culture and Public Action*, pp. 59–84. Delhi: Permanent Black.

Appadurai, Arjun, Frank J. Korom, and Margaret A. Mills, (eds). 1991. *Gender, Genre, and Power in South Asian Expressive Traditions*. Philadelphia: University of Pennsylvania Press.

Arambam, Lokendra. 2008. 'The Politics of National Patronage: Shaping a Theatre Modernism for the Periphery, The Manipur Experience'. Paper presented at 'Reviewing Disciplinary Agendas in Theatre Studies: Cultural Arena Policies Institutions', 23–25 January, Institute of Economic Growth, New Delhi.

Araghi, Farshad. 2000. 'The Local in the Global', *International Journal of Sociology of Food and Agriculture*, vol. 8, pp. 111–25.

Arrighi, Giovanni. 1994. *The Long Twentieth Century: Money, Power and the Origins of Our Times*. Verso: New York.

Asad, Talal. 2003. *Formations of the Secular: Christianity, Islam, Modernity*. Palo Alto: Stanford University Press.

Auslander, Philip. 1994. 'Boal-Blau-Brecht: the Body', in Jan-Cohen Cruz and Mady Schutzman (eds), *Playing Boal*, pp. 124–33. New York: Routledge.

Badiou, Alain. 2008. 'The Communist Hypothesis', *New Left Review*, 49: 29–42.

Bagchi, Jasodhara, (ed.) 2005. *The Changing Status of Women in West Bengal, 1970–2000: The Challenge Ahead*. New Delhi: Sage Publications.

Bagchi, Jasodhara, and Jaba Guha. 2005. 'Education', in Jasodhara Bagchi (ed.), *The Changing Status of Women in West Bengal, 1970–2000*, pp. 49–70. New Delhi: Sage Publications.

Balagopalan, Sarada. 2005. 'An Ideal School and a Schooled Ideal: Education at the Margins', in Radhika Chopra and Patricia M. Jeffery (eds), *Educational Regimes in Contemporary India*, pp. 83–98. New Delhi: Sage Publications.

Banerjee, Nirmala and Mukul Mukherjee. 2005. 'Demography', in Jasodhara Bagchi (ed.), *The Changing Status of Women in West Bengal, 1970–2000*, pp. 21–33. New Delhi,: Sage Publications.

Banerjee, Nirmala and Poulomi Roy. 2004. 'What does the State do for Indian Women', *Economic and Political Weekly*, 39(44): 4831–837.

Banerjee, Partha Sarathi. 2008. 'The Party and the *Panchayats* of West Bengal', *Economic and Political Weekly*, 43(24): 17–19.

Banerjee, Sumanta. 1989. *The Parlour and the Streets: Elite and Popular Culture in Nineteenth Century Calcutta*. Calcutta: Seagull Books.

———. 2006. 'Elections, *Jatra* Style, in West Bengal', *Economic and Political Weekly*, 41(9): 864–866.

Bannerjee, Mukulika. 2007. 'Sacred Elections', *Economic and Political Weekly*, 42(17): 1556–562.

Bannerji, Himani. 1998. *The Mirror of Class: Essays on Bengali Theatre*. Calcutta: Papyrus.

———. 2002. *Inventing Subjects: Studies in Hegemony, Patriarchy, and Colonialism*. London: Anthem Press.

Barton, David, and Mary Hamilton. 1998. *Local Literacies: Reading and Writing in One Community*. London: Routledge.

Basu, Amrita. 1992. *Two Faces of Protest: Contrasting Modes of Women's Activism in India*. Berkeley: University of California Press.

Basu, Dipankar 2001. 'Political Economy of "Middleness": Behind Violence in Rural West Bengal', *Economic and Political Weekly*, 36(16): 1333–344.

Basu, Partha Pratim. 2007. '"Brand Buddha" in India's West Bengal: The Left Reinvents Itself', *Asian Survey*, 47(2): 288–306.

Baviskar, Amita. 1995. *In the Belly of the River: Tribal Conflicts over Development in the Narmada Valley*. Delhi: Oxford University Press.

Baviskar, A. and Nandini Sundar. 2008. 'Democracy versus Econo-mic Transformation?', *Economic and Political Weekly*, 43(46): 87–89.

Beck, Andrew. 2003. *Cultural Work: Understanding the Culture Industries*. London: Routledge.

Benjamin, Walter. 1968. *Illuminations*, trans. Harry Zohn, ed. Hannah Arendt. New York: Schoken Books.

Becker, Howard S. 1982. *Art Worlds*. Berkeley: University of California Press.

Bennett, Tony. 2007. 'The Work of Culture', *Cultural Sociology*, 1(1): 31–47.

Bernstein, Henry. 2006. 'Is There an Agrarian Question in the 21st Century?', *Canadian Journal of Development Studies*, 27(4): 449–60.

———. 2008. 'Agrarian questions from transition to globalisation', in A.H. Akram-Lodhi and C. Kay (eds), *Peasants and Globalization: Political Economy, Rural Transformation and the Agrarian Question*, pp. 239–61. London: Routledge.

Besnier, Niko. 1995. *Literacy, Emotion, and Authority: Reading and Writing on a Polynesian Atoll*. Cambridge: Cambridge University Press.

Beverley, John. 2004. 'Subaltern Resistance in Latin America: A Reply to Tom Brass', *Journal of Peasant Studies*, 31(2): 261–275.

Bhaduri, Amit. 2007. 'Alternatives in Industrialisation', *Economic and Political Weekly*, 42(18): 1597–1601.

Bharucha, Rustom. 1983. *Rehearsals of Revolution: The Political Theater of Bengal*. Honolulu: University of Hawaii Press.

———. 1996. 'Somebody's Other: Disorientations in the cultural politics of our Times', in Patrice Pavis (ed.), *The Intercultural Performance Reader*, pp. 196–212. London: Routledge.

———. 1993. *Theatre and the World: Performance and the Politics of Culture*. London: Routledge.

———. 1999. *In the Name of the Secular: Contemporary Cultural Activism in India*. New York: Oxford University Press.

———. 2000. *The Politics of Cultural Practice: Thinking Through Theatre in an Age of Globalization*. Hanover: Wesleyan University Press.

Bhatia, Nandi. 2004. *Acts of Authority/Acts of Resistance: Theater and Politics in Colonial and Postcolonial India*. Ann Arbor: University of Michigan Press.

Bhattacharya, Buddhadeb. 2007. 'We Cannot Fail People's Expectations', in *People's Democracy: Weekly Organ of the Communist Party of India (Marxist)*, XXXI (3): January 21. http://pd.cpim.org/2007/0121/01212007_buddhadeb's%20letter.htm (accessed on 14 April 2007).

Bhattacharya, Harihar. 1998. *Micro Foundations of Bengal Communism*, pp. 179–80. Delhi: Ajanta Books International.

Bhattacharya, Malini. 1983. 'The IPTA in Bengal', *Journal of Arts and Ideas*, January–March, 2: 5–22.

———. 1989. 'The Indian People's Theatre Association: A Preliminary Sketch of the Movement and the Organization', *Sangeet Natak*, October–December, 94: 3–25.

Bhattacharya, Malini. (ed.) 2004. 'Globalization, Modernity, and the Woman Rural Artist', *Globalization*, pp. 158–168. Delhi: Tulika Books.

Bhattacharya, Moitree. 2002. *Panchayati Raj in West Bengal*. New Delhi: Manak Publications.

Bhattacharyya, Dwaipayan. 1999. 'Politics of Middleness: The Changing Character of the Communist Party of India (Marxist) in rural West Bengal (1977-90)', in Ben Rogaly, Barbara Hariss-White and Sugata Bose(eds), *Sonar Bangla?: Agricultural Growth and Agrarian Change in West Bengal and Bangladesh*, pp. 279–300, New Delhi: Sage Publications.

———. 2001. 'Civic Community and its Margins: School Teachers in Rural West Bengal', in *Economic and Political Weekly*, 36 (8): 673–83.

Bhattacharyya, Sudipta. 2001. 'Capitalist Development, Peasant Differentiation and the State: Survey Findings from West Bengal', *The Journal of Peasant Studies*, 28(4): 95–126.

Biswas, Bulbuli and Paramita Banerjee. 1997. 'Street Theatre in Bengal: A Glimpse', *Seagull Theatre Quarterly*, 16: 31–7.

Boal, Augusto. 1979. *The Theatre of the Oppressed*. NY: Urizen Books.

———. 1998. *Legislative Theatre: Using Performance to Make Politics*. London: Routledge.

Bose, Pratim Ranjan. 2004. 'P & O to Develop Bengal's Kulpi Port', *The Hindu Business Line*, http://www.thehindubusinessline.com/2004/08/12/stories/2004081202760600. (accessed on 1 May 2008).

Bose, Sugata. 1997. 'Instruments and Idioms of Colonial and National Development: India's Historical Experience in Comparative Perspective', in Frederick Cooper and Randall Packard (eds), *International Development and the Social Sciences: Essays on the History and Politics of Knowledge*, pp. 45–63. Berkley: University of California Press.

Bourdieu, Pierre. 1977 (trans. by Richard Nice). *Outline of a Theory of Practice*. Cambridge: Cambridge University Press.

Brass, Tom. 2002. 'On which side of what barricade? Subaltern resistance in Latin America and elsewhere', *Journal of Peasant Studies*, 29(3): 336–99.

Breman, Jan. 1996. *Footloose Labour: Working in India's Informal Economy*. Cambridge: Cambridge University Press.

———. 1999. 'Silencing the Voice of Agricultural Labourers in South Gujarat', *Modern Asian Studies*, 33(1): 1–22.

Butler, Judith. 1990. 'Performative Acts and Gender Constitution', in Sue-Ellen Case (ed.), *Performing Feminisms: Feminist Critical Theory and Theatre*, pp. 270–82. Baltimore: Johns Hopkins University Press.

———. 1992. 'Contigent Foundations: Feminism and the Question of Postmodernism', in Judith Butler and Joan W.Scott (eds), *Feminists Theorise the Political*, pp. 3–21. London: Routledge.

———. 1998. 'Marxism and the Merely Cultural', in *New Left Review*, 1(227): 33–34.

———. 1999. *Gender Trouble: Feminism and the Subversion of Identity*, 2nd edn. New York: Routledge.

———. 2008. 'Sexual Politics, Torture and Secular Time', *British Journal of Sociology*, 59 (1): 1–23.

Calclini, Nestor Garcia. 1995. *Hybrid Cultures: Srategies for Entering and Leaving Modernity*. Minnesota: University of Minnesota Press.

Caraway, Nancie. 1991. *Segregated Sisterhood: Racism and the Politics of American Feminism*. Knoxville: University of Tennessee Press.

Chakrabarty, Dipesh. 2000. *Provincializing Europe: Postcolonial Thought and Historical Difference*. Princeton, N.J.: Princeton University Press.

Chambers, Robert. 1997. *Whose Reality Counts?: Putting the First Last*. London: Intermediate Technology Publications.

Chandrasekhar, C.P. 2009. 'Learning Nothing, Forgetting Everything', *Frontline*, 26 (1). http://www.frontlineonnet.com/fl2601/stories/20090116260113100.htm (accessed on 13 January 2009).

Chatterjee, Partha. 1993. *The Nation and Its Fragments: Colonial and Postcolonial Histories*. Princeton, N.J.: Princeton University Press.

———. 1997. *The Present History of West Bengal: Essays in Political Criticism*. Delhi: Oxford University Press.

———. 2000. 'Two Poets and Death: On Civil Society and Political Society in the Non-Christian World', in Timothy Mitchell (ed.), *Questions of Modernity*, pp. 35–48. Minneapolis: University of Minnesota Press.

———. 2004. *The Politics of the Governed*. New Delhi: Permanent Black.

———. 2008a. 'Democracy and Economic Transformation in India', *Economic and Political Weekly*, 43(16): 53–62.

———. 2008b. 'Class, Capital, and Indian Democracy', *Economic and Political Weekly*, 43(46): 89–93.

Chatterjee, Sudipto. 2007. *The Colonial Staged: Theatre in Colonial Calcutta*. Calcutta: Seagull Books.

Chattopadhyay, Raghabendra and Esther Duflo. 2004. 'Impact of Reservation in Panchayati Raj: Evidence from a Randomized Experiment', *Economic and Political Weekly*, 39(9): 979–86.

Chaudhuri, Una. 1998. 'Working Out (of) Place: Peter Brook's Mahabharata and the Problematics of Intercultural Performance', in Jeanne Colleran and Jenny S. Spencer (eds), *Staging Resistance: Essays on Political Theater* pp. 77–97. Ann Arbor: Michigan University Press.

Chopra, Radhika. 2005. 'Sisters and Brothers: Schooling, Family, and Migration', in Radhika Chopra and Patricia M. Jeffery (eds), *Educational Regimes in Contemporary India*, pp. 299–315. New Delhi: Sage Publications.

Clarke, Gerard. 2007. 'Agents of Transformation? Donors, Faith-based Organisations and International Development', *Third World Quarterly*, 28(1): 77–96.

Collins, James. 1995. 'Literacy and Literacies', *Annual Review of Anthropology*, 24: 75–93.

Collins, Patricia Hill. 1990. *Black Feminist Thought: Knowledge, Consciousness, and the Politics of Empowerment*. Boston: Unwin Hyman.

Comaroff, Jean. 1985. *Body of Power, Spirits of Resistance: The Culture and History of a South African People*. Chicago and London: University of Chicago.

Comaroff, Jean and John Comaroff (eds). 1993. *Modernity and Its Malcontents: Ritual and Power in Postcolonial Africa*. Chicago and London: University of Chicago Press.

———. 2000. 'Millennial Capitalism: First Thoughts on a Second Coming', *Public Culture* 12(2): 291–343.

Commission on Human Security. 2002. 'Workshop on Education, Equity, and Security'. Report of the conference at Kolkata, India, 2–4 January. http://www.humansecurity-chs.org/activities/outreach/kolkatarep.pdf.(accessed on 25 August 2004).

Cook, Bill and Uma Kothari (eds). 2001. *Participation, The New Tyranny?* London: Zed.

Cooper, Frederick, and Ann Laura Stoler (eds). 1997. *Tensions of Empire: Colonial Cultures in a Bourgeois World*. Berkeley, Los Angeles, London: University of California Press.

Cooper, Frederick, and Randall Packard. (eds) 1997. *International Development and the Social Sciences*. Berkeley: University of California Press.

Corbridge, Stuart, Glyn Williams, Manoj Srivastava and René Véron. 2005. *Seeing the State: Governance and Governmentality in India*. Cambridge: Cambridge University Press.

Corrigan, Philip and Derek Sayer. 1985. *The Great Arch: English State Formation as Cultural Revolution*. London: Basil Blackwell.

Cowen, Michael P. and Robert W. Shenton. 1998. 'Agrarian doctrines of development: Part I', *Journal of Peasant Studies*, 25(2): 49–76.

———. 1998. 'Agrarian doctrines of development: Part II', *Journal of Peasant Studies*, 25(3): 31–62.

Crow, Brian and Chris Banfield (eds). 1996. 'Badal Sircar's Third Theatre of Calcutta', in *An Introduction to Post-Colonial Theatre*, pp. 112–35. Cambridge: Cambridge University Press.

Crush, Jonathan. 1995. *The Power of Development*. New York and London: Routledge.

Da Costa, Dia and Philip McMichael. 2007. 'The Poverty of the Global Order', *Globalizations*, 4(4): 588–602.

Da Costa, Dia. 2007a. 'Tensions of Neo-liberal Development: State Discourse and Dramatic Oppositions in West Bengal', *Contributions to Indian Sociology*, 41(3): 287–320.

Da Costa, Dia. 2007b. 'Mirrors of Value?: Advertising and Political Theatre in the Hegemonic Constructions of Women in India', in Sudhanva Deshpande (ed.), *Theatre of the Streets*, pp. 132–55. New Delhi: Jan Natya Manch.

Dalmia, Vasudha. 2006. *Poetics, Plays, and Performances: The Politics of Modern Indian Theatre*. New York: Oxford University Press.

Das, Raju J. 2007. 'Looking, but not seeing: The state and/as class in rural India', *Journal of Peasant Studies*, 34(3): 408–40.

Das Veena, 1995. *Critical Events: An Anthropological Perspective on Contemporary India*. Delhi: Oxford University Press.

Dasgupta, Manasi and Mandakranta Bose, 2000. 'The Goddess-Woman Nexus in Popular Religious Practice', in Mandakranta Bose (ed.), *Faces of the Feminine in Ancient, Medieval, and Modern India*, pp. 148–61. Oxford: Oxford University Press.

Das Gupta, Ranajit. 1998. 'Elections in West Bengal', *Economic and Political Weekly*, 33(19): 1113–118.

Das Sharma, Biren. 1995. 'How political is a cultural policy? The NSD example', *Seagull Theatre Quarterly*, 6: 8–12.

De Bruin, Hanne M. 2001. 'The History of Rural Natakam or "Drama" in North Tamil Nadu', *Seagull Theatre Quarterly*, 31: 56–74.

de Haan, Arjaan, and Ben Rogaly. 2002. 'Migrant Workers and Their Role in Rural Change', *Journal of Development Studies*, 38(5): 1–14.

Dean, Mitchell. 1999. *Governmentality: Power and Rule in Modern Society*. London: Sage Publications.

Deshpande, Govind Purushottam. 1985. 'Fetish of Folk and Classic', *Sangeet Natak*, July–December, No. 77–78: 47–50.

Desmarais, Annette Aurelie. 2007. *La Vía Campesina: Globalization and the Power of Peasants*. London: Fernwood Books & Pluto Press.

Dharwadker, Aparna Bhargava. 2005. *Theatres of Independence: Drama, Theory, and Urban Performance in India Since 1947*. Iowa City: University of Iowa Press.

Dimock, Edward. C. Jr. 1962. 'The Goddess of Snakes in Medieval Bengali Literature', *History of Religions*, 1(2): 307–21.

Dimock, Edward C. Jr. and Attipat Krishnaswami Ramnujan. 1964. 'The Goddess of Snakes in Medieval Bengali Literature, Part II', *History of Religions*, 3(2): 300–22.

Dirks, Nicholas, (ed.) 1992. *Colonialism and Culture*. Ann Arbor: University of Michigan Press.

———. 2001. *Castes of Mind: Colonialism and the Making of Modern India*. Princeton.: Princeton University Press.

Dolan, Jill. 2005. *Utopia in Performance: Finding Hope at the Theater*. Ann Arbor: University of Michigan Press.

Drèze, Jean and Amartya Sen (eds). 1997. *Indian Development: Selected Regional Perspectives*. New Delhi: Oxford University Press.

Dube, Saurabh. 2002a. 'Introduction: Enchantments of Modernity', *The South Atlantic Quarterly*, 101(4): 729–55.

Dube, Saurabh. 2002b. 'Presence of Europe: An Interview with Dipesh Chakrabarty', *The South Atlantic Quarterly*, 101(4): 859–68.

Durkheim, Emile. 1995. (1912) (trans. by Karen E. Fields) *The Elementary Forms of Religious Life*. New York: Simon Schuster.

Elson, Diane, (ed.) 1995. *Male Bias in the Development Process*. Manchester: Manchester University Press.

Elyachar, Julia. 2002. 'Empowerment Money: The World Bank, Non-Governmental Organizations, and the Value of Culture in Egypt',*Public Culture*, 14(3): 493–513.

———. 2005. *Markets of Dispossession: NGOs, Economic Development, and the State in Cairo*. Durham: Duke University Press.

Escobar, Arturo. 1995. *Encountering Development: The Making and Unmaking of the Third World*. Princeton: Princeton University Press.

Feldman, Shelley. 1997. 'NGOs and Civil Society: (Un)stated Contradictions', *Annals of the American Academy of Political and Social Science*, 554: 46–65.

Ferguson, James. 1994. *The Anti-Politics Machine: "Development", Depoliticization, and Bureaucratic Power in Lesotho*. Minneapolis: University of Minnesota Press.

———. 1997. 'Anthropology and Its Evil Twin', in Frederick Cooper and Randall Packard (eds), *International Development and the Social Sciences*, pp. 150–75. Berkeley: University of California Press.

Ferguson, James and Akhil Gupta. 2002. 'Spatializing States: Toward an Ethnography of Neoliberal Governmentality', *American Ethnologist*, 29(4): 981–1002.

———. 2006. *Global Shadows: Africa in the Neoliberal World Order*. Durham: Duke University Press.

Fernandes, Leela. 1997. 'Beyond Public Spaces and Private Spheres: Gender, Family, and Working Class Politics in India', *Feminist Studies*, 23(3): 525–47.

Fisher, Berenice. 1994. 'Feminist Acts: Women, Pedagogy, Theatre of the Oppressed', in Mady Schutzman and Jan Cohen-Cruz (eds), *Playing Boal: Theatre, Therapy, Activism*, pp. 185–97. London: Routledge.

Ford, Andrew. 1995. 'Katharsis: the Ancient Problem', in Andrew Parker and Eve Kosofsky Sedgwick (eds), *Performance and Performativity* pp. 109–32. London: Routledge.

Forester, John. 1996. 'Beyond Dialogue to Transformative Learning: How Deliberative Rituals Encourage Political Judgment in Community Planning Processes', *Democratic Dialogues: Theories and Practices*, pp. 295–233. Atlanta, Ga: Rodopi.

Foucault, Michel. 1991. 'Governmentality', in Graham Burchell, Colin Gordon and Peter Miller (eds), *The Foucault Effect*, pp. 87–104. Chicago: University of Chicago Press.

Freeman, Carla. 2001. 'Is Local: Global as Feminine : Masculine? Rethinking the Gender of Globalization', *Signs: Journal of Women in Culture and Society*, 26 (4):1007–37.

Freire, Paulo. 2000. *Pedagogy of the Oppressed*, 30th Anniversary Edition. New York: Continuum Publishing.

Fruzetti, Lina M. 1990. *The Gift of a Virgin: Women, Marriage, and Ritual in a Bengali Society*. New Delhi: Oxford India Paperbacks.

Ganguly, Sanjoy. 1988–89. 'Theatre for Change Project Documentation', *Seagull Theatre Quarterly*, 20/21, December 98–March 99.

———. 2004. 'Theatre a space for empowerment: celebrating Jana Sanskriti's experience in India', in Richard Boon and Jane Plastow (eds.), *Theatre and Empowerment: Community Drama on the World Stage*, pp. 220–57. Cambridge: Cambridge University Press.

Garnham, Nicholas. 1995. 'Political Economy and Cultural Studies: Reconciliation or Divorce?', *Critical Studies in Mass Communications*, 12(1): 62–71.

Geertz, Clifford. 1973. *The Interpretation of Cultures: Selected Essays*. New York: Basic Books.

———. 1981. *Negara: The Theatre State in Nineteenth-Century Bali*. Princeton, N.J.: Princeton University Press.

Ghatak, Maitreya and Maitreesh Ghatak. 2000. 'Grassroots Democracy: A Study of the Panchayat System in West Bengal'. Paper presented at the conference on 'Experiments in Empowered Deliberative Democracy', January 2000, Wisconsin–Madison. http://www.ssc.wisc.edu/~wright/ghatak.pdf (accessed on 8 July 2008).

———. 2002. 'Recent Reforms in the Panchayat System in West Bengal: Towards Greater Participatory Governance', *Economic and Political Weekly*, 37(1): 45–57.

Ghatak, Ritwik. 2006. *'On the Cultural "Front": A Thesis Submitted by Ritwik Ghatak to the Communist Party of India in 1954*. Kolkata: Ritwik Memorial Trust.

Giddens, A. 1998. *The Third Way: The Renewal of Social Democracy*. Oxford: Polity Press.

Ghosh, Amitav, and Dipesh Chakrabarty. 2002. 'A Correspondence on Provincializing Europe', *Radical History Review*, 83(Spring): 146–72.

Gidwani, Vinay and K. Sivaramakrishnan. 2003. 'Circular Migration and the Spaces of Cultural Assertion', *Annals of the Association of American Geographers*, 93(1): 186–213.

Gluckman, Max. 1963. 'Rituals of Rebellion in South-East Africa', in *Order and Rebellion in Tribal Africa: Collected Essays*, pp. 110–36. London: Cohen & West.

Gold, Ann Grodzins. 2002. 'New Light in the House: Schooling Girls in Rural North India', in *Everyday Life in South Asia*, Diane P. Mines and Sarah Lamb (eds), pp. 86–99. Bloomington: Indiana University Press.

———. 2009. 'Tasteless Profits and Vexed Moralities: Assessments of the Present in Rural Rajasthan', *Journal of the Royal Antropological Institute*. 15(2): 365–85.

Gold, Ann Grodzins and Bhoju Ram Gujar. 2002. *In the Time of Trees and Sorrows: Nature, Power, and Memory in Rajasthan*. Durham: Duke University Press.

Goswami, Manu. 2004. *From Colonial Economy to National Space*. Chicago and London: University of Chicago Press.

Gramsci, Antonio. 1971. *Selections from the Prison Notebooks of Antonio Gramsci* Ed. and trans. by Quintin Hoare and Geoffrey Nowell Smith. New York: International Publishers.

Grell, Ole Peter and Andrew Cunningham 1996. *"Religio Medici": Medicine and Religion in Seventeenth-Century England*. Aldershot: Scholar Press.

Griswold, Wendy. 1987. 'The Fabrication of Meaning: Literary Interpretations in the US, Britain, and the West Indies', *American Journal of Sociology*, 92(5): 1077–117

Guha, Prabir. 1996. 'Invisible Theatre', *Seagull Theatre Quarterly*, 12: 60–63.

Guha, Ranajit. 1974. 'Neel-darpan: The image of a peasant revolt in a liberal mirror', *Journal of Peasant Studies*, 2(1): 1–46.

———. 1983. *Elementary Aspects of Peasant Insurgency in Colonial India*. Delhi: Oxford University Press.

Gupt, Somnath and Kathryn Hansen (Translator) 2005. *The Parsi Theatre*. Calcutta: Seagull Books.

Gupta, Akhil. 1992. 'The Reincarnation of Souls and the Rebirth of Commodities: Representations of Time in "East" and "West"', *Cultural Critique*, 22: 187–211.

———. 1995. 'Blurred Boundaries: The discourse of corruption, the culture of politics, and the imagined state', *American Ethnologist*, 22(2): 375–402.

———. 1998. *Postcolonial Developments: Agriculture in the Making of Modern India*. Durham: Duke University Press.

———. 2002. 'Reliving Childhood? The Temporality of Childhood and Narratives of Reincarnation', *Ethnos*, 67(1): 33–55

Gupta, Akhil and James Ferguson. 1997. *Culture Power Place: Critical Explorations in Anthropology*. Durham: Duke University Press.

Gupta, Dipankar. 2005. 'Whither the Indian Village: Culture and Agriculture in Rural India', *Economic and Political Weekly*, 40(8): 751–58.

Gupta, Jayoti. 2002. 'Women Second in the Land Agenda', *Economic and Political Weekly*, 37(18): 1746–54.

Gupta, Manjari, and Ratnabali Chattopadhyay. 2005. 'Law and Violence against Women', in Jasodhara Bagchi (ed.), *The Changing Status of Women in West Bengal, 1970–2000: The Challenge Ahead*, pp. 111–29. New Delhi: Sage Publications.

Guss, David. 2000. *The Festive State: Race Ethnicity and Nationalism as Cultural Performance*. Berkeley: University of California Press.

Hall, Stuart. 1981. 'Notes on Deconstructing the "Popular"', in Raphael Samuel (ed.), *People's History and Socialist Theory*, pp. 227–39. London: Routledge and Kegan Paul.

Hall, Stuart and Tony Jefferson (eds). 1990. *Resistance through Rituals: Youth Subcultures in Post-war Britain*. London and New York: Routledge.

Hansen, Kathryn. 1991. *Grounds for Play: The Nautanki Theater of North India*. Berkeley: University of California Press.

Hansen, Thomas Blom. 2001. *Wages of Violence: Naming and Identity in Postcolonial Bombay*. Princeton, NJ: Princeton University Press.

Hansen, Thomas Blom and Finn Stepputat. 2001. 'Introduction: States of Imagination', in Thomas Blom Hansen and Finn Stepputat (eds), *States of Imagination: Ethnographic Explorations of the Postcolonial State*, pp. 1–38. Durham: Duke University Press.

Hardiman, David. 1985. 'From Custom to Crime: The Politics of Drinking in Colonial South Gujarat', in Ranajit Guha (ed.), *Subaltern Studies IV*, pp. 165–228. Delhi: Oxford University Press.

Harraway, Donna. J. 1991. 'Situated Knowledges: The Science Question in Feminism and the Privilege of Partial Perspective', in *Simians, Cyborgs, and Women: The Reinvention of Nature*, pp. 183–202, New York: Routledge.

Harris, John. 1993. 'What is Happening in Rural West Bengal? Agrarian Reform and Distribution', *Economic and Political Weekly*, 18(24): 1237–247.

Hart, Gillian. 1991. 'Engendering Everyday Resistance: Gender, Patronage Production Politics in Malaysia', *Journal of Peasant Studies*, 19(1): 93–121.

———. 1998. 'Multiple Trajectories: A Critique of Industrial Restructuring and the New Institutionalism', *Antipode*, 30(4): 333–56.

Harvey, David. 1992. *The Condition of Postmodernity: An Enquiry into the Origins of Cultural Change*. Massachusetts: Wiley-Blackwell.

———. 2000. *Spaces of Hope*. Berkeley: University of California.

———. 2003. 'Accumulation by Dispossession', in *The New Imperialism*, pp. 137–82. Oxford: Oxford University Press.

Hooks, Bell. 1989. *Talking Back: Thinking Feminist, Thinking Black*. Cambridge, MA: South End Press.

Hopkins, Terence K. 1979. 'The Study of the Capitalist World-Economy: Some Introductory Considerations', in Walter Goldfrank (ed.), *The World System of Capitalism: Past and Present*, pp. 21–52. Beverly Hills: Sage Publications.

Hindu Business Line. 2003. 'Entry tax reintroduced; liquor licensing liberalised', 21 March. http://www.blonnet.com/2003/03/21/stories/2003032101681700.htm (accessed on 14 September 2005).

Herring, Ronald J. 1983. *Land to the Tiller: The Political Economy of Agrarian Reform in South Asia*. New Haven: Yale University Press.

Horkheimer, Max and Theodor Adorno. 2002 (1944). 'The Culture Industry: Enlightenment as Mass Deception', in Gunzelin Schmid Noerr (ed.) and Edmund Jephcott (trans.), *Dialectic of Enlightenment: Philosophical Fragments*, pp. 94–136. Stanford, C.A.: Stanford University Press.

I-Maritime Research and Consulting Division. 2003. *India Port Report: Ten Years of Reforms and Challenges Ahead*, Mumbai. http://www.imaritime.com/backoffice/published_files/India_Port_Report_Numbered.pdf (accessed on 1 May 2008).

Iyengar, Sameera. 1999. 'Theatre as a Magnifying Lens: A Participant/Observer Report', *Seagull Theatre Quarterly*, 20&21: 10–23.

Jackson, Cecile. 1999. 'Men's Work, Masculinities and Gender Divisions of Labour', *Journal of Development Studies*, 36 (1): 89–108.

Jamil Ahmed, Syed. 2002. 'Wishing for a World without "Theatre for Development": Demystifying the Case of Bangladesh', *Research in Drama Education* 7(2): 207–19.

Jassal, Smita Tewari. 2003. 'Bhojpuri songs, women's work and social control in Northern India', *Journal of Peasant Studies*, 30(2): 159–206.

Jeffery, Patricia. 2005. 'Introduction: Hearts, Minds, and Pockets', in Radhika Chopra and Patricia M. Jeffery (eds), *Educational Regimes in Contemporary India*, pp. 13–38. New Delhi: Sage Publications.

Jeffery, Patricia, and Roger Jeffery. 1998. 'Silver Bullet or Passing Fancy? Girls' Schooling and Population Policy', in Cecile Jackson and Ruth Pearson (eds), *Feminist Visions of Development: Gender Analysis and Policy*, pp. 239–58. London: Routledge.

Jeffrey Craig. 2007. *Degrees Without Freedom: Education, Masculinities and Unemployment in North India*. Palo Alto: Stanford University Press.

Jeffrey, Craig, Roger Jeffery, and Patricia Jeffery. 2004. 'Degrees Without Freedom: The Impact of Formal Education on Dalit Young Men in North India', *Development and Change*, 35(5): 963–86.

———. 2007. *Degrees Without Freedom: Education, Masculinities and Unemployment in North India*. Palo Alto: Stanford University Press.

Jeffrey, Robin. 1992. *Politics, Women, and Well-Being: How Kerala Became "a Model"*. London: Macmillan.

Joseph, Gilbert M. and Daniel Nugent. 1994. *Everyday Forms of State Formation: Revolution and the Negotiation of Rule in Modern Mexico*. Durham and London: Duke University Press.

Kamath, Shyam J. 1999. 'Indian Development and Poverty: Making Sense of Sen et al', *Critical Review* 13 (3–4): 315–36.

Kandiyoti, Deniz. 1998. 'Gender, Power and Contestation: "Rethinking Bargaining with Patriarchy"', in Cecile Jackson and Ruth Pearson (eds), *Feminist Visions of Development: Gender Analysis and Policy*, pp. 135–52. London: Routledge.

Kapoor, Ilan. 2008. *The Postcolonial Politics of Development*. London: Routledge.

Kapur, Anuradha. 2006. *Actors, Pilgrims, Kings and Gods: The Ramlila of Ramnagar*. Calcutta: Seagull Books.

Katyal, Anjum 1996. '"A Coming Together: An Affirmation; A Sharing Kulavai: A Report"', *Seagull Theatre Quarterly*, 9: 41–53.

Kaviraj, Sudipta. 1989. 'A Critique of the Passive Revolution', *Economic and Political Weekly*, 23(45-47): 2429–444.

Kerr, David. 2002. 'Art as Tool, Weapon or Shield? Arts for Development Seminar, Harare', in Biodun Jeyifo (ed.), *Modern African Drama: backgrounds and criticism*, pp. 486–493. New York: W.W. Norton.

Kershaw, Baz. 1999. *The Radical in Performance: Between Brecht and Baudrillard*. London: Routledge.

Kidd, Ross. 1983. 'Popular Theatre and Popular Struggle in Kenya: The Story of *Kamiriithu*', *Race and Class*, 24(3): 287–304.

Klenk, Rebecca M. 2003. 'Difficult Work: Becoming Developed', in K. Sivaramakrishnan and Arun Agrawal (eds), *Regional Modernities: The Cultural Politics of Development in India*, pp. 99–121. Stanford: Stanford University Press.

———. 2004. '"Who Is the Developed Woman?", Women as a Category of Development Discourse, Kumaon, India', *Development and Change*, 35(1): 57–78.

Kohli, Atul. 1987. 'West Bengal: Parliamentary Communism and Reform from above', in his *The State and Poverty in India: The Politics of Reform*, pp. 95–143. Cambridge: Cambridge University Press.

———. 2006. 'Politics of Economic Growth in India, 1980–2005, Part II: The 1990s and Beyond', *Economic and Political Weekly*, 41(14): 1361–369.

Kumar, Nita. 2000. *Lessons from Schools: The History of Education in Banaras*. New Delhi: Sage Publications.

Lamb, Sarah. 2000. *White Saris and Sweet Mangoes: Aging, Gender, and Body in North India*. Berkeley: University of California Press.

Laurie, Nina. 2005. 'Establishing Development Orthodoxy: Negotiating Masculinities in the Water Sector', *Development and Change*, 36(3): 527–49.

Levinson, Bradley A., Douglas E. Foley, and Dorothy C. Holland (eds). 1996. *The Cultural Production of the Educated Person: Critical Ethnographies of Schooling and Local Practice*. Albany: SUNY Press.

Li, Tania Murray. 1999a. 'Compromising Power: Development, Culture, and Rule in Indonesia', *Cultural Anthropology*, 14(3): 295–322.

———. 1999b. 'Development, Culture, and Rule in Indonesia', *Cultural Anthropology*, 14 (3): 295–322.

Liechty, M. 2005. 'Carnal Economies: The Commodification of Food and Sex in Kathmandu', *Cultural Anthropology*, 20(1): 1–38.

Lieten, Georges Kristoffel. 1990. 'Depeasantisation Discontinued: Land Reforms in West Bengal', *Economic and Political Weekly*, 15(35): 2265–271.

———. 1994. 'For a new debate on West Bengal', *Economic and Political Weekly*, 24(29): 1835–838.

———. 2003. *Power, Politics, and Rural Development: Essays on India*. New Delhi: Manohar Publishers.

Ludden, David. 1992. 'India's Development Regime', in Nicholas Dirks (ed.), *Colonialism and Culture*, pp. 247–88. Ann Arbor: Michigan University Press.

———. 2001. 'India's development regime', in Nicholas Dirks (ed.), *Colonialism and Culture*, pp. 247–88. Ann Arbor: University of Michigan Press.

Mahmood, Saba. 2005. *Politics of Piety: The Islamic Revival and the Feminist Subject*. Durham: Duke University Press.

Mallick, Ross. 1993. *Development Policy of a Communist Government: West Bengal Since 1977*. Cambridge: Cambridge University Press.

Mangai, V. Padma. 2000. 'Representing Protest and Resistance on Stage: *Avvai*', *Indian Journal of Gender Studies*, 7(2): 217–30.

Marriott, McKim (ed.) 1990. *India through Hindu Categories*. London: Sage Publications.

Martin, Randy. 1994. *Socialist Ensembles: Theater and State in Cuba and Nicaragua*. Minneapolis: University of Minnesota Press.

———. 2006 'Staging the Political: Boal and the Horizons of Theatrical Commitment', in Jan Cohen-Cruz and Mady Schutzman (eds), *A Boal Companion: Dialogues on Theatre and Cultural Politics*, pp. 23–32. New York: Routledge.

Marx, Karl. 1852. *Eighteenth Brumaire of Louis Bonaparte*. Moscow: Progress Publishers. http://marxists.org/archive/marx/works/1852/18th brumaire index.htm (accessed on 26 May 2005).

———. 1857. *Grundrisse*. http://www.marxists.org/archive/marx/works/1857/grundrisse (accessed on 21 March 2008).

Marx, Karl and Frederic Engels. 1848 (1998). *The Communist Manifesto*. New York: Penguin.

———. 1967. *Capital: A Critique of Political Economy*. New York: International Publishers.

McMichael, Philip. 2003. 'Food Security and Social Reproduction', in S. Gill and I. Bakker (eds), *Power, Production and Social Reproduction*, pp. 169–88. New York: Palgrave MacMillan.

———. 2006. 'Peasant Prospects in an Age of Neo-Liberalism', *New Political Economy*, 11(3): 407–18.

———. 2008. 'Food sovereignty, social reproduction, and the agrarian question', in Haroon Akram-Lodhi and Christobal Kay (eds), *Peasant Livelihoods, Rural Transformation and the Agrarian Question*, pp. 288–312. Routledge: United Kingdom.

McRobbie, Angela. 1999. *In the Culture Society: Art, Fashion and Popular Music*. London: Routledge.

———. 2000. 'Feminism and the Third Way', in *Feminist Review* 64 (Spring): 97–112.

Menon, Dilip. 2008. 'The Idea of Development as Governance: India in the first decade of independence'. Paper presented at 'Reviewing

Disciplinary Agendas in Theatre Studies: Cultural Arena Policies Institutions', 23–25 January, Institute of Economic Growth, New Delhi.
Menon, Nivedita. (ed.) 1999. *Gender and Politics in India*. Delhi: Oxford University Press.
———. 2005. 'Between the Burqa and the Beauty Parlor? Globalization, Cultural Nationalism, and Feminist Politics', in Ania Loomba, Suvir Kaul, Matti Bunzl, Antoinette Burton and Jed Esty (eds), *Postcolonial Studies and Beyond*, pp. 206–29. Durham: Duke University Press.
Menon, Nivedita and Aditya Nigam. 2007. *Power and Contestation: India Since 1989*. Halifax and Winnipeg: Fernwood Publishing.
Mitchell, Timothy. 1988. *Colonising Egypt*. Berkeley: University of California Press.
———. 1991a. 'America's Egypt: Discourse of the Development Industry', *Middle East Report*, No. 169, Crossing the Line (Mar–Apr), 18–34+36
———. 1991b. 'The Limits of the State: Beyond Statist Approaches and the Critics', *American Political Science Review*, 85(1): 77–96.
———. 1999. 'Society, Economy and the State Effect', in G. Steinmetz (ed.), *State/Culture: State-Formation after the Cultural Turn*, pp. 76–97. Ithaca: Cornell University Press.
———. 2002. *Rule of Experts: Egypt, Techno-Politics, Modernity*. Berkeley: University of California Press.
Mitra, Subrata. 2001. 'Making local government work: Local elite, *panchayati raj*, and governance in India', in Atul Kohli (ed.), *The Success of India's Democracy*, pp. 103–26. Cambridge: Cambridge University Press.
Mohan, D. 2003. 'Scripting Power and Changing the Subject: Jana Sanskriti's Political Theatre in rural north India'. Ph. D. Thesis, Cornell University.
———. 2004. 'Reimagining Community: Scripting Power and Changing the Subject through Jana Sanskriti's Political Theatre in Rural North India', *Journal of Contemporary Ethnography*, 33 (2): 178–217.
Mohanty, Mritiunjoy. 2007. 'Political Economy of Agrarian Transformation: Another View of Singur', *Economic and Political Weekly*, 42 (9): 737–41.
Morarji, Karuna. 2005. 'The Moral of the Story: Schooling, Development, and State Formation in India'. Master's thesis, Cornell University.
———. 2007. '"Where does the rural educated person fit?" Negotiating values of education and development in contemporary India'. Paper presented at the conference on 'Neoliberalism in Contention: A Social Movement Analysis', 28 September, Robert and Ruth Polson Institute for Global Development, Cornell University, Ithaca, New York.
Mukherjee, Nivedita. 2008. 'Country Roads', *India Today*, pp. 40–42, 18 August.
Mukherji, Chandra. 2007. 'Cultural Genealogy: Method for a Historical Sociology of Culture or a Cultural Sociology of History', *Cultural Sociology*, 1: 49–71.

Mukhopadhyay, Ishita. 2005. 'Economic Empowerment', in Jasodhara Bagchi (ed.), *The Changing Status of Women in West Bengal, 1970–2000*, pp. 71–80. New Delhi: Sage Publications.

Munshi, Vidya. 2005. 'Political Participation', in Jasodhara Bagchi (ed.), *The Changing Status of Women in West Bengal 1970–2000: The Challenge Ahead*, pp. 81–95. New Delhi: Sage Publications.

Nagar, Richa. 2000. 'Mujhe Jawab Do! (Answer me!): Women's grass-roots activism and social spaces in Chitrakoot (India)', *Gender, Place and Culture*, 7(4): 341–62.

———. 2002. 'Women's Theater and the Redefinitions of Public, Private, and Politics in North India', *ACME: An International E-Journal for Critical Geographers*, 1(1): 55–72.

Needham, Anuradha Dingwaney and Rajeswari Sunder Rajan (eds). 2007. *The Crisis of Secularism in India*. Durham and London: Duke University Press.

Nicholas, Ralph W. 1981. 'The Goddess Sitala and Epidemic Smallpox in Bengal', *The Journal of Asian Studies*, 41 (1): 21–44.

Nigam, A. 2000. 'Secularism, Modernity, Nation: Epistemology of the Dalit Critique', *Economic and Political Weekly*, 35(48): 4256–268.

———. 2006. *The Insurrection of Little Selves: The Crisis of Secular-Nationalism in India*. Delhi: Oxford University Press.

Obeyesekere, Ranjini. 1999. *Sri Lankan Theater in a Time of Terror: Political Satire in a Permitted Space*. New Delhi: Sage Publications.

O'Hanlon, Rosalind. 2001 (1988). 'Recovering the Subject: Subaltern Studies and Histories of Resistance in Colonial South Asia', in David Ludden (ed.), *Reading Subaltern Studies: Critical History, Contested Meaning, and the Globalisation of South Asia*, pp. 135–86. Delhi: Permanent Black.

Ong, Aihwa. 1987. *Spirits of Resistance and Capitalist Discipline*. Albany: State University of New York Press.

Otero, Gerardo. 2008. 'Contesting neoliberal globalism in Mexico: Challenges for the political and the social left', in Paul Bowler, Ray Broomhill, Teresa Gutienez-Haces and Stephen McBride (eds), *International Trade and Neoliberal Globalism: Towards Re-Peripheralization in Australia, Canada and Mexico*, pp. 163–77. London: Routledge.

Pedersen, Jorge Dige. 2001. 'India's Industrial Dilemmas in West Bengal', *Asian Survey*, 41 (4): 646–68.

Pigg, Stacey Leigh. 1996. 'The Credible and the Credulous: The Questions of "Villagers' Beliefs" in Nepal', *Cultural Anthropology*, 11(2): 160–201.

Pigg, Stacey Leigh. 1997. '"Found in Most Traditional Societies": Traditional Medical Practitioners between Culture and Development', in Frederick Cooper and Randall Packard (eds), *International Development and the Social Sciences: Essays on the History and Politics of Knowledge*, pp. 259–90. Berkeley: University of California Press.

Plastow, Jane. 1998. 'Uses and Abuses of Theatre for Development: Political struggle and development theatre in the Ethiopia-Eritrea war', in Kamal Salhi (ed.), *African theatre for development: art for self-determination*, pp. 97–113. Chicago: University of Chicago Press.

Polanyi, Karl. 1957. *The Great Transformation: The Political and Economic Origins of Our Time*. Boston: Beacon Press.

Pradhan, Sudhi (ed.) (1979, 1982, 1985). *Marxist Cultural Movement in India: Chronicles and Documents 1936–1947*, vols. *I–III*. Calcutta: Pustak Bipani .

Prashad, Vijay. 2005. 'American Grand Strategy and the Assassination of the Third World', *Critical Asian Studies*. 37(1): 117–27.

Prashad, Vijay and Teo Ballve. 2006. *Dispatches from Latin America: On the Frontlines against Neoliberalism*. Cambridge: South End Press.

Rademacher, Anne and Raj Patel 2002. 'Retelling worlds of poverty: Reflections on transforming participatory research for a global narrative', in K. Brock and R. McGee (eds), *Knowing Poverty: Critical Reflections on Participatory Research and Policy*, pp. 166–88. London: Earthscan Publications.

Radway, Janice A. 1991. *Reading the Romance: Women, Patriarchy, and Popular Literature*. Berkeley: University of North Carolina Press.

Raheja, Gloria Goodwin and Ann Grodzins Gold. 1994. *Listen to the Heron's Words: Reimagining Gender and Kinship in North India*. Berkeley: University of California Press,

Rajagopal, Arvind. 2001. *Politics After Television: Religious Nationalism and the Reshaping of the Public in India*. Cambridge: Cambridge University Press.

Rajan, S. Irudaya, Mala Ramanathan and U. S. Mishra. 1996. 'Female Autonomy and Reproductive Behaviour in Kerala: New Evidence from the Recent Kerala Fertility Survey', in *Girls' Schooling, Women's Autonomy, and Fertility Change in South Asia*, Roger Jeffery and Alaka M. Basu (eds), pp. 269–87. Thousand Oaks, CA: Sage.

Rana, Kumar, Abdur Rafique, and Amrita Sengupta. 2002. *The Pratichi Education Report*. Number 1. New Delhi: TLM Books.

Rana, Kumar and Liby T. Johnson. 2003. 'Hot-Tempered "Cold Fever": Illness and Impoverishment among Adivasis in Jharkhand', *Economic and Political Weekly*, 38(15): 1451–454.

Rastogi, Anupam. 2006. 'The Infrastructure Sector in India 2006', http://www.3inetwork.org/reports/IIR2007/01-The%20Infrast.pdf (accessed on 1 May 2008).

Rawal, Vikas. 2001. 'Agrarian Reform and Land Markets: A Study of Land Transactions in Two Villages of West Bengal 1977–1995', *Economic Development and Cultural Change*, 49 (3): 611–30.

Rockwell, Elsie. 1994. 'Schools of the Revolution: Enacting and Contesting State Forms in Tlaxcala, 1910–1930', in Gilbert M. Joseph and Daniel

Nugent (eds), *Everyday Forms of State Forma-tion: Revolution and the Negotiation of Rule in Modern Mexico*, pp. 170–208. Durham, NC: Duke University Press.

Rogaly, Ben. 1998. 'Containing Conflict and Reaping Votes: Management of Rural Labour Relations in West Bengal', *Economic and Political Weekly*, 33(42–43): 2729–739.

Rogaly, Ben, Barbara Harriss-White and Sugata Bose. 1999. *Sonar Bangla?: Agricultural Growth and Agrarian Change in West Bengal and Bangladesh*. New Delhi: Sage Publications.

Roy, Dayabati. 2007. 'Politics at the Margin: A Tale of Two Villages', *Economic and Political Weekly*, 42(32): 3323–329.

———. 2008. 'Whither the Subaltern Domain? An Ethnographic Enquiry', *Economic and Political Weekly*, 43(2): 31–38.

Ruud, Arild Engelsen. 1997. 'Of Novels and Dramas: Engaging with Literature in Bengal and the making of a modern village leader', *South Asia Research*, 17(1): 70–92.

———. 1999. 'From Untouchable to Communist: Wealth, Power and Status among Supporters of the Communist Party (Marxist) in Rural West Bengal', in Ben Rogaly, Barbara Harriss-White and Sugata Bose (eds), *Sonar Bangla?: Agricultural Growth and Agrarian Change in West Bengal and Bangladesh*, pp. 253–78. New Delhi, Thousand Oaks, London: Sage Publications.

———. 2003. *The Poetics of Village Politics: The Making of West Bengal's Rural Communism*. New Delhi and New York: Oxford University Press.

Sadasivam, Bharati. 2000. 'Community Justice: West Bengal's Women Draw on Village Tradition to Stop Domestic Violence', Ford Foundation Report: Winter.

Saha, Sambit. 2007. 'Prohibiting the use of agricultural land for industries is ultimately self-defeating', Interview with Amartya Sen, *The Telegraph*, 23 July. http://www.telegraphindia.com/1070723/asp/nation/story_8094453.asp (accessed on 10 June 2008).

Sahlins, Marshall. 1976. *Culture and Practical Reason*. Chicago: University of Chicago Press.

Salverson, Julie. 1994. 'The Mask of Solidarity', in Mady Schutzman and Jan Cohen-Cruz (ed.), *Playing Boal: Theatre, Therapy, Activism*, pp. 157–70. London and New York: Routledge.

Sanyal, Kalyan. 2007. *Rethinking Capitalist Development: Primitive Accumulation, Governmentality and Post-Colonial Capitalism*. New Delhi: Routledge.

Sarangapani, Padma. 2003. *Constructing School Knowledge: An Ethnography of Learning in an Indian Village*. New Delhi: Sage Publications.

Sarkar, Abhirup. 2007. 'Development and Displacement: Land Acquisition in West Bengal', *Economic and Political Weekly*, 42(16): 1435–442.

Sarkar, Sumit. 1998. *Writing Social History*. Delhi: Oxford University Press.

Sarkar, Tanika. 1984. 'Politics and Women in Bengal: The conditions and meaning of participation', *Indian Economic and Social History Review*, 21(1): 91–101.

Sayer, Andrew. 2005. *The Moral Significance of Class*.Cambridge: Cambridge University Press.

Schechner, Richard. 1983. *Performative Circumstances from the Avant-garde to the Ramlila*. Calcutta: Seagull Books.

———. 1986. 'Victor Turner's Last Adventure', in Victor Turner (ed.), *The Anthropology of Performance* pp. 7–20. New York: PAJ Publications.

Schechner, Richard and Willa Appel (eds) 1990. *By Means of Performance: Intercultural Studies of Theatre and Ritual*. Cambridge: Cambridge University Press.

Scott. James C. 1976. *The Moral Economy of the Peasant: Rebellion and Subsistence in Southeast Asia*. New Haven: Yale University Press.

———. 1987. *Weapons of the Weak: Everyday Forms of Peasant Resistance*. New Haven: Yale University Press.

———. 1990. *Domination and the Arts of Resistance: Hidden Transcripts*. New Haven: Yale University Press.

Scott, Joan W. 1992. 'Experience', in Judith Butler and Joan Scott (eds), *Feminists Theorize the Political*, pp. 22–40. New York: Routledge.

———. 1994. 'Deconstructing Equality-versus-Difference: Or, the Uses of Poststructuralist Theory for Feminism', in Anne C. Herrmann and Abigail J. Stewart (eds), *Theorizing Feminism: Parallel Trends in the Humanities and Social Sciences*, pp. 254–70. Boulder: Westview Press.

Schutzman Mady, and Jan Cohen-Cruz. 1994. 'Introduction' in Mady Schutzman and Jan Cohen-Cruz (eds), *Playing Boal: Theatre, Therapy, Activism*, pp. 1–16. London: Routledge.

Seagull Theatre Quarterly, 1998–99. Theatre for Change Project Documentation, (December-March).

Seizer, Susan. 2000. 'Roadwork: Offstage with Special Drama Actresses in Tamilnadu, South India', *Cultural Anthropology*, 15 (2): 217–59.

———. 2005. *Stigmas of the Tamil Stage: An Ethnography of Special Drama Artists in South India*. Durham: Duke University Press.

Sen, Amartya. 1999. *Development as Freedom*. New York: Knopf.

———. 2002. 'Introduction', in Kumar Rana, Abdur Rafique and Amrita Sengupta (eds), *The Pratichi Education Report*, pp. 1–12. Delhi: TLM Books.

———. 2003. 'The Importance of Basic Education'. *Guardian*, 28 December. http://education.guardian.co.uk/schools/story/0,5500,1072739,00.html. (accessed on 24 April 2005).

———. 2004. 'How Does Culture Matter?', in Vijayendra Rao and Michael Walton (eds), *Culture and Public Action*, pp. 37–58. Delhi: Permanent Black.

Sen Gupta, Prasanta. 1989. 'Politics in West Bengal: The Left Front Versus the Congress (I)', *Asian Survey*, 29(9): 883–97.

Shramajibee Mahila Samity. 2003. 'Shalishi in West Bengal: A Community-based Response to Domestic Violence', *Economic and Political Weekly*, 38(17): 1665–673.

Sinha, Aseema. 2005. *The Regional Roots of Developmental Politics in India: A Divided Leviathan*. Bloomington: Indiana University Press.

Sivaramakrishnan, K. 1999. *Modern Forests: Statemaking and Environmental Change in Colonial Eastern India*. Stanford: Stanford University Press.

Sivaramakrishnan and Arun Agrawal (eds). 2003. *Regional Modernities: The Cultural Politics of Development in India*. Stanford: Stanford University Press.

Skaria, Ajay. 2002. 'Gandhi's Politics: Liberalism and the Question of the Ashram', *South Atlantic Quarterly*, 101 (4): 954–86.

Soman, Krishna. 2002. 'Rural Health Care in West Bengal', *Economic and Political Weekly*, 29 July.

Spivak, Gayatri Chakravarty. 1988. 'Can the Subaltern Speak?', in Cary Nelson and Lawrence Grossberg (eds), *Marxism and the Interpretation of Culture*, pp. 271–315. Urbana, IL: University of Illinois Press.

Steinmetz, George. 1999. *State/Culture: State Formation After the Cultural Turn*. Ithaca: Cornell University Press.

Stoler, Ann Laura. 1995. *Race and the Education of Desire: Foucault's History of Sexuality and the Colonial Order of Things*. Durham: Duke University Press.

———. 2006. 'On Degrees of Imperial Sovereignty', *Public Culture*, 18(1): 125–46.

Strauss, Julia and Donal B. Cruise O'Brien. 2007. *Staging Politics: Power and Performance in Asia and Africa*. London: I. B. Tauris.

Street, Brian V. 1984. *Literacy in Theory and Practice*. Cambridge: Cambridge University Press.

Subramanian, Ajantha. 2002. 'Community, Place and Citizenship', *Seminar* (www.india-seminar.com).

———. 2003. 'Mukkuvar Modernity: Development as a Cultural Identity', in K. Sivaramakrishnan and Arun Agrawal (eds), *Regional Modernities: The Cultural Politics of Development in India*, pp. 262–85. Stanford: Stanford University Press.

Swidler, Ann. 1986. 'Culture in Action: Symbols and Strategies', *American Sociological Review*, 51: 273–86.

Taylor, Diana. 1991. *Theatre of Crisis: Drama and Politics in Latin America*. Lexington: The University Press of Kentucky.

———. 1997. *Disappearing Acts: Spectacles of Gender and Nationalism in Argentina's "Dirty War"*. Durham: Duke University Press.

———. 2003. *The archive and the repertoire: Performing cultural memory in the Americans*. Durham: Duke University Press.

Taussig, Michael. 1980. *The Devil and Commodity Fetishism in South America*. Chapel Hill: University of North Carolina Press.

Taussig, Michael and Richard Schechner. 1994. 'Boal in Brazil, France, the USA', in Mady Schutzman and Jan Cohen-Cruz (eds), *Playing Boal: Theatre, Therapy, Activism* pp. 17–34. London: Routledge.

The Times of India, 2002. 'Faulty Policies Hurt Liquor Trade in State', 1 October. http://timesofindia.indiatimes.com/articleshow/23898459.cms (accessed on 14 September 2005).

Thompson, E. P. 1971. 'The Moral Economy of the English Crowd in the 18th Century', *Past & Present*, 50: 76–136.

———. 1966. *The Making of the English Working Class*. New York: Vintage.

Trivedi, Lisa. 2003. 'Visually Mapping the "Nation": Swadeshi Politics in Nationalist India, 1920–1930', *Journal of Asian Studies*, 62(1): 11–41.

Trouillot, Michel-Rolph. 2002. 'North Atlantic Universals: Analytical Fictions, 1492–1945', *South Atlantic Quarterly*, 101 (4): 839–58.

Tsing, Anna Lowenhaupt. 1993. *In the Realm of the Diamond Queen: Marginality in an Out-of-the-Way Place*. Princeton : Princeton University Press.

Tucker, Robert C. (ed.) 1978. *The Marx-Engels Reader*. New York: W.W. Norton.

Turner, Victor Witter. 1975. *Dramas, Fields and Metaphors: Symbolic Action in Human Society*. Ithaca: Cornell University Press.

———. 1995. *The Ritual Process: Structure and Anti-Structure*. Reprint Edition. New York: Aldine.

Walton, Michael and Vijayendra Rao (eds). 2004. *Culture and Public Action*. Stanford: Stanford Social Sciences.

UNDP (United Nations Development Programme). 2004. *West Bengal Human Development Report, 2004*. Development and Planning Department, Government of West Bengal. http://data.undp.org.in/shdr/wb/WBHDR.pdf (accessed on 25 May 2006).

UNESCO. 2000. 'The Dakar Framework for Action: Education for All. Meeting our Collective Commitments'. http://www.unesco.org/education/efa/ed_for_all/dakfram_eng.shtml (accessed on 23 May 2008).

van Erven, Eugene. 1992. *The Playful Revolution: Theatre and Liberation in Asia*. Bloomington: Indiana University Press.

Van Hollen, Cecilia. 2003. *Birth on the Threshold: Childbirth and Modernity in South India*. Berkeley, Los Angeles, London: University of California Press.

Wallerstein, Immanuel. 1974. *The modern world-system*. New York: Academic Press.

———. 1989. '1968, Revolution in the World-System', *Theory and Society*, 28(4): 431–49.

Wa Thiong'o, Ngugi. 1998. *Penpoints, Gunpoints, and Dreams: Towards a critical theory of the arts and the state in Africa.* New York: Oxford University Press.

Weiss, Brad. 2004. *Producing African Futures: Ritual and Reproduction in a Neoliberal Age.* Leiden: Brill.

White, Christine Pelzer. 1986. 'Everyday Resistance, Socialist Revolution, and Rural Development: The Vietnamese Case', *Journal of Peasant Studies,* 13(2): 49–63.

Williams, Glyn. 1999. '*Panchayati Raj* and the Changing Micro-Politics of West Bengal', in Ben Rogaly, Barbara Harriss-White and Sugata Bose (eds), *Sonar Bangla?: Agricultural Growth and Agrarian Change in West Bengal and Bangladesh,* pp. 229–52. New Delhi: Sage Publications.

Williams, Raymond. 1973. *The Country and the City.* New York: Oxford University Press.

———. 1977. *Marxism and Literature.* Oxford: Oxford University Press.

Willis, Paul. 1977. *Learning to Labour: How Working Class Kids Get Working Class Jobs.* Farnborough: Saxon House.

Wolford, Wendy 2005. 'Agrarian moral economies and neoliberalism in Brazil: Competing worldviews and the state in the struggle for land', *Environment and Planning A,* vol. 37, 241–61.

———. 2007. 'Land Reform in the Time of Neoliberalism: A Many-Splendored Thing', *Antipode,* 39 (3): 550.

World Commission on Culture and Development. 1996. 'Our Creative Diversity', http://unesdoc.unesco.org/images/0010/001055/105586E.pdf (accessed on 22 July 2005).

Yúdice, George. 2003. *The Expediency of Culture: Uses of Culture in the Global Era.* Durham: Duke University Press.

Zalik, Anna. 2007. 'Armed Struggle as Election? Social Protest, Extractive Security, and the De/legitimation of Civilian Transition'. Paper presented at the conference on 'Neoliberalism in Contention: A Social Movement Analysis', 28 September, Robert and Ruth Polson Institute for Global Development, Cornell University, Ithaca, New York.

Zook, Darren C. 2001. 'The Farcical Mosaic: The Changing Masks of Political Theatre in Contemporary India', *Asian Theatre Journal,* 18 (2): 174–199.

Index